Asian Americans
Emerging Minorities

Harry H. L. Kitano
University of California, Los Angeles

Roger Daniels
University of Cincinnati

PRENTICE HALL
Englewood Cliffs, New Jersey 07632

Library of Congress Cataloging-in-Publication Data

Kitano, Harry H. L.
  Asian Americans.

  Bibliography: p.
  Includes index.
  1. Asian Americans.   I. Daniels, Roger.   II. Title.
E184.06K57 1987   973'.0495   87-25933
ISBN 0-13-049164-0

For Lynn and Judith

Cover design: Photo Plus Art
Cover photo: New York Convention and Visitors Bureau
Manufacturing buyer: Raymond Keating
Interior design and production supervision: Scott Huler

Extract on pp. 141–142 from *American Mosaic: The Immigrant Experience in the Words of Those Who Lived It* by Joan Morrison and Charlotte Zabusky. Copyright © 1980 by Joan Morrison and Charlotte Fox Zabusky. Reprinted by permission of the publisher, E. P. Dutton, a division of NAL Penguin, Inc.

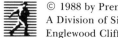 © 1988 by Prentice-Hall, Inc.
A Division of Simon & Schuster
Englewood Cliffs, New Jersey 07632

Printed in the United States of America
10 9 8 7 6 5 4 3 2 1

ISBN 0-13-049164-0

Prentice-Hall International (UK) Limited, *London*
Prentice-Hall of Australia Pty. Limited, *Sydney*
Prentice-Hall Canada Inc., *Toronto*
Prentice-Hall Hispanoamericana, S.A., *Mexico*
Prentice-Hall of India Private Limited, *New Delhi*
Prentice-Hall of Japan, Inc., *Tokyo*
Simon & Schuster Asia Pte. Ltd., *Singapore*
Editora Prentice-Hall do Brasil, Ltda., *Rio de Janeiro*

Contents

Preface

Almost two decades ago, in an earlier collaboration, we were chiefly concerned with the nature of prejudice.[1] This work, at least in part, is the story of victories—or partial victories—over prejudice. We could not imagine then that Asian Americans would be as numerous as they are now: an authoritative estimate projects some 6.5 million Asian Americans by 1990. Nor could we have guessed at the tremendous growth of some of the newer Asian American groups. We pointed out then that Asian Americans—we called them "Orientals"—were "the most successful, the most middle-class, the most respected" of non-Caucasian groups in the nation. That trend has largely continued. We also noted—not decisively enough, we now think—that some economic and other discriminations persisted; that phenomenon has continued as well.

Most surprising today, as compared with the end of the 1960s, is the variety of the Asian American experience. Then we wrote primarily about Chinese and Japanese, with a brief treatment of Filipinos and just glancing mentions of "East Indians" and Koreans. Of this book, however, less than half is devoted to Chinese and Japanese. The Census Bureau now enu-

1. Roger Daniels and Harry H. L. Kitano, *American Racism: Exploration of the Nature of Prejudice* (Englewood Cliffs, NJ: Prentice-Hall, 1970).

merates and identifies seventeen Asian American groups and nine groups of Pacific Islanders. The newer Asian and Pacific Islander immigrants are much less culturally homogenous than their predecessors. Whereas the overwhelming majority of pre–World War II Asian immigrants were of peasant stock (with a smattering of intellectuals and political dissidents), today the range is from premodernized groups, such as the Hmong, to medical professionals from the Philippines and Ph.D.s from India.

This transformation is the result of changes in American foreign and domestic policy, the war in Vietnam (which we mentioned only in passing in our earlier work), and changes in U.S. immigration and refugee policy that we did not discuss at all. In the previous book one of our unstated assumptions was that, for all intents and purposes, large-scale immigration had come to a halt. Today that is clearly not the case, and we find it necessary to devote an entire chapter to the evolution of our immigration laws and regulations.

Such, of course, are the dangers of writing about the very recent past and discussing the present. Undoubtedly, in a couple of decades, we will see weaknesses in the current work that are not now apparent. But we do not believe, with Hegel, that "the owl of Minerva rises only at dusk"—that intelligent accounts can be written only long after the fact. All things considered, we believe that our earlier book stands up pretty well, and anyone who chooses to compare the two will find many more continuities than changes.

The present work, we hope, will provide a guide to the bewildering proliferation of Asian American groups. Like any pioneering work, this book has deficiencies, but we think that it has two chief virtues. First, it is an interdisciplinary approach, using the insights of both history and social science. Second, it is comparative: it tries to portray the experience of each group not only individually but as part of that essentially artificial construct, the Asian American experience.

This work was jointly conceived and executed: although each author has had different primary responsibilities, each chapter as well as the whole is a mutual production. What follows is solely our own responsibility, but we have had assistance of all kinds from more persons than we can possibly acknowledge here. Nonetheless, we must thank one person, Kriste Lindenmeyer Dick, who helped to prepare the index.

Even more important, we must acknowledge the ways in which our students—graduate and undergraduate—have contributed to our education and thus to this book. Their keen awareness of subtle changes in the ethnocultural climates of opinion, both in the majority and minority communities, has kept us more alert and up to date than we would have been otherwise. Each of us continues to participate in a variety of ethnic community–based activities and gains more from those encounters than he contributes. As we noted in our earlier book: "Research and teaching, theory and practice, contemplation and action are not the dichotomies that so many superficial observers suppose; on the contrary, they represent linked aspects of meaningful, contemporary academic experience." The merits of this work flow largely, we believe, from our participation in both sides of that experience.

Harry H. L. Kitano
Roger Daniels
Los Angeles and Cincinnati

1

Introduction

The standard images associated with immigrants are of crowded boats, the Statue of Liberty, Ellis Island, poverty, hard work, night school, and the Americanization of succeeding generations. This process, often referred to as the "European model" or "straight line" theory,[1] includes voluntary immigration, acculturation, integration, assimilation, and eventual absorption into the dominant society. This theory assumes that given sufficient time anyone can become a part of the American mainstream by working hard, learning English and the American way, participating in the community, and blending into the mainstream. Those who do not are looked upon as somehow lacking the motivation to become American.

But this scenario is a narrow one and may reflect an idealized vision of the past, reserved primarily for those of "proper" Caucasian background. Not all immigrants were welcome; many did not possess the desired attributes or background for easy blending, and many came with different notions of the meaning of America. Until after World War II, for example, many immigrants from Asia were kept not on Ellis Island, in the shadow of the Statue of Liberty, but in the detention barracks on Angel Island, near San Francisco's Alcatraz, a notorious prison. In the wooden barracks-prison, which can still be visited, some Chinese detainees whiled away the time by carving poems in Chinese characters into the soft wood of the walls. One poem read:

> There are tens of thousands of poems composed on these walls,
> They are all cries of complaint and sadness.
> The day I am rid of this prison and attain success,
> I must remember that this prison once existed.
>   . . .
> All my compatriots please be mindful,
> Once you have some small gains, return home early.
>
> *By one from Xiangshan*[2]

Present-day migration provides different symbols and images. Some newcomers simply walk across the border, while others arrive in jet aircraft; the new ports of entry include major airports and overcrowded border cities in Texas and California. But despite these differences, a number of similar questions may be asked about both the older and present-day immigrants, however they arrive.

Why and how did they come to the United States? What skills, resources, values, cultures and life-styles did they bring with them? Did they have family and community support? And—most important for peoples who have faced much discrimination—how were they received by the host society? Were they welcome or unwelcome?

Asian migration to the United States provides a rich source of data regarding these questions. Some Asians came as contract laborers and as sojourners with the expectation of returning to their home country; others arrived with the hope of permanent residence. Many came for economic and educational opportunities and with the expectation of participating in the American dream. Others fled for personal and political reasons. Some Asians carefully planned their move to the new country; others, forced to flee at a moment's notice, arrived as refugees.

They came to America at different periods of time. After a period of "free immigration," the early immigrants faced steep barriers, which virtually forced a separatist and less-than-equal existence. But at other periods the barriers were lowered, and Asians integrated and acculturated more fully. It is the interaction between the dominant society and the immigrant group that determines outcomes, with the direction of change controlled largely by the group with more power and resources.

We perceive a relationship between the motivations for migration, the reactions of the host society, and the adaptive patterns of the migrants. The state of an immigrant group is the result of the interaction of factors within the ethnic group and the reactions of the host society. In addition, relationships between ethnic groups are significant.

Factors internal to the ethnic group include:

1. Historical circumstances, including motivations for migration, goals, and expectations.
2. Demographic factors, such as number, age, sex ratio, education, training, and skills.
3. Cultural factors, including language, values, social class background, urban-rural experiences, religion and life-styles.
4. Family and community cohesion, resources, power, and alternative opportunities.
5. Home-country factors, such as power, stage of development, and status of the mother country.

The host society provides the context for immigrant group adaptation through such factors as:

1. Governmental policies.
2. The raising of barriers, including prejudice and discrimination.
3. The relationship of the host nation with the mother country.
4. The reactions of other ethnic groups.
5. International, national, and local economic factors.

WHO IS AN AMERICAN?

One of the critical factors affecting the ability of immigrants from Asia to participate as equals in American society has been the varying definitions of who is an American. If being an American is defined in terms of race then the question of Asians belonging becomes difficult.[3] If being an American is determined by nationality and country of origin, or by religion and culture, then those who do not fit into the white, European Protestant or Catholic mode will again face difficulty. However, if being an American is defined on the basis of a belief in the American system, or by the needs of the economy, or by relatives already in residence, then Asians will find an easier fit. At different periods of our history, the question of who could become an American has had different answers. Asian immigrants were deeply affected by these changes in definition, as reflected in our national policies. The question of who could become an American is analyzed in Chapter 2.

For example, in the mid-19th century (1840s–1870s), there was no formal immigration policy—those who were willing to contribute their labor were welcome. Chinese laborers filled a critical labor gap, working the mines and building the railroads, but when their labor was no longer needed, their race and nationality became an issue. In 1882, Chinese laborers were no longer allowed to immigrate to this country. Race and nationality as criteria for becoming American were reinforced in 1917 and 1924, when immigration policy extended discrimination to almost all Orientals (as they were known in those days).

There was little immigration from Asian countries from then until World War II, when China was an American ally. To defuse Japanese arguments about a race war, it was felt that it would be politically sound to grant a token immigration quota and the right of naturalization to our friends. Current immigration legislation gives preferences to immigrants with special skills or capital: Qualified Asian immigrants are welcome. Thus, a review of our immigration policy is a reflection of changes in orientation toward immigrants.

Gleason indicates that although colonial America was populated primarily by immigrants from Great Britain, the early American identity was based more on abstractions, such as liberty, equality, and a belief in the republic, than on any particular language, religion, nationality, or ethnic background.[4] But in spite of these idealistic abstractions, a two-tiered system, or a system of "Iron Cages," developed in America.[5] One system was free, open, and reserved for whites; the other, a step below, was for American Indians and blacks. A belief in liberty and justice was insufficient for Indians and blacks to participate in the society, whereas "pure" Caucasian ancestry meant that one could become a part of the mainstream. Asians were soon to join other "non-whites" in the second-class section of the social structure.

WHO WANTS TO BE AN AMERICAN?

Another related, but often unasked, question is, Who wants to become an American? The apparently simple question turns out to be difficult and complicated, since it involves different "Americas." If becoming an American means full acceptance and the chance for equal participation in the mainstream, most immigrants would answer with a resounding yes. If becoming American means giving up one's cultural heritage in order to participate in the mainstream, the affirmative responses of some immigrants might have a lower intensity. And if it means domination and a second-class role, then some immigrants would not wish to become Americans.

Some Asians prefer to retain strong ethnic ties, and hence their definition of an American lies in a pluralistic model. They may see themselves primarily as Asians, believing that the meaning of America lies in its recognition of diversity. Others may prefer to live their lives within ethnic boundaries because they feel that America will never accept people of color as equals.

These various definitions are not static. There is constant change, both in the immigrant group and the host society. American society is and has been characterized by change. Present-day America is significantly different from the nation that existed at the beginning of the century. For example, a book about Asian Americans in 1910 or even 1950 might have dealt with only two groups, the Chinese and the Japanese. They would be seen as "problem minorities"; they did not fit into the then-existing definition of who could become an American. The solution to the problem was simple: there would be discriminatory legislation prohibiting further immigration and, for those already here, barriers to equal participation.

But in the 1980s, there are many diverse Asian American groups. Their estimated population in 1985 was 5.1 million, which included Chinese, Filipinos, Japanese, Vietnamese, Koreans, Indians, Laotians, Kampucheans, and others.[6] (See Appendix for population data.)

The growth of Asian American groups has been varied. Japanese Americans, the most numerous as recently as 1970, were third in 1980 and may be sixth by the year 2000. The cause of this decline is the very low rate of emigration from Japan; its workers now stay home and send products abroad. One population projection guesstimates that by the year 2000 there will be almost ten million Asian Americans, led be two million Filipinos, more than a million and a half Chinese and Vietnamese, a million and a third Koreans, one million Asian Indians, and only 850,000 Japanese. That would represent annual growth rates over 1980 figures of less than 1 percent for Japanese, over 5 percent for Chinese, 8 percent for Asian Indians, over 8 percent for Filipinos, over 13 percent for Koreans, and 27 percent for Vietnamese.

But leaving projections and estimates aside, the 1980 data show that the Asian American population is changing rapidly. Where once almost all lived in the West, by 1980 just over one-half did. Only a minority of Koreans and Vietnamese live in the West, and fewer Asian Indians live in the West than in the Northeast, South, or Midwest.

In terms of age, there is more variety. The median age for the Japanese was 33.5 years, distinctly above the national median of 30.0. Asian Indians were almost exactly at the national median. The median age for the Chinese was 29.6 years; Filipinos, 28.5 years; and Koreans, 26 years. These figures are below the national median, but above the medians for blacks, 24.9 years, and Hispanics, 23.2 years. The white median age was 31.3 years. Finally, the median age for the Vietnamese, 21.5 years, was significantly below that of other groups. Similarly, the birth rates of every major Asian group, except the Vietnamese, were below those of the white population. The Vietnamese birth rates were similar to, but slightly below, those of blacks and Hispanics.

Occupational data from the census suggest that, in some ways at least, most Asian American groups have higher occupational status than whites, not to speak of Hispanics and blacks; the data also show that some foreign-born Asian groups have higher occupational status than native-born members of the same groups.

What this and other recent data demonstrate is that the old stereotypes, even the informed ones, no longer apply, and that increasing variety is the hallmark of the contemporary Asian American experience.

Their absolute numbers are relatively small in a country with more than 240 million inhabitants, but Asians are among the fastest-growing minorities. Their relative growth is largely due to immigration, since fertility rates of most Asian American groups are well below national norms.

MODELS OF IMMIGRANT GROUPS

Because we are a nation of immigrants, much attention has been paid to the experiences of immigrant groups. One widely used model was developed by Gordon, who sees different types or stages in the assimilation of various groups.[7] Cultural assimilation or acculturation means taking on the ways of the host society, such as in dress, diet, and life-style; other types of assimilation include structural, marital, identificational, and civic. The critical entry for minority groups is structural assimilation. Once a group enters into the social clubs, cliques, and institutions of the core society at the primary group level, it will inevitably lead to marital assimilation. According to Gordon,

> If children of different ethnic backgrounds belong to the same play group, later the same adolescent cliques and at college the same fraternities and sororities; if the parents belong to the same country club and invite each other to their homes for dinner; it is completely unrealistic not to expect these children, now grown, to love and marry each other, in spite of ethnic extraction.[8]

Gordon also predicts that all of the other types of assimilation will follow once structural assimilation is achieved. The price of such assimilation is the disappearance of the ethnic group as a separate entity and the loss of its distinctive values. Given this perspective, different groups can be located at different stages of the assimilative process. Blacks are culturally but not structurally assimilated; Jews still retain some cultural and structural distinctiveness. Asians may have acculturated but remain structurally separate.

A model proposed by Blauner provides a contrasting perspective.[9] Not all groups have followed the immigration, acculturation, assimilation theme. The key points to Blauner's model include:

1. Forced involuntary entry.
2. Impact of interaction that is much more dramatic than the natural pace of acculturation.

3. Rule of group by outsiders.
4. Racism against group.

Blauner titles his model domestic, or internal, colonialism and likens the relationship of America's racial minorities to the dominant society to the practices of the European colonial powers over their conquered populations in Africa and Asia. The conquered population is forced to participate in someone else's society, whether they wish to or not; they are subjected to a wide number of restrictions in their social, economic, and political mobility, and their culture and social institutions are attacked, often to the point where they are forced to give up their own "inferior" ways and accept the ways of their "superiors."

Asian experiences lie somewhere between the assimilation model of Gordon and the domestic colonial model of Blauner, especially since Asian immigration has covered a wide span of years and faced a number of different Americas. For example, many early Asian migrants came as contract laborers, with the view of returning at the end of their contract period. Thus, they were not truly voluntary immigrants, striving to assimilate into the dominant society, nor was their migration totally involuntary. Early Asian immigrants to Hawaii lived on separate ethnic plantations, ruled by "outsiders."[10] For the majority, acculturation was primarily functional—they learned enough about the new culture to survive, but most retained their Asian cultural ways, reinforced by the hostility of the American society. There were restrictions on their social, economic, and political mobility, and there was racism.

For example, as an early progressive and well-educated California editor put it early in this century:

> Race counts more than anything else in the world. It is the mark God placed on those whom he put asunder.... An educated Japanese would not be a welcomed suitor for the hand of any American's daughter, but an Italian of the commonest standing would be a more welcomed suitor than the finest gentleman of Japan.... If we deal with the Japanese question now, our descendants will have no race questions to deal with. If not, they, like antebellum South Carolinians, will leave a race question which their descendants will have to deal with, and against which they will be helpless.[11]

But at other times, Asian experiences were different; thus, no one model can encompass the experiences of all Asian groups. Racism is most effective if the dominant group is successful in convincing a dominated group that there are "superiors" and "inferiors." It is to the credit of America's racial minorities and to the American system that its racial minorities have never fully accepted a permanent inferior position.

Most of the generalizations concerning Asians concentrate on the male population. Very little information concerning the role of Asian females is available, yet if life for men in the early days was difficult, then the lives of women must have been doubly difficult. Stories of women going back to work alongside their men almost immediately after childbirth are commonly heard. Glenn sees the Asian females of that period as victims of triple oppression—trapped in the most menial types of work, such as houseworker or seamstress; subjected to institutional racism; and subordinated at home by a patriarchical family system.[12]

PURPOSES OF THIS BOOK

This book has a number of purposes. One is to place in one volume the material on Asian Americans that is currently scattered in widely disparate sources. Another is to provide a cohesive, interdisciplinary account, tying in historical and social psychological perspectives.

The book includes separate chapters on most Asian American groups and examines their different patterns of adaptation, based on the interaction of what they brought with them and the reactions of the host society. Prior to the presentation of each group, there is an overall look at immigration legislation (Chapter 2), since legislative acts have been and will continue to be crucial to any understanding of Asians in America.

Chapters 3 and 4 are devoted to the Chinese; Chapters 5 and 6, to the Japanese. These two groups represent the "old" immigrants—the ones who arrived in the nineteenth century. (Chinese immigration still continues at a heavy pace.)

Chapter 7 focuses on the Filipino. Although a current spelling is Pilipino, we are using the old spelling, primarily because the vast majority of our historical references use it. (But we understand why the newer term, Pilipino, is in use—many older terms, used by colonial powers, have been replaced throughout the third world, as Rhodesia has become Zimbabwe, and so on.)

Chapter 8 deals with the Asian Indians—a group that represents the second most populous country in Asia but is often omitted when Asian Americans are discussed. The Asian Indians are a sizable Asian American minority, but little has been written about them.

Chapter 9 is about the Koreans, one of the fastest-growing Asian groups. Their migration is still in progress, but there is a significant literature about them, particularly from the social sciences.

Chapter 10 covers a "hidden" minority, the Pacific Islanders. This chapter looks at the Samoans, the Guamanians, and the native Hawaiians. They do not readily fit as Asian Americans but have been placed in the category by federal authorities, albeit as Asian American/Pacific Islanders.

Chapter 11 presents information on the immigrants from Southeast Asia—Vietnamese, Laotians, and Cambodians. They have come largely as refugees, as differentiated from regular immigrants, but their processes of dealing with the new culture appear similar to those of other immigrants.

Chapter 12 presents data on the current status of Asian Americans, reporting on their socioeconomic accomplishments and taking note of the fields in which they are not doing so well. Chapter 13, the final chapter, presents a model for analyzing Asian American adaptation to America.

NOTES

1. Neil Sandberg, *Jewish Life in Los Angeles* (Lanham, Md.: University Press of America, 1986).
2. Him Mark Lai, Ginny Lim, and Judy Yung, *Island: Poetry and History of Chinese Immigrants on Angel Island, 1910–1940* (San Francisco: San Francisco Study Center, 1980).
3. A scientific definition of race is difficult to defend, especially when one talks about "pure races." Much of the literature speaks of four or five races, popularly known as "whites," "blacks," "yellows," "reds," and sometimes "browns" for Caucasian, Negroid, Mongoloid, Amerindian, and Malaysian.
4. Philip Gleason, "American Identity and Americanization," in Stephan Thernstrom et al., eds., *Harvard Encyclopedia of American Ethnic Groups* (Cambridge, Mass.: Harvard University Press, 1980), pp. 31–58.
5. Ronald Takaki, *Iron Cages* (New York: Alfred Knopf, 1979).
6. See Chapter 12 for demographic data from the U.S. Census and other sources.
7. Milton Gordon, *Assimilation in American Life* (New York: Oxford University Press, 1964).
8. Ibid., p. 80.
9. Robert Blauner, *Racial Oppression in America* (New York: Harper and Row, 1972). See also Harry H. L. Kitano, *Race Relations,* 3rd ed. (Englewood Cliffs, N.J.: Prentice-Hall, 1985), Chapter 5.
10. Ronald Takaki, *Pau Hana* (Honolulu: University of Hawaii Press, 1983).
11. Roger Daniels, *The Politics of Prejudice* (Berkeley and Los Angeles: University of California Press, 1962), pp. 23–24.
12. Evelyn Nakano Glenn, *Issei, Nisei, War Bride* (Philadelphia: Temple University Press, 1986).

2

Immigration Laws and Their Effects

Discrimination against Asians has been evident from the very early years of their migration to America, although there have been changes in recent years. Nevertheless, "Asian bashing," a relatively modern but appropriate term, most often directed against a specific group, has never fully disappeared. One major issue has been immigration, which has led to restriction and exclusion and raised barriers to Asian "equality," whether immigrant or native born. Words such as yellow hordes, pagans, and unassimilable were indicative of majority group feelings against immigrants from across the Pacific, and these prejudices led to anti-Asian legislation. Legalized discrimination took many forms, but immigration and naturalization legislation was especially critical. Thus, a review of that legislation will serve as a background to some of the major problems that Asian immigrants faced.

Many recent historians divide the history of immigration into six periods: (1) the colonial period, during which neither Great Britain nor the American colonies had effective control of immigration and when the overwhelming number of all immigrants came from the British Isles and were Protestant; (2) the era of the American Revolution and beyond (1775–1820), when war, both here and in Europe, inhibited immigration; (3) the era of the "old" immigration (1820–ca. 1880), in which most immigrants came from the British Isles, Germany, and Scandinavia and were primarily Protestant Christians (large numbers of Irish and Germans were Roman Catholic); (4) the era of the "new" immigration (ca. 1880–1924), when most immigrants came from central, southern, and eastern Europe and were largely Roman Catholic, Greek Orthodox, and Jewish; (5) the era of the national-origins quota system (1924–65), in which rigorous regulation reduced the volume of immigration greatly, and most immigrants were from the countries of the "old" immigration or the quota-free new world; (6) the era of liberalized restrictions (1965 to the present), in which most immigrants have come from Asia and Latin America, or, as Reimers would put it, the "Third World."[1] The 1986 Immigration Reform Act focused primarily on the "undocumented" problem from south of the border.

There was no significant immigration legislation before the passage of the Chinese Exclusion Act in 1882. Some eastern states had attempted to stop with restrictive laws what they had considered the flood of undesirable immigration from Ireland and Germany in the 1830s and 1840s, but the United States Supreme Court in the *Passenger Cases* of 1849 ruled that such laws were unconstitutional because the commerce clause of the Constitution gave the federal government preemptive control over "domestic and foreign commerce," and immigration, the court ruled, was "foreign commerce."[2] The adoption of the Fourteenth Amendment in 1868 made "all persons born . . . in the United States" citizens (this would later have a tremendous impact on the lives of native-born Asian Americans, although the amendment was concerned solely with blacks). Two years later, in a revision of the naturalization statutes, Congress accordingly made "white persons and persons of African descent" eligible for citizenship. Attempts by Charles Sumner, the radical Republican Senator from Massachusetts, and a few others to make naturalization color-blind were overwhelmingly voted down by Congress. Therefore, the definition of who could become American by naturalization barred only Asians.[3]

It should be noted, however, that naturalization procedures were not uniform, and some judges allowed individual Asians—Chinese, Japanese, and Asian Indians—to become citizens. The question was finally settled in two Supreme Court cases, *Ozawa v. U.S.* in 1922 and *Thind v. U.S.* in 1923. These cases made it clear that Asians of any hue could not become naturalized. Although since 1870 the Constitution has guaranteed citizenship to persons who are born in the United States, naturalization is governed by statute and, as we shall see, has been modified often.

UP TO 1924

Direct federal discrimination against Asian immigration began in 1882. In that year Congress passed the first significant restrictive immigration law, the Chinese Exclusion Act, whereby the immigration of Chinese laborers was suspended for ten years. In 1892 the Geary Act extended these exclusion laws for another decade, and in 1902 the exclusion of Chinese immigrants was extended indefinitely.

It is clear that the actions taken against the Chinese were a culmination of a host of anti-Chinese actions, which included lynchings, murders, and race riots. Although there were never more than 125,000 Chinese in the whole United States—almost all of them in the Far West—the fear of massive Chinese immigration and of economic competition, as well as the racism of the majority of whites, was sufficient to offset more moderate voices. *Exclusion,* rather than *restriction,* became the law of the land.

Sizable, but still relatively small, amounts of Japanese immigration began shortly after the Chinese exclusion laws became effective. Similar feelings about their undesirability soon arose; in 1907–08 there was a diplomatic "Gentlemen's Agreement" between the United States and Japan by which Japan agreed to limit the number of laborers emigrating to the United States.

In 1917, Congress created a "barred zone," whereby natives of China, South and Southeast Asia, the Asian part of Russia, Afghanistan, Iran, part of Arabia, and the Pacific and Southeast Asian Islands not owned by the United States were declared inadmissible. Japan, for diplomatic reasons, was left out of the barred zone. Filipinos and some Samoans were allowed to enter as U.S. nationals, but they could not be naturalized.

Racial, national, and ethnic discrimination was broadened and codified in the Immigration Act of 1924. Japanese were added to the barred list. Europeans were given national quotas. Northern and western Europeans were given relatively large quotas—in 1931, for example, the quota for Great Britain and Northern Ireland was 65,000, Ireland almost 18,000, and Germany nearly 26,000. Eastern and southern European countries received relatively small quotas—in 1931, Poland and Italy got about 6,000 each. Originally Congress spoke of making the admissions representative of the ethnic mix of the current population, but when the majority discovered that this would give relatively large quotas to countries like Italy and Poland, it pushed the determining date of quotas back to the census of 1890. The blatant bias of the act is clear. A person of Chinese ancestry, for example, who was born in England and was a British subject, was still barred as an "alien ineligible for citizenship"; similarly, although Japan and other Asian countries were given token annual quotas of 100, no person of discernible Asian ancestry could enter on those quotas. They were reserved for "white persons" who happened to be born in Asia. (In theory, persons of "African descent" were also eligible to use quota spaces, but there were few, if any, of them.)

Except for Japanese, who were barred by the unilateral abrogation of the gentlemen's agreement that the 1924 act effected, Asians were not really affected by the 1924 act. They were already effectively excluded. The main brunt of the act was borne by southern and eastern Europeans. The whole anti-immigrant movement was based on a number of factors: fear of foreigners, at first Asians but soon after Europeans with different and supposedly inferior cultures and genes; economic fears of being outworked and undercut by those with a lower standard of living; fears, particularly after the Russian Revolution of 1917, of incoming radicals; and a racism that was directed not only against "non-whites" but that also found one white ethnic type—variously styled "Anglo-Saxon" or "Nordic"—superior to all the rest. In the 1930s, Adolf Hitler and others would take such notions a step further. Nazi theories of a "master race" resulted in the Holocaust, in which not only millions of Jews but also Poles, Gypsies, and other "inferior types" were put to death. While not going that far, the overwhelming majority of Americans "knew" that it was the "white culture" that had built the country, and the notion that the "yellow races" in particular could ever assimilate was felt to be preposterous.

The sobering generalization concerning this era comes from the work of Higham, who found that it was not only the crackpots or extremists, although they were certainly involved, but also people of the American mainstream who wished to close America's doors.[4]

THE 1930s

The Great Depression had no legislative effect on the national-origins law of 1924, but it did reduce immigration generally, with many immigrants returning to their native lands for economic reasons. It seemed as if the exclusion of Asians would remain a permanent part of American policy. Further legislation was enacted to close a loophole concerning the Filipinos, who, after the American conquest of the Philippines in 1898, were legally American nationals, not aliens, and were therefore free to enter the United States. The loophole was closed by a curious nativist solution. Philippine independence was backed, and a 1934 law promised Philippine independence in 1945. The law gave the islands an annual quota of fifty, as opposed to the unlimited ability to enter that their former status as "nationals" had provided. In addition, two subsequent statutes, in 1935 and 1939, enabled any Filipino living in the United States to return to the Philippines at public expense.[5]

The end of the 1930s and the beginning of the 1940s saw a "refugee problem." Many Jews and others sought to flee the Nazis, but except for a fortunate few, the barriers were not dropped. The thinking that was behind the 1924 act prevailed; the fear of foreigners and the desire to maintain an immigration status quo led to a hands-off policy. Very little assistance was given to the refugees, and, as Vice-President Walter Mondale observed in 1979, we could have provided asylum, but we "failed the test of civilization."[6]

THE 1940s

The years of World War II saw a few changes in immigration policy; the most important change for Asians was the repeal of Chinese exclusion. Just as the Chinese Exclusion Act in 1882 saw the inauguration of race- and ethnicity-related immigration restrictions, the repeal of Chinese exclusion in 1943 was the start of a legislative process that would end with the removal of race and ethnicity as immigration and naturalization criteria.

The 1943 repeal, however, maintained racist elements. For example, although it set a quota of 105 annually, a Chinese born in Canada would still be charged to the Chinese quota, whereas a white native of Canada could enter as a nonquota immigrant.

The basic reason behind the legislation was China's status as an ally in World War II. President Roosevelt, in signing the legislation, talked about the affection and regard that tied the two countries together and stated that "an unfortunate barrier" had been removed between allies and that the "war effort in the Far East" would be pursued with "a greater vigor" because of it.[7]

The idea that a quota could be granted only to "good governments" does not stand for a principled policy, and there were a few pleas to treat all Asians equally. Owen Lattimore even suggested privately that a repeal of Japanese exclusion, though Japan was then our wartime enemy, would be a message that "we were fighting against Japanese militarism and imperialism, not the Japanese people." However, he realistically saw the difficulty of getting such a proposal passed.[8]

In 1946, Congress extended the privilege of naturalization to Filipinos and "persons of races indigenous to India" and gave a small quota to the latter.[9] President Truman raised the Filipino quota to 100 by proclamation.[10]

Other Asians, including Japanese and Koreans, were still ineligible for naturalization and thus barred as immigrants. However, in 1946, Congress approved a law that placed Chinese wives of American citizens on a nonquota basis, and in 1950 the law was liberalized to give spouses and minor children of members of the armed forces the same rights.[11] These rights were extended to Japanese and other Asians after 1952.

There was also a continuing liberalization of other immigration policies. In 1948, the first of two Displaced Persons Acts was passed, which marked the beginning of a positive policy toward refugees. The United

States accepted the International Refugee Organization definition of "displaced persons" as those who were

> victims ... of the nazi or fascist ... or ... quisling regimes ... or Spanish Republicans and other victims of the Falangist regime in Spain ... (or) persons who were considered refugees before the outbreak of the second world war, for reasons of race, religion, nationality, or political opinion ... who (have) been deported, or obliged to leave (their) country of nationality or of former habitual residence.[12]

1950–1965

The McCarran-Walter Act of 1952 was the first general immigration act since 1924. In most ways it was a continuation of the national-origins model, with several major innovations. It removed all racial and ethnic bars to immigration and naturalization and provided for family unification. Female citizens were permitted to bring alien husbands to America on a nonquota basis. But the act retained enough of the old injustices that one scholar wrote: "Into this omnibus bill, Congress packed all the hypocrisy, the malevolence, the arrogance, the racial resentments of earlier laws and earlier moods."[13]

However, this was probably an overreaction, since race was dropped as a restriction. This was the main reason that many Japanese Americans supported the bill. For the first time, Japan was given a quota of 185 immigrants per year, and Japanese residents, heretofore classified as "aliens ineligible for citizenship," were now able to obtain naturalization. As a consequence, the Japanese American Citizens League lobbied for the legislation and supported an override of President Truman's veto.

Between 1952 and 1964, nearly 63,000 Japanese, more than 5,000 a year, were able to immigrate to the United States. Most of them came as nonquota immigrants, that is, as parents, spouses, children, or siblings of United States citizens. Similarly, more than 30,000 Chinese women, many of whom had been separated from their husbands for decades, entered as nonquota immigrants by 1960.

The Commission on Immigration and Naturalization, appointed by President Truman, issued a report shortly before the end of his administration that was highly critical of the 1952 act. The report made a number of recommendations, including the abolition of the national-origins system. It recommended a unified quota system that would allocate visas without regard to national origin, race, creed, or color. Such a system would be based on five principles: the right of asylum, reunion of families, needs in the United States, needs in the "Free World," and general immigration. The report also proposed the annual admission of 100,000 refugees, expellees, escapees, and remaining displaced persons.[14] Many of these recommendations were implemented twelve years later in the Immigration Act of 1965. The Refugee Relief Act of 1953 authorized the admission of 205,000 nonquota persons for the next two and a half years. Reflecting the Cold War atmosphere, a refugee was then defined as

> any person in a country or area which is either Communist or Communist-dominated, who because of persecution, fear of persecution, natural calamity or military operation is out of his usual place of abode and is unable to return thereto, who has not been firmly resettled, and who is in urgent need of assistance for the essentials of life or for transportation.

A new feature in this legislation was the inclusion, for the first time, of refugees of Chinese origin, as long as they were vouched for by the Nationalist Chinese government.[15]

THE 1965 IMMIGRATION ACT

The 1965 Immigration Act abolished the national-origins system and substituted hemispheric quotas. Western hemispheric immigration, up to then unlimited, was to be limited to 120,000 annually after 1968, without limitation by country. The eastern hemisphere quota was set at 170,000, with a limit of 20,000 from any one country. President Lyndon B. Johnson, in signing this important piece of legislation, said, "This bill that we will sign today is not a revolutionary bill. It does not affect the lives of millions. It will not reshape the structure of our daily lives, or really add importantly to our wealth or our power."[16]

President Johnson was no doubt accurately portraying the intent of Congress. As Reimers indicates, the legislators thought that southern and eastern European immigration would grow and did not anticipate the tremendous growth of Asian immigration. In his speech, Johnson stressed the wrong done to immigrants from southern and eastern Europe, and although he did mention "developing continents," there was no other reference to Asian or Third World immigration.

The 1965 act gave high priority to the reunification of families, which has largely become a chain migration. An immigrant family arrives, puts down roots, acquires permanent residence and then citizenship, and brings eligible relatives into the country. Another priority was given to skilled and unskilled workers deemed to be in short supply in the United States. The act also included a large number of qualitative restrictions regarding mental retardation, insanity, addiction, prostitution, and radicalism.

The most visible beneficiaries of the preference provisions of the 1965 law, as amended, have been Asians, especially Chinese, Koreans, Asian Indians, Filipinos, Vietnamese, and other Southeast Asian ethnic groups. In

1940 the Asian American population was about 250,000, with about the same number in Hawaii; in 1960 the figure was 900,000 (including those in Hawaii). But by 1980 the Asian American population had boomed to nearly 3.5 million, and in 1985 the population reached an estimated 5.1 million. Thus, the group that was singled out for exclusion in the early part of the century now finds that it has become the prime beneficiary of legislation passed in the latter part of the century.

In late 1986, after years of acrimonious debate, the Immigration Reform Act was passed. It seems unlikely that this new law will affect immigration from Asia significantly, although some "undocumented" Asian American aliens may be able to regularize their status under the act's complex and controversial amnesty provisions. Some earlier "reform" proposals would have reduced the number of "slots" available to relatives under the preference provisions; this reduction would have adversely affected the number of Asians able to come here, but none of these provisions survived into the final measure.

In summary, there has been a considerable change in American immigration policy toward Asians. The Chinese, the first group to be legally excluded, years later were the first formerly excluded Asian group to be legally admissible. Other Asian groups have had similar experiences—legal exclusion, then token quotas, and finally admission through "normal" immigration procedures. Naturalization procedures were more tolerant. First-generation Asians were denied naturalization privileges until the 1940s and 1950s, but their American-born children were, after 1870, automatically American citizens.

The changes in law have changed the composition of our immigrant population. Asian Americans, including those arriving as refugees, have become the fastest-growing group of immigrants to America.

A more detailed account of recent refugee legislation and its affect on Asian immigration appears in Chapter 11.

NOTES

1. The best recent history of immigration is Thomas Archdeacon, *Becoming American: An Ethnic History* (New York: The Free Press, 1983). For a survey of the period after 1965, David M. Reimers, *Still the Golden Door: The Third World Comes to America* (New York: Columbia University Press, 1985), is first rate.
2. For brief surveys of constitutional issues and legislation, see Roger Daniels, *Racism and Immigration Restriction* (St. Charles, Mo.: Forum Press, 1974), and Roger Daniels, "Changes in Immigration Law and Nativism Since 1924," *American Jewish History* 76 (1986): 158–80.
3. Act of July 4, 1870.
4. John Higham, *Strangers in the Land* (New Brunswick, N.J.: Rutgers University Press, 1955).
5. Philippine Independence Act, 48 Stat. 456 (Mar. 24, 1934); To Provide Means by Which Certain Filipinos Can Emigrate from the United States, 49 Stat. 478 (July 10, 1935); and Emigration of Filipinos from the United States, 53 Stat. 1133 (July 27, 1939).

6. Mondale speech text, released by the vice-president's press secretary, Saturday, July 21, 1979.

7. Samuel I. Rosenman, ed., *The Public Papers and Addresses of Franklin D. Roosevelt,* 1943 volume (New York: Harper, 1950), 548.

8. Lattimore letter (Mar. 3, 1942), as cited in Fred W. Riggs, *Pressures on Congress: A Study of the Repeal of Chinese Exclusion* (New York: King's Crown, 1950), p. 49.

9. Act of July 2, 1946, 60 Stat. 416.

10. President's Proclamation No. 2696 of July 4, 1946, 11 Fed. Reg. 7,517 (July 9, 1946).

11. Act of Aug. 9, 1946, 60 *Stat.* 975, and Act of Aug. 14, 1950, 64 *Stat.* 464.

12. Constitution of the International Refugee Organization, annex I, secs. A and B.

13. J. Campbell Bruce, *The Golden Door: The Irony of Our Immigration Policy* (New York: Random House, 1954).

14. President's Commission on Immigration and Naturalization, *Whom We Shall Welcome* (Washington, D.C.: Government Printing Office, 1953).

15. 67 Stat. 401.

16. *Public Papers of the Presidents, Lyndon B. Johnson, 1965,* "Remarks at the Signing of the Immigration Bill, Liberty Island, New York, Oct. 3, 1965" (Washington, D.C.: Government Printing Office, 1966), pp. 1037–40.

3

The Chinese:
The Early Years

No one is sure when the first Chinese came to America. Isolated navigators may have crossed the Pacific before the voyages of Columbus. We know that a few Chinese were in Mexico in the 17th century and that some Chinese seamen were in northeastern U.S. ports such as Philadelphia and Boston in the late 18th century. But the first trans-Pacific immigrants from China almost certainly came to San Francisco just before the fabled Gold Rush of 1849. By 1860 there were more than 30,000 Chinese in the United States, almost all of them in California. Who were these Asian argonauts, and what drew them 7,000 miles from home?

THE SOJOURNER PATTERN

The second question is easier to answer than the first. The Chinese, along with hundreds of thousands of others, were drawn to California by gold and the economic boom that its discovery set off. Between 1850 and 1860, California's population more than quadrupled, to nearly 400,000. Almost all of the Chinese were from one small part of South China, Kwangtung, and more than 90 percent of them were adult males. Most of them probably intended to come to the "Gold Mountain"—as the Chinese characters for

California can be translated—work for a time, and then return home "rich," which meant by Chinese standards a few hundred dollars. This has caused some scholars to label Chinese as "sojourners" and thus not immigrants, and to proceed to blame many of the troubles the Chinese encountered in America on their refusal to assimilate. This "blaming the victim" for discrimination is an old and ongoing device used by groups in power to excuse their own behavior. The question must be asked, How different were the Chinese from other immigrants to this country?

A recent student of immigration, Professor Thomas Archdeacon, has made it very clear that Chinese sojourners had their counterparts in other ethnic groups.

> The Chinese thought of themselves as sojourners who would return with honor after spending their working years in America. Among members of many European groups . . . the hope became to earn enough money in a brief period to secure the family's farmstead, to provide dowries for female relatives, or to reestablish themselves solidly in the mother country. For these people, migration to the United States became an extension of the international seasonal migrations that were becoming common in Europe.[1]

Archdeacon also shows that many ethnic groups had very heavy male migration (Scandinavians, 61.3 percent; Italians, 74.5 percent; and Greeks 87.8 percent) and a high rate of return migration (Scandinavians, 15.4 percent; Italians, 45.6 percent; Greeks, 53.7 percent).

Thus, the sojourner pattern was common to many immigrant groups, European as well as Asian. What made the Chinese experience in America unique were three other factors: (1) their race, (2) the region to which they came, and (3) the fact that in 1882 they became the first group of voluntary immigrants ever to be shut out by the American government. Their continued immigration to America, despite undisguised and brutal discrimination, reflects the often wretched conditions under which they lived at home. China, a once great and powerful empire, was by the mid-19th century in a long period of decline.

THE CHINESE DIASPORA

South China, the home of almost all of the Chinese immigrants to America, had a long tradition of both political rebellion and emigration. South China was the springboard from which most of the worldwide diffusion of Chinese—what can be called the Chinese diaspora—began and continued. It was also the main contact point for British, Americans, and other Westerners and the region of their first concessions. Places such as Hong Kong and Macao became ports through which not only foreign goods like opium came in, but also from which Chinese people embarked for new worlds.

The labor migration of Asians outside of Asia—what the British scholar Hugh Tinker has called "a new system of slavery"—began a little earlier in the 19th century with the bringing of indentured workers from India to work the sugar fields of Mauritius. The indentured Indians, used largely in the British Empire, were soon followed by Chinese who were taken to places like Cuba and Peru under abominable conditions in what came to be known as the "coolie trade." Later in the 19th century and on into the 20th, Japanese, Filipinos, Koreans, Southeast Asians, and even a few thousand Indonesians were brought under semifree conditions of indenture to labor in the plantation and extractive economies of the Indian Ocean, East and Southern Africa, the Pacific, and the Caribbean.[2] While some of these Asian workers entered willingly into their contracts or indentures, others were kidnapped or "shanghaied," a word that came into the English language in 1871. Still others were tricked into going where they did not want to go. One American consular report from the mid-19th century speaks of Chinese being lured onto ships that took them to work in the deadly guano fields of Peru's Pacific islands or the sugar plantations of Cuba; the Chinese believed that they were being taken to the gold fields of California or Australia. As we shall see, most of the early Asian immigrants to Hawaii, both Chinese and Japanese, were brought in as indentured laborers. Some immigrants to the United States proper, immigrants from both Europe and Asia, came as contract laborers, but such contracts, after the abolition of slavery, were all but impossible to enforce.

The coolie trade did not come to America. Tens of thousands of Chinese, and later other Asians, were too willing to come to the United States to make their "fortunes" for coercion to be necessary. Most of them went into debt to come here. In the 1850s, for example, Chinese in Hong Kong who wanted to come to America could borrow the equivalent of $70—$50 for passage and $20 for expenses—if they would obligate themselves to repay $200. This "credit ticket system" continued for almost a century; its persistence is the best evidence that the Chinese were free immigrants and that most borrowers paid back their loans.[3]

ANTI-CHINESE SENTIMENT

In the first two decades of Chinese immigration—the census of 1870 found some 60,000 Chinese, with almost 50,000 in California—Chinese worked at gold mining, in agriculture, at various urban occupations, and, most spectacularly, as the builders of the western leg of the first transcontinental railroad. After an initial welcome, the Chinese soon became the targets of both legal and extralegal harassment and, beyond that, of sometimes murderous violence. The California Foreign Miners Tax, originally directed at Hispanics, soon had Chinese miners as its chief target. In San Francisco, which became the metropolis of Chinese America, a variety of municipal ordinances put special taxes on their livelihood, fined them for living in overcrowded tenements, and even required arrested Chinese to have their heads shaved. That most of these regulations as well as many anti-Chinese statutes passed by the state legislature were eventually declared unconstitutional by various courts is beside the point. The fact of the matter was, as an early California historian noted, that "the legislation on Oriental labor sprang from the people." The new California constitution, adopted by a popularly elected convention in 1879, was loaded with specifically anti-Chinese provisions, which sought, among other things, to bar the Chinese from employment and ownership of land. As one delegate noted, some sections of this document amounted to "starvation by constitutional provision."[4]

Even worse was the fact that Chinese were often defenseless targets for all kinds of violence, ranging from casual abuse on city streets to mass murder. Until well after the Civil War, California courts refused to accept the testimony of blacks, American Indians, or Chinese; even when Chinese testimony was admitted, testimony against whites was almost always ignored by juries. From Los Angeles to Seattle and as far east as Denver and Rock Springs, Wyoming, Chinese were run out of town or beaten and killed by mobs whose members were almost never brought to justice. The worst atrocities were in Los Angeles in 1871, where between eighteen and twenty-one Chinese were hanged or burned to death; in Rock Springs in 1885, where at least twenty-eight Chinese coal miners were shot to death; and in desolate Hell's Canyon, on the Idaho-Oregon border, in 1887, where thirty-one Chinese gold miners were robbed and murdered. At least some of the killers were caught but not convicted. As a contemporary white rancher noted, "I guess if they had killed 31 white men something would have been done about it, but none of the jury know the Chinamen or cared much about it, so they turned the men loose."[5]

During the 1870s the Chinese population in America increased by about two thirds, to just over 100,000, with more than 95 percent in the far western states. This decade witnessed the development of the anti-Chinese political movement in California and throughout the West, sparked by working-class agitation led by a recent Irish immigrant, Dennis Kearney. The 1870s were a time of economic hardship in the Far West, and the Chinese made convenient scapegoats. Kearney's Workingman's Party demanded a whole range of economic and social reforms, but the one demand that dominated the movement was that "The Chinese Must GO!" As an 1877 party manifesto put it:

> before the world we declare that the Chinaman must leave our shores. We declare that white men, and women, and boys, and girls, cannot live as the people of the great republic should live and compete with the single Chinese coolie in the labor market. We declare that we cannot hope to drive the China-

man away by working cheaper than he does. None but an enemy would expect it of us; none but an idiot could hope for success; none but a degraded coward and slave would make the effort. To an American, death is preferable to life on a par with the Chinaman.[6]

The economic radicalism of the Kearneyites never prevailed, although its anti-Chinese sentiments were shared by the overwhelming majority of the population. Some employers of labor insisted that the Chinese presence was necessary for economic growth, and a few Christian missionaries pointed out that their soul-saving endeavors in Asia would be hampered if Chinese here were ill-treated. In addition, the recently negotiated Burlingame Treaty with China (1868), which gave great advantages to American merchants and shippers hungry for the China market, had guaranteed Chinese the right of immigration.

CHINESE EXCLUSION

These obstacles were soon surmounted. A new treaty was negotiated with China in 1880, giving the United States the right to "regulate, limit or suspend" Chinese immigration, but not to prohibit it absolutely. After some political maneuvering, including a presidential veto, the Chinese Exclusion Act of 1882 was adopted, which barred the immigration of Chinese laborers for ten years. (The act was renewed in 1892 for another ten-year term and made "permanent" in 1902.)

It can be argued that the Chinese Exclusion Act was the hinge on which all American immigration policy turned. Prior to 1882 there were no significant legal inhibitions to immigration. From that time until 1924, progressively stricter immigration laws were passed, excluding not only other Asian ethnic groups—Asian Indians, Japanese and Koreans—but greatly reducing the immigration of most Europeans as well. In addition, moral, medical, ideological, and economic barriers were raised so that by the mid-1920s and until after World War II the once wide-open golden door of immigration was all but closed. In fact, in some years of the Great Depression of the 1930s, more people emigrated *from* the United States than immigrated to it.

THE STRUCTURE OF CHINESE AMERICAN SOCIETY

When the Chinese Exclusion Act was passed in 1882 there were perhaps 125,000 Chinese in the United States. From that time until sometime in the 1920s, Chinese population in the United States steadily declined (see Table 3–1).

TABLE 3-1   Chinese in the United States, 1890-1940

YEAR	POPULATION
1890	107,620
1900	89,863
1910	71,531
1920	61,639
1930	74,954
1940	77,504

Source: U.S. Census data.

A major reason for this decline was the heavily imbalanced sex ratio in the Chinese American community. In 1890, for example, only 3,868 Chinese females were recorded by the census; there were 26.8 males for every female. This ratio went down steadily, and by 1940 there were 2.9 Chinese American males to every female. In 1940 citizen Chinese for the first time outnumbered alien Chinese, 40,262 to 37,242. But it is necessary to look more closely at the demographic data to get a true picture of the Chinese American community in the years before World War II. Let us take 1920 for our example (see Table 3-2). It is necessary to examine the age structure of the sexes to complete our picture. Chinese males had a median age of 42 years; the largely citizen females, a median age of just 19 years. The largest single five-year cohort of Chinese males, 5,850, were 50–54 years of age; the largest single five-year cohort of females, 1,418, were under 5 years of age. If we subtract all Chinese, male and female, under 10 years of age in 1920, we find that there were almost ten males to every female—9.84 to be precise.

If one were trying to create a population model that would be likely to resist acculturation, one could do a lot worse than to use the reality of Chinese America. Add to that a heavily male-dominated culture, a history of brutal discrimination, extreme residential segregation, and a high degree of cultural differentiation between Chinese and most other Americans, and one can begin to understand why acculturation took relatively long for Chinese Americans as a community. Individual Chinese, of course, successfully acculturated from almost the beginning of Chinese American history. Perhaps the earliest example was Yung Wing (1828–1912), who was born in

TABLE 3-2   Chinese American Population, 1920

	MALE	FEMALE	TOTAL	MALES:FEMALES
All Chinese	53,891	7,748	61,639	7.0:1
Alien	40,573	2,534	43,107	16.0:1
Citizen	13,318	5,214	18,532	2.6:1

Source: U.S. Census data.

southeast China, near Macao. He attended a missionary school in Hong Kong and came to America in 1847. Three years later he entered Yale College and, in 1854, became its first Chinese graduate. In the meantime he had become a Christian and, in spite of the law, a naturalized citizen of the United States. He married an American woman and had a long and distinguished career in both China and America.[7]

CHINESE AMERICAN INSTITUTIONS

As the small but growing native-born segment of the population evolved, it began to form its own American-oriented organizations. The most notable of these was the Native Sons of the Golden State, an organization that was founded in San Francisco in 1895 and that evolved into the Chinese American Citizens Alliance in 1915. The Americanizing thrust of this organization can be seen by the following clause from its first constitution: "It is imperative that no member shall have sectional, clannish, Tong or party prejudices against each other or to use such influence to oppress fellow members. Whoever violates this provision shall be expelled. . . . "[8]

Most Chinese Americans, however, were part of the largely unacculturated "bachelor society" that dominated the Chinatowns of America until World War II. The major institutions of that society were oriented towards China rather than America. Most, if not all, American ethnic groups have had some kind of organizational focus. For many European immigrant groups, much of the focus was provided by ethnic or ethnically oriented churches. Since traditional Chinese religions tended to be familial rather than societal, religion was not a unifying communitywide force, except for the minority who were or became Christians. For most immigrant Chinese the family association, or clan (that is all those who had a common last name and thus a putative common ancestor), was the primary associational focus. Originally village oriented and representing real blood relationships, the clan system was adapted by overseas Chinese to fit conditions wherever Chinese settled. Outside of San Francisco, or "dai fou" (big city) as the Chinese called it, one clan tended to dominate the smaller Chinatowns. Thus, in Pittsburgh, Yees predominated; in Chicago, Moys; and in Denver, Chins. A Moy in Pittsburgh, for example, whose mother or wife had been a Yee, could affiliate himself with and expect support from the powerful Yee clan there.

An even more complex arrangement, called the four-clan association, also arose. Professor Rose Hum Lee has described such a situation in Butte, Montana, whose 710 Chinese residents were in 1880 more than a fifth of the population. There, two four-clan associations arose, and almost all Chinese residents were considered members of one group or the other. The associations were used to settle disputes between individuals and functioned as a kind of court; a loser in a local dispute could always make an appeal back to headquarters in San Francisco. The functions of the family associations were similar to those of the benevolent and protective societies of other ethnocultural groups, sometimes called generically *landsmanschaften*. They tendered protection and mutual aid to members. The family associations, however, went far beyond most other such societies, as they were considered extended family groups. Chinese Americans, many of whom had no blood relatives in this country, would speak of all other members of their association as "clan cousins." A wife was considered a member of her husband's clan. If, however, he predeceased her, often she would be financially assisted by her own clan, as her husband's clan might regard her and her children as not being entitled to the clan's scarce resources. Although they were not "incest groups," marriages within clans and clan associations were discouraged. Thus, in Butte, according to Professor Lee, where there were special tensions between the two four-clan associations, not one of the ninety-nine members of the Chinese American community born in Butte had married a fellow resident of Butte as late as the mid-1940s![9]

In addition to being a member of a clan, each Chinese, at least in theory, belonged to a district association. Originally based on regional districts of Kwangtung Province, the ancestral home of most Chinese immigrants, the associations were eventually governed by an umbrella group, the Chinese Consolidated Benevolent Association, popularly known as the Six Chinese Companies. The Six Companies also resembled *landsmanschaften*, having benevolent and protective functions. They also acted as agents of social control and served as the community's voice to white America. That later capacity was exercised as early as 1853, when Company heads (there were then only four) appeared before a committee of the California legislature. The Companies often hired white lawyers to serve as their spokesmen before national, state, and local governing bodies and courts, and, especially, before the administrative authorities who governed immigration.

In addition, their agents met incoming ships, arranged for the initial housing and employment of migrants, organized medical treatment for the sick, and performed other welfare functions. They also helped to arrange for the shipment of the bones of the dead for burial in China and arbitrated disputes between individual members. In an age when government assumed none of the responsibilities of what is now called the welfare state, ethnic organizations all over the United States performed similar functions.

The Six Companies also came to exert a very high degree of social control over the lives of American Chinese and, in this, were quite unlike most other immigrant community organizations. The association's chief beneficiaries were the merchants who came to dominate it. In China merchants had little prestige and authority; China was governed by a gentry-dominated scholar officialdom whose ideology placed the merchant at the bottom of the social scale. But gentry did not emigrate—the merchants did and quickly turned their economic power into social and political power within the Chinese American community. In addition to trade, merchants derived some of their income from the credit ticket system and from services performed as labor contractors. As the leading lights of the district associations, the merchants used the associations as a mechanism to make sure that individuals not only settled their debts but also paid their share of the Chinese American welfare system. Every Chinese who returned to China was supposed to be checked at the dock to make sure that his debts had been paid. In addition, each returnee was assessed a "tax" to support the welfare functions of the district associations. While, of course, the system was far from 100 percent effective, the fact that it continued to function for decades suggests that it was more than marginally so. Since most Chinese in America thought of themselves as sojourners who would return to China, any system that affected that return was an ideal mechanism for social control.

But parallel to these "establishment" organizations, there developed an "antiestablishment" form of social organization centered around the tongs, or secret societies. Tongs had flourished as illegal opposition to the establishment in China since at least the 14th century and, as happens in nations where political opposition is illegal, often operated in that gray area between political opposition and crime. The Chinese American tongs were patterned on, and probably had some direct relation with, the Triad Society, an anti-Manchu, antiforeign society based in Kwangtung. Unlike the family and district associations, which were universal (all Chinese in America theoretically belonged), the tongs were particularistic. No one knows how many Chinese Americans belonged to tongs. As Chinese were debarred from American political life, the criminal aspect of the tongs predominated here, although it is clear that the tongs played an antiestablishment role within Chinese American society. Eventually some merchants managed to gain membership and influence in some tongs, and some tong leaders gained respectability among the establishment. After 1900, Dr. Sun Yat-sen's revolutionary movement (which became the Kuomintang) found its chief support among American Chinese in the antiestablishment tongs: It was clearly more expedient to support a revolutionary movement through a secret organization. After the Kuomintang became the government of China, of course, the Chinese American establishment embraced it publicly.

The tongs were also involved in criminal activities that preyed on rather than protected the immigrant community. As Daniel Bell has noted, speaking only of European ethnic groups here, crime has been an "American way of life" for many immigrants and second-generation ethnics. For Chinese criminals, the nature of their crime was dictated largely by the nature of their community. The immigrant working men and petty entrepreneurs wanted recreation that could only be provided within the immigrant community. The most popular entertainment seems to have been gambling, chiefly fan-tan, faro, and lottery; as a testimony to Americanization, poker had become popular by 1900. Opium rather than alcohol seems to have been the favored narcotic, although there is no way of determining what percentage of Chinese used the drug. In addition, Chinese brothels and, to a lesser degree, opium-smoking establishments were frequented by whites. Such establishments were quite numerous in Chinese American communities of any size. Since these activities were illegal, lucrative, and semipublic, it is clear that police and politicians in the white community were involved in sanctioning and profiting from them. Competition for scarce commodities—narcotics and Chinese women—often sparked murderous "tong wars," in which all or almost all of the casualties were Chinese. One such war, between the Hip Sings and the Bing Kungs, began with four assassinations in Butte, Montana, in 1922, and quickly spread to every Chinatown in North America and entailed dozens of killings.[10]

In 1921, as Loren Chan has told us, a tong quarrel that started in San Francisco spread throughout northern California and even to Nevada. On the night of August 27, 1921, a 74-year-old laundry proprietor and nominal member of the Bing Kung tong answered a knock at his door in tiny Mina, Nevada. He was shot to death with a Colt .38 by a 29-year-old Canton-born hit man from San Francisco named Gee Jon, who had come to the United States in either 1907 or 1908. The finger man was Hughie Sing, 19 years old and perhaps U.S. born. Sing had been educated in the Nevada public schools and knew the victim well, having been apprenticed to him for two years. Because the perpetrators were arrested and convicted and because they talked—none of which usually happened in tong killings—we know some of the details.[11]

URBAN CHINESE AMERICA

But most Chinese were not hit men—or "hatchet men" as the sensation-seeking white media liked to call them—and their only connection with tongs was as customers of their illegal establishments. Although agriculture, mining, and railroad building were the chief occupations of Chinese Americans until about the 1880s, after that time urban service occcupations—laundries, restaurants, grocery stores—became the pursuits of the majority. Unlike most modern immigrant groups, Chinese were initially found largely in rural and small-town America. In 1880, for example, only about a fifth of all Chinese Americans lived in cities with populations over 100,000. This percentage increased with every census, with close to half of Chinese Americans living in such cities by 1910 and more than seven out of ten by 1940. At first almost all large-city Chinese lived in San Francisco, but by 1940 fewer than one in three did. According to the 1940 census, San Francisco had a Chinese American population of 17,782, with another 3,000 living across the bay in Oakland. There were more than 12,000 Chinese Americans in New York, nearly 5,000 in Los Angeles, and just over 2,000 in

Chicago; Seattle, Portland, Sacramento, and Boston each had between 1,000 and 2,000 Chinese.

While it is customary today to write off such ethnic enclaves as ghettos—and the Chinatowns of America certainly had many of the worst characteristics of ghettos—there was, for many of the Chinese immigrants and Chinese Americans of later generations, a positive aspect of these urban neighborhoods. One Chinatown resident remarked in the 1920s:

> Most of us can live a warmer, freer and a more human life among our relatives and friends than among strangers. . . . Chinese relations with the population outside Chinatown are likely to be cold, formal, and commercial. It is only in Chinatown that a Chinese immigrant has society, friends and relatives who share his dreams and hopes, his hardships, and adventures. Here he can tell a joke and make everybody laugh with him; here he may hear folktales told which create the illusion that Chinatown is really China.[12]

The shift to larger cities, coupled with a shrinking total population, meant not only disappearance or near disappearance of many smaller Chinatowns (Butte's shrank from 710 in 1880 to 88 in 1940) but also a sharp reduction of the percentage of Chinese found in California and the West in general. Although the Golden State contained an absolute majority of Chinese Americans in every census of the period, save that of 1920, within California the incidence of Chinese in the population contracted drastically. In 1860, Chinese had made up 9.2 percent of California's population; in 1940 they represented about 0.6 percent. In some other western states, particularly Idaho, Montana, and Nevada, Chinese population was once quite high. The Idaho Territorial Census of 1870 reported them as 28.5 percent of the population; in that year they were 9.5 percent of the population of neighboring Montana. A decade later Chinese made up 8.7 percent of the population of Nevada. Each of those figures declined rapidly as Chinese were either eliminated from the mining industry or the mining industry declined. These Chinese pioneers have largely been written out of the histories of the western states. When Chinese do appear in them it is as exotic curiosities or as victims. Their pioneering role as developers of the economy of the West has simply been ignored.

The heart of Chinese America was San Francisco, whose Chinatown contained between an eighth and a fifth of all Chinese Americans during the years under discussion. But the city was much more important to the Chinese than mere numbers indicated. As one Chinese American recently remembered about his father's experience early in this century, San Francisco was always his home base, the "safest place," although his work took him up and down California's valleys and as far away as Alaska, where he packed salmon.[13]

San Francisco was the cultural, economic, and administrative hub of Chinese America, the entrepôt through which Chinese goods and services were distributed, the communications center through which information and people passed back and forth between the old world and the new. And, despite Chinese exclusion, large numbers of persons did continue to go back and forth across the Pacific, legally, illegally, and extralegally. Until 1924, American law did not exclude Chinese per se but rather "Chinese laborers." In addition to diplomats and students, who were not technically immigrants (but many of them did stay here), Chinese merchants, or "treaty merchants" as they are sometimes called, and members of their families were admissible. A 1893 law specifically and insultingly defined a merchant and required that the status of any Chinese merchant had to be sworn to "by the testimony of two credible witnesses other than Chinese." Chinese were held up until 1910 in a grim facility on the San Francisco waterfront called The Shed; after that they were kept in the special detention facility in the bay on Angel Island. A missionary described the Shed around 1900 as a place where

> merchants, laborers are all alike penned up, like a flock of sheep . . . often weeks at their own expense . . . while the investigation of their cases moves its slow length along. . . . A man is imprisoned as a criminal who has committed no crime, but has merely failed to find a white man to prove his right to be here.[14]

Even bona fide, upper-class students were often detained. One of the famous Soong sisters, Ailing, was held for more than two weeks when she arrived to attend college even though she was traveling with two white American missionaries and had influential persons intercede for her. As an articulate Chinese diplomat, Wu Ting-fang, put it to New York reporters in 1901: "Why can't you be fair? Would you talk like that if mine was not a weak nation? Would you say it if the Chinese had votes?"[15]

OUTWITTING THE IMMIGRATION LAWS

In addition to the hundreds who came in legally, if with difficulty, there were uncounted others who jumped ship or sneaked across the border; the Puget Sound region, the Mexican border, and Florida seem to have been the most favored places. But perhaps most numerically important of all were the thousands who came in extralegally, that is, by successfully claiming a status they were not entitled to. A combination of circumstances, including incompetent and venal federal employees and the 1906 San Francisco earthquake and fire that destroyed many birth and other records, made it possible for many Chinese men to obtain documents falsely indicating that they were native-born American citizens. If such persons traveled to China and fathered children there, the children were eligible to enter the United States. Those who came in falsely were known in the community as "paper sons." Years later, after a federal amnesty program, begun in the 1950s, was in place, some paper sons were willing to talk. One of them described the process:

> In the beginning my father came in as a laborer. But the 1906 earthquake came along and destroyed all those immigration things. So that was a big chance for a lot of Chinese. They forged themselves certificates saying that they were born in this country, and when the time came they could go back to China and bring back four or five sons just like that! They might make a little money off it, but the main thing was to bring a son or nephew or a cousin in. Now my father thought he was even smarter than that. When he came the second time he didn't use that native-born certificate he had. He got a certificate saying he was a student. But that didn't make sense at all. He thought he was smart being a student, but then, if you came in as a student, how could you bring a son into this country? If he had used his birth certificate, I could have come in as a native son. Instead we had to go back to the same old thing, "paper son." They had to send me over not as my own father's son, but as the son of another cousin from our village.[16]

Another paper son, Jim Quock, told interviewers in 1979 that

> I came to America because my grandfather was here during the Gold Rush times, the 1860s. Somebody robbed him and he got killed and they never found the body or anything. My grandmother told us that grandpa had a lot of gold, made quite a bit of money, you know. So that's what got in my mind, "Oh, this is a fortune. I'm going over to America to make money." Only fifteen at the time. So the only way I could come is to buy a paper, buy a citizen paper. I paid quite a bit of money, too. I paid $102 gold! That's quite a bit of money at that time in China.[17]

Immigration officials quickly caught on to the paper son and other gambits and subjected Chinese applicants for admission to detailed and quite prolonged interrogations. Ironically, some of the first Chinese to get federal jobs were employed to help discover illegal immigrants. The immigrants, of course, developed elaborate countermeasures. As Jim Quock told it:

> They give you a book of about 200 pages to study—all your life, your family, your brother's name, the whole village, almost. They ask you all kinds of questions when you get to the United States, the immigration (station) at Angel Island. . . . I was there for three weeks. They ask you how many steps in your house? Your house had a clock? Questions like that. You got to remember all this. They asked me, "Where do you sleep at your house?" I said, "I sleep with my grandmother and my brother." They say, "Okay which position do you sleep? All kinds of questions, you got to think. But, I'm pretty smart. I said, "Tonight I sleep over here, tomorrow I sleep over there, it doesn't matter."

Archivists have discovered "crib sheets," obviously written for paper sons, that describe in detail some Chinese village. It is clear that most of the thousands of successful paper sons were intelligent, alert, and more than marginally literate.

U.S. immigration records show almost 95,000 individual entries of Chinese "immigrants" between 1883 and the end of Chinese exclusion in 1943, an average of about 1,500 a year. Many of these were former residents returning, and many individuals came several times. Until 1924, when the immigration law made it impossible, perhaps 150 Chinese women per year were admitted as wives of either citizens or treaty merchants. A 1930 act relaxed this ban, as long as the marriage had taken place before the 1924 law went into effect, and allowed an average of sixty women a year until the Japanese attack on Pearl Harbor. Thus, the sexual imbalance of Chinese immigration was reinforced by Chinese custom and American law.

Obviously, large numbers of the "bachelor" immigrants to the United States had wives in China. The 1930 census, for example, showed four times as many married Chinese men here as married Chinese women. These separated families, called "mutilated families" by the sociologist Charles Frederick Marsden, far outnumbered "normal," united families in the Chinese American community until well after the end of World War II. A similar condition prevailed for the same basic reasons in Canada. Peter S. Li's study of the pattern of Chinese marriage in Canada is more thorough than any study done for the United States. Of 22,777 Chinese Canadian families in 1941, Li found only 1,177 "intact conjugal families" (5.2 percent); 1,459 "broken families" (6.4 percent), in which one or both partners were widowed or divorced; and 20,141 "mutilated families" (88.4 percent), with the wife outside of Canada.

The data for the United States are surely similar. Because of this pattern of family life, the acculturation of many Chinese Americans, including many putative native-born citizens, was retarded. Many immigrant "bachelors" of several generations could spend most of a lifetime in American Chinatowns without learning more than a handful of English phrases. Conversely, of course, there were many thousands of second-generation Chinese Americans who broke through at least some of the ethnic barriers and achieved real acculturation.[18]

The contrast is well illustrated in one of the most annoying Chinese American cultural stereotypes, the Charlie Chan movies, rightly resented by most Chinese Americans today. Yet even stereotypes have their value, and the contrast between the wise, inscrutable Chinese American detective— always played by Caucasian actors—and his wisecracking, shallow number one and number two sons—played by skilled Chinese American actors such as Keye Luke and Victor Sen Yung—is not unrelated to the reality of generational conflict in the Chinese American community in the pre–World War II years. A more sophisticated treatment of the generation gap may be found in the autobiographies of Jade Snow Wong, *Fifth Chinese Daughter*

(1950) and *No Chinese Stranger* (1975), and of Pardee Lowe, *Father and Glorious Descendant* (1943).

The Chinese American community was clearly undergoing great change in the years just before the Japanese attack on Pearl Harbor. The rise of the native-born community, although overstated by the enumeration of paper sons, and the dying off of the older generation were pushing the community, as a whole, toward greater acculturation. But World War II, which changed the lives of most Americans, accelerated change within the Chinese and other Asian American communities even more rapidly than for most of the rest of the nation.

SUMMARY

There is no question that the Chinese talked, dressed, and acted differently from the "preferred" norms of the "Anglo" society, but so did members of almost every other immigrant group. More critical was that the Chinese "looked different," which ran into the rampant racism that was a part of the United States at the end of the 19th and the beginning of the 20th century. It is from this background that the adaptation of the Chinese becomes understandable.

Acculturation works most readily for the young, for those who have an opportunity to go through the American school system and for those with an expectation of participating in the mainstream. It does not work as well for those who are isolated and denied access, the segregated, those who are older, and those who expect to return to the home country. A pluralistic adaptation, it is hoped, of some degree of equality seems more appropriate.

Acculturation, integration, and participation in the mainstream are also appropriate for those who come in families. Thus, although parents may never become full participants, it is their expectation that their children will. Being American is also for those who can become citizens and where citizenship means access to economic, political, and social opportunities. It means justice and equality; it means a full identity. It does not mean second-class citizenship.

As we have seen, most of the early Chinese did not easily acculturate, integrate, or participate in the American society. The majority were single males. If married, their families were left behind in China. They could not become citizens; prejudice, discrimination, and segregation kept them apart from the mainstream. Jobs were largely limited to the lower part of a dual labor market; social and political opportunities were limited to their own communities. They were "outsiders"; what wealth and leadership qualities they had could only be used from the "outside looking in." They were hemmed in by their own needs and the walls erected by the dominant community. They were identified as Chinese and foreigners; they were not viewed as Americans. It was a pluralistic adaptation, less than equal and primarily involuntary. It was only with changes in their demographic structure and changes in the American society that we begin to see a break away from a segregated existence.

NOTES

1. Thomas Archdeacon, *Becoming American: An Ethnic History* (New York: Free Press, 1983), pp. 138–39. Table V-4, at p. 139, which treats twenty-five groups, shows a high Pearson product-moment correlation of .689.
2. Hugh Tinker, *A New System of Slavery: The Export of Indian Labour Overseas, 1820–1920* (London: Oxford University Press, 1974). For a worldwide survey of indentured labor, see W. Klosterboer, *Involuntary Labour Since the Abolition of Slavery: A Survey of Compulsory Labour Throughout the World* (The Hague: Mouton, 1960).
3. The best brief description is in Kil Young Zo, "Credit Ticket System for the Chinese Emigration into the United States," *Journal of Nanyang University* 8/9 (1974–75): 129–38.
4. Elmer C. Sandmeyer, *The Anti-Chinese Movement in California* (Berkeley: University of California Press, 1939); Lucille Eaves, *A History of California Labor Legislation* (Berkeley: University of California Press, 1910), p. 115; *Debates and Proceedings of the Constitutional Convention of the State of California*, Vol. 1 (Sacramento, 1881), p. 630.
5. Roger Daniels, ed., *Anti-Chinese Violence in America* (New York: Arno Press, 1978); David H. Stratton, "The Snake River Massacre of Chinese Coal Miners, 1887," in Duane A. Smith, ed., *A Taste of the West* (Boulder: Pruett, 1981), p. 125.
6. Sandmeyer, *Anti-Chinese Movement*, p. 65.
7. Yung Wing, *My Life in China and America* (New York: Holt, 1909); Edmund H. Worthy, Jr., "Yung Wing in America," *Pacific Historical Review* 39 (1965): 265–87.
8. Sue Fawn Chung, "The Chinese American Citizens Alliance: An Effort in Assimilation" (honors thesis, UCLA, 1965).
9. Rose Hum Lee, *The Growth and Decline of Chinese Communities in the Rocky Mountain Region* (New York: Arno Press, 1978).
10. Daniel Bell, *The End of Ideology* (Glencoe, Ill.: The Free Press, 1960); Ching-Chao Wu, "Chinatowns: A Study in Symbiosis and Assimilation" (Ph.D. diss. University of Chicago, 1928), pp. 213–14, 232.
11. Loren Chan, "Example for the Nation: Nevada's Execution of Gee Jon," *Nevada Historical Society Quarterly* 18 (1975): 90–106.
12. Wu, "Chinatowns," p. 158.
13. Victor G. Nee and Brett de Bary Nee, *Longtime Californ'* (New York: Pantheon, 1973), p. 22.
14. Ira M. Condit, *The Chinaman As We See Him* (Chicago: Revell, 1900), pp. 86–87.
15. As cited by Delber L. McKee, *Chinese Exclusion Versus the Open Door Policy, 1900–1906* (Detroit: Wayne State University Press, 1977), p. 51.
16. Nee and Nee, *Longtime Californ'*, p. 63.
17. Diane Mei Lin Mark and Ginger Chih, *A Place Called Chinese America* (Dubuque, Iowa: Kendall/Hunt, 1982), pp. 47–48.
18. Peter S. Li, "Immigration Laws and Family Patterns: Some Demographic Changes Among Chinese Families in Canada, 1885–1971," *Canadian Ethnic Studies* 12, No. 1 (1980): 58–73.

4

The Chinese After 1943

Although it is quite clear that World War II marked a crucial turning point in the lives of Chinese Americans, it is also clear that significant changes were occurring even before the war began to dominate the thoughts and actions of most Americans at the end of the 1930s. First of all, as we have seen, significant demographic changes had begun in the peaceful 1920s and 1930s. The long population decline that was triggered by the passage of the Chinese Exclusion Act had ended, and a small upturn due to natural increase and ingenuity in evading immigration regulations had set in. Between 1920 and 1940 the census recorded an increase of 25 percent, from 61,000 to 77,000, in the Chinese American population. (This does not take into account the 28,000 Chinese who lived in Hawaii in 1940; residents of Hawaii were counted in national population figures only after statehood in 1959.) Even more significant than the turnaround in sheer numbers was the fact that by 1940 citizen Chinese Americans for the first time outnumbered the alien segment of the community. If we look at the population breakdown for 1940 in Table 4–1, we will see the effect of the paper sons phenomenon.

The fact that there were 75 percent more citizen and presumably native-born Chinese American males than females is probably the best pos-

TABLE 4-1   Chinese American Population, 1940

	MALE	FEMALE	TOTAL	MALES:FEMALES
All Chinese	57,389	20,115	77,504	2.9:1
Alien	31,687	5,555	37,242	5.7:1
Citizen	25,702	14,560	40,262	1.8:1

Source: U.S. Census data.

sible numerical index to the number of paper sons in the population, although not all of the difference can be so explained.

CHANGES IN IMAGE

By the time citizens outnumbered aliens—and we must remember that many of the citizens were small children, meaning that among adults aliens continued to predominate—the image of the Chinese was beginning to change, however slowly. Even before Americans began to see the Chinese people as heroic resisters and victims of Japanese aggression, the picture most Americans had of China and her people was being altered by the daughter of a missionary, Pearl S. Buck (1892–1973). In a whole series of immensely successful novels, beginning with the Pulitzer Prize–winning *The Good Earth* (1931), Ms. Buck dealt with all levels of Chinese society, but her focus was on "the character of the Chinese peasant . . . hardworking, strong, persevering . . . kind toward children, respectful toward elders, all in all an admirable [and] warmly lovable character."[1] This idealized image, which was even more unreal in the popular movies made from *The Good Earth* and its sequel, *Dragon Seed*, which dealt with peasant resistance and suffering under Japanese attack, was an important element in making the period after 1937 one that the social scientist Harold Isaacs, in his study of American *Images of Asia*, called an "Age of Admiration." According to Isaacs, Pearl Buck "'created' the Chinese" for a whole generation of Americans, "in the same sense that Dickens created . . . the people who lived in the slums of Victorian England."[2] At a lower level of culture the cartoonist Milton Caniff created *Terry and the Pirates*, a popular adventure comic strip set in war-torn China, in which American heroes helped the Chinese fight the Japanese.

The Japanese attack on Pearl Harbor made the United States and China allies, and to the growing positive stereotype of the noble Chinese peasant was added the grossly distorted favorable picture of a great democratic leader, Generalissimo Chiang Kai-shek and his Christian, American-educated bride, usually referred to as Madame Chiang Kai-shek. In addition to receiving favorable media treatment, the couple was lauded by American political leaders. One public message from Franklin Delano Roosevelt proclaimed that "all the world knows how you have carried on that fight which is the fight of all mankind."

In China, however, the knowledgeable American ambassador wrote a private memorandum, noting realistically that

> it is unfortunate that Chiang and the Chinese have been "built up" in the United States to a point where Americans have been made to believe that China has been "fighting" the Japanese for five years, and that the Generalissimo, a great leader, has been directing the energetic resistance of China to Japan and is a world hero. Looking the cold facts in the face, one could only dismiss this as "rot."[3]

Although in the long run this false image had unfortunate consequences—it helped make it easy for demogogues in the 1950s to convince many Americans that their country had somehow "lost China"—in the short run it was useful to the Chinese American community. But not all of the improvements in the position of Chinese Americans were based on false images. Other important factors included real changes in the nature of the Chinese American community, changes in the attitudes of the larger society, and the real accomplishments of Chinese Americans. In addition, the favorable wartime climate of opinion was manipulated to bring about significant and lasting changes in American immigration and nationality law, modifications that at first affected only Chinese Americans, but that, we can now see, marked a crucial turning point in overall American immigration policy.

DEMOGRAPHIC CHANGES

The demographic changes of the 1940s were quite pronounced. Nearly 20,000 Chinese American babies were born during the decade; for the first time in history the most numerous five-year cohort of Chinese Americans was persons under five years of age. Total population jumped some 40,000, aided, as we shall see, by a relaxation in immigration laws. Large numbers of younger American citizen adults—the children born or brought over in the 1910s and 1920s—assisted by the wartime boom that improved the economic circumstances of almost every group in American society, were able to move outside of the ethnic economy. By the end of the decade about 7 percent of all Chinese workers were in professional jobs, although most employed Chinese were in service, managerial, clerical, and sales positions. The educational achievement of Chinese Americans, once well below the norm, was by 1950 at about the level of the general population: Median years completed were 8.4 for males and 10.3 for the younger and more predominantly native-born females.

Within the larger society the war years had the effect of minimizing, but certainly not eliminating, racism as a stated value in American society. As Philip Gleason has written:

> For a whole generation, the question "What does it mean to be an American?" was answered primarily by reference to "the values America stands for": democracy, freedom, equality, respect for individual dignity and so on. Since these values were abstract and universal, American identity could not be linked exclusively with any single ethnic derivation. Persons of any race, color, religion or background could be, or become, Americans.[4]

While Gleason may be overstating somewhat the pervasiveness of cultural pluralism, it was quite pronounced during the war years, especially among the elite movers and shakers of American society. Nothing more clearly indicates this than the successful campaign for the repeal of Chinese exclusion, a campaign mounted, not by members of the Chinese American community, but rather by members of what can be called the white establishment.

The successful campaign was studied at length years ago as a classic example of "pressures on Congress." The key figure was a New York publisher, Richard J. Walsh, who was also the husband of Pearl Buck. Walsh was the major force behind the Citizens Committee to Repeal Chinese Exclusion and Place Immigration on a Quota Basis. The more than 150 names on the committee's letterhead represented a broad group of the American upper class and intellectuals, from Roger Baldwin of the American Civil Liberties Union on the left to Henry Luce of *Time, Life,* and *Fortune* on the right. Assisted by bipartisan allies in Congress—Democrat Emanuel Celler and Republican Clare Boothe Luce led the way—and by a strong message from President Roosevelt, the fifteen separate laws that had effected Chinese exclusion were repealed in December 1943. The new law was a simple one, in three sections. Section one repealed the old acts. Section two gave a quota to "persons of the Chinese race," later set at 105 per year. The quota retained overt racist features: a Chinese born anywhere in the world would be charged to the Chinese quota rather than to the country of birth or nationality. Section three amended the nationality act to make "Chinese persons or persons of Chinese descent" eligible for naturalization on the same terms as other aliens. Two and a half years later, Congress, feeling that the phrase "Chinese person" was inexact, defined it as "any person who is as much as one-half Chinese blood."[5]

President Roosevelt made it clear in statements urging and then celebrating passage that repeal was essentially a foreign policy matter. He told Congress that the legislation was "important in the cause of winning the war and of establishing a secure peace." FDR admitted that "it would give the Chinese a preferred status" vis-à-vis other Asians but argued that "their great contribution to the cause of decency and freedom entitles them" to it. When he signed the bill, he remarked, "An unfortunate barrier between

TABLE 4-2   Immigration of Chinese by Sex, 1945-53

YEAR	MALE	FEMALE	PERCENT FEMALE	TOTAL
1945	45	64	59	109
1946	71	162	69	233
1947	142	986	87	1,128
1948	257	3,317	92	3,574
1949	242	2,248	90	2,490
1950	110	1,179	92	1,289
1951	126	957	89	1,083
1952	118	1,034	90	1,152
Total	1,111	9,947	90	11,058

Source: Immigration and Naturalization Service, *Annual Reports.*

allies has been removed. The war effort in the Far East can now be carried on with greater vigor and a larger understanding of our common purpose."[6]

Nothing more clearly indicates the lack of concern for Chinese Americans, as opposed to China, than the way that Congress and President Roosevelt ignored bills introduced in Congress that would have allowed the alien wives of Chinese American citizens to enter as nonquota immigrants. Family reunification, later to become a prime factor in our immigration legislation, was not considered important in 1943, at least not for Asian American families. Nevertheless, the repeal of Chinese exclusion was important, both because it reversed the trend of American immigration naturalization law as it related to Asians and because within three years bars would be similarly lowered, as we shall see, for Filipinos and "natives of India," and in nine years for all otherwise eligible Asians.

But for tangible, as opposed to symbolic, importance to the Chinese American community, a little noted act passed in 1946 was actually more immediately significant. It simply made Chinese alien wives of American citizens, native born or naturalized, admissible on a nonquota basis. This set off a minor boom in the legal migration of Chinese women and is an example of how, once given a quota, a group, no matter how tiny, could under immigration law and without subterfuge greatly exceed that quota. For the eight years from 1945 to 1952, there was a total of 840 Chinese quota spaces; as Table 4-2 shows, that quota was all but meaningless.

This migration of almost 10,000 females in eight years, almost all of them after the provisions of the 1946 act and almost all of them adults, had tremendous impact on the structure of Chinese American society, which contained, as late as 1950, only 28,000 women fourteen years of age and older. One must remember that the impact of this relatively large number of adults would serve, in the short run at least, to reinforce Chinese as opposed to Chinese American culture.

Other changes during the war included a significant but little remarked contribution to the war effort. Almost 16,000 Chinese Americans served in the armed forces between 1940 and 1946. Unlike the Japanese, the Chinese were not placed in segregated units. About 1,600 served, including some as officers, in the more restrictive Navy, which took no Japanese Americans at all. William Der Bing, who became the head of protocol and community affairs for NASA in the 1970s, described some of the obstacles he overcame to become a naval aviator in wartime.

> They were reluctant to give me the application forms. I said, "Either I can get them here or I can get them from my Congressman." The minute I mentioned "Congressman," the next thing I know I had a pile of papers. Even in the Navy there were some real good men, but the majority didn't want a "Chinaman" in their outfit. They made every remark possible to harass you.
> Personally, I was told that "No Chinaman will ever fly in my outfit." I was told that by a doctor—a Navy doctor. He gave me a physical. He said, "I want you to know that I would do anything I can to fail you in your physical." I looked at him and said, "If you do, it would be the most dishonest thing that an officer in this United States Navy would ever do to another member of the United States Navy." I put it just this way.[7]

The bittersweet nature of increasing Chinese American success during the war continued in the immediate postwar years, as the following incidents—trivial in themselves—illustrate. They are the kinds of things that could happen only when successful middle-class Chinese began to move out of the Chinatowns. In San Francisco a former Kuomintang officer, Sing Sheng, moved into the middle-class San Francisco suburb of Southwood. After some turmoil about his presence, an informal neighborhood referendum found 174 persons voted against his staying, 28 voted for his continuing, and 14 had no opinion. Yet, when the story received widespread publicity, Sheng and his family received invitations to move into scores of communities across the nation. Sheng eventually settled peacefully in Sonoma, in northern California. In the Midwest a fraternity at elite Northwestern University revoked the bid it made to Sherman Wu, the son of a former Nationalist officer, because at least seven Caucasian pledges said that they would not join if Wu was accepted. Again publicity brought a counterreaction: Two other fraternities at Northwestern offered to pledge the young Chinese American, who understandably, was hesitant. "If they are sincere enough," the *New York Times* reported him as saying, "I may join one. I don't know yet."

THE COLD WAR

But as World War II eased into the Cold War—and in Asia the crucial event was the victory of the communist forces of Mao Tse-tung in 1949—the

American image of China was again transformed. Harold Isaacs's "Age of Admiration" degenerated into first a brief "Age of Disenchantment" (1944–49), then quickly into an "Age of Hostility." The latter lasted until 1971–72, when "Ping-Pong diplomacy" and President Richard Nixon's trip to China, spectacularly covered on television, ushered in a new wave of good feeling toward China. Knowing that in the past attitudes toward China had quickly been translated into worse or better treatment for Chinese in America, many in the Chinese community were nervous about their possible fate after 1949. The nervousness increased when China intervened against American troops in Korea in late 1950. Many feared that Chinese Americans would be placed in concentration camps as Japanese Americans had been just eight years previously.

That, happily, did not happen, and the American view of China *and* Chinese became plural. Just as, in World War II, United States policy and ideology had carefully differentiated between "good" and "bad" Germans, in the Cold War era distinctions were made between "good" and "bad" Asians as well. There were now, for most Americans, two Chinas: Mao Tse-tung's communist, pagan, and threatening China and Chiang Kai-shek's capitalist, Christian, and supportive China. The clearest example of this new attitude can be seen in our insistence during the long negotiations at Panmunjon, which finally brought the fighting in Korea to an end, that Chinese prisoners of war had the right to choose to go back to China or to Chiang's regime on Taiwan. This was a new "right" and one we had denied to the Soviet prisoners of war we had liberated in Europe in 1944–45. Even more significant for Asian Americans would be the way in which the Cold War would modify our immigration and refugee policies.

The Cold War came to Chinese Americans, too. The Kuomintang had enjoyed overwhelming support in America's Chinatowns, before and during the war, as Overseas Chinese here and elsewhere were important mobilizers of support for China in her struggle against Japan. However, slowly but surely, most Chinese Americans—including many who were refugees from communist rule—have come to support or at least be reconciled to the People's Republic, which has, after all, "the mandate of heaven."

One is tempted to say that, just as international developments produced two Chinas, domestic developments produced two Chinese Americas. But that would be a gross oversimplification. As Dr. Rose Hum Lee pointed out in the mid-1950s, about half of the Chinese American population was native born, and this segment of the population, reinforced by elite émigrés from Nationalist China, was becoming increasingly middle class, disassociating itself from the concerns of the American Chinatowns and striving for acculturation, if not assimilation, into American society.

Other positive effects of the Cold War in Asia for Chinese Americans can be seen in changing refugee policy. The 1950 Displaced Persons Act had reserved 4,000 spaces for "European refugees from China," largely White

Russians and members of the Shanghai Jewish community, and provided no spaces for Asians. In 1953, for the first time, Asians were designated admissible refugees, and 2,000 visas were reserved for "refugees of Chinese origin." These had to be vouched for by the government on Taiwan, because of the fear in the United States in the 1950s and 1960s about the danger of letting in "red" Chinese. This tiny trickle was the start of a flow, which by the late 1970s became, with the so-called boat people and other Southeast Asian refugees, a major component of American immigration.[9]

Another gain from the Cold War was the permanent addition to the American population of a few thousand "stranded" Chinese. When China "fell" there were perhaps 5,000 Chinese nationals resident in the United States on non-immigrant visas. A majority of them had come as undergraduate and graduate university students; others were highly trained professionals. They represented very different elements of Chinese society from most of the previous immigrants, who had been largely southern peasants. One student, Donald Tsai, who had come to study at Pomona College in 1941 and went on to do graduate work at M.I.T., recently told interviewers:

> Many students came from China on scholarships from the Chinese government, although I myself did not come as a scholarship student. Those were very difficult scholarships to obtain, through competitive examinations, and so on. And the reason why you see so many Chinese people in the United States who are eminent professionals, teachers, and so forth is that many of these were, indeed, the scholarship students. . . . When they arrived, the war occurred and they were either cut off or decided not to return, and they have indeed made out very well. . . . I went to M.I.T. [which] was my father's school also. He studied mining engineering there in 1910. . . . All of the students were planning to go back to China. There was no thought of staying.[10]

Yet, as things turned out, a majority of these students did stay, making them the first important segment of the postwar brain drain, which saw more and more technical and professional personnel from lesser developed countries migrate to the United States and other advanced nations. Some of the students did "return," but to Taiwan, rather than China. A very few did choose to go to the People's Republic; the most prominent was physicist Dr. Hsue-shen Ts'ien, who is considered to be the father of the first Chinese satellite.

Although the worst fears of Chinese Americans in the 1950s were not realized—none were sent to concentration camps—they did suffer from domestic aspects of the Cold War. Some of the most traditional and conservative Chinese institutions in America, such as the family associations that united all persons sharing the same last name, ran afoul of J. Edgar Hoover's FBI and other "red-hunting" organizations because of their continuing communications with related clan groups in mainland China. As late as

1969, long after the peak of the Cold War hysteria, Hoover testified before a congressional committee that

> Red China has been flooding the country with propaganda and there are over 300,000 Chinese in the United States, some of whom would be susceptible to recruitment either through ethnic ties or hostage situations because of relatives in Communist China. . . . In addition up to 20,000 Chinese immigrants can come into the United States each year and this provides a means to send illegal agents into our Nation.[11]

Another onslaught on the Chinese American community came in late 1955 from the American consul general in Hong Kong, Everett F. Drumwright. He made a report to the State Department about what he called "a fantastic system of passport and visa fraud" and later argued that Chinese communists were using the system to infiltrate agents into the United States. (Ironically, the only spy for China we know of, Larry Wu-tai Chin, who committed suicide after apprehension in 1985, was brought into this country by the CIA.) In March 1956, in an apparent follow-up to Drumwright's charges, agents of the Immigration and Naturalization Service (INS) conducted a series of raids to seize illegal immigrants in the Chinatowns of both the East and West coasts. The major protest of the Chinese American establishment, interestingly enough, stressed economic losses rather than human rights violations. In a complaint couched to appeal to the Eisenhower administration, New York City Chinese leaders claimed that the immigration raids were costing merchants there $100,000 a week in lost sales.

But even some of the "humane" reforms of immigration procedures could be twisted and used as weapons in the Cold War. The government provided an amnesty program, the "confession system," to regularize the status of long-established illegal immigrants, the paper sons of Chinese America. Written into the statute books in 1957 after a trial period as an administrative innovation, the program provided that illegal Chinese immigrants *might* be able to regularize their status if a close relative—spouse, child, or parent—were a citizen of the United States or a permanent resident alien. Because of the climate of fear engendered by the Cold War and because much discretion was placed in the hands of officials of the INS, an agency Chinese Americans had learned to distrust, most potential beneficiaries probably were not willing to utilize the program. In some cases the government used information gained under the confession program selectively hoping to get rid of those who favored the People's Republic of China. Many Chinese Americans also believe that the INS was abetted by informers in the service of the Chinese Nationalist regime. Maurice Chuck, the publisher of a left-wing newspaper, the San Francisco *Journal,* reported an eventually unsuccessful attempt to deport him:

> My grandfather used the name of Chuck to come to this country, so naturally my father was under the same name and became a citizen of this country.... What happened was [that my father confessed and] they arrested me and tried me and used my father's confession as evidence against me. They didn't use it against my father.... They tried to deport me to Taiwan but my activities here in this country were so totally against the Chiang Kai-shek government, it's like sending me to a firing squad.[12]

Obviously there was, and continues to be, illegal immigration, and the Chinese, as the first group to be shut out, were pioneers in developing methods and techniques of entry. No one who has read Maxine Hong Kingston's marvelous book *The Woman Warrior*, with its evocations of "ghost" names and dual lives, can underestimate the impact that illegal status has had on the Chinese American community.[13] But from the 1950s on, illegality was surely less and less important, both statistically and psychologically, as more and more of the Chinese American population was native born or became naturalized and as more humane American immigration legislation and procedures allowed greater numbers of Chinese to enter the United States legally.

Further psychological strength resulted from the admission of Hawaii as a state in 1959. Hawaii had a majority of non-whites in its population—almost all of them Asian or Pacific peoples. One of its first senators was the Chinese American banker, Hiram Fong, who served in the United States Senate until he retired in 1977. The fear of having Asian Americans in Congress had been a major factor in the inordinate delay in the grant of statehood to Hawaii. Statehood bills had passed the House in 1947, 1950, and 1953, but in each instance they were bottled up in the race-conscious Senate. Senator Strom Thurmond of South Carolina, for example, quoted Rudyard Kipling with approval, "East is East and West is West and never the twain shall meet," and stressed the "impassable difference" between the majority of Hawaiians whose ancestors came from Asia and the majority of Americans whose ancestors came from Europe.

By 1960 natural increase and continued, relatively small-scale immigration had changed significantly the Chinese American profile. Including Hawaii, which had 38,000 Chinese Americans, the census recorded a total Chinese American population of 236,000. While still a male-dominated community—males outnumbered females in every five-year census cohort—that dominance was reduced to 57.4 percent. Just over 60 percent of Chinese Americans were native born. Three fifths of all Chinese were located in the four Pacific states of California, Hawaii, Washington, and Oregon; more than 90 percent were found in just thirteen states and the District of Columbia. The age distribution still reflected the bachelor-society pattern established in the 19th century. With a median age of 28.3 years for the whole Chinese American population, men were significantly older than women, 30.9 to 25.2 years. Urban centers away from the Pacific coast tended to be more heavily male: The Chinese population in the cities of New York, Chicago, Boston, Washington, D.C., and Boston was between 58.3 and 62.2 percent male.

Education and income data show a Chinese American community that was increasingly becoming two communities: one educated, relatively affluent, and becoming acculturated to American society; the other largely uneducated, distinctly nonaffluent, and still retaining much of its traditional culture. Some who have written about Chinese Americans have been misled by the median figures, which show for education a number close to the national average—11.1 years—and show females as somewhat better educated than males—11.7 years to 10.7 years. But a close look at the data shows that rather large numbers of Chinese had either a great deal of education or none. In addition, the advantages females had disappears when we look only at the well educated. At the upper end of the spectrum, just under half of all Chinese Americans were high school graduates, 48.3 percent of the women and 44.1 percent of the men. At the very top of the spectrum, more than a sixth of all Chinese American men and an eighth of Chinese American women were listed as having college degrees. At the very bottom of the educational spectrum, about a seventh of the adult population (14.7 percent for males, 15.2 percent for females) was recorded as having no formal schooling.

Given the number of well- and relatively well-educated adults, the income figures for Chinese Americans were quite low. Chinese American men earned an annual average of $3,471; Chinese women earned only about three-fifths of that amount, $2,067. It is relatively easy to explain the reasons for the depressed earnings of Chinese Americans. Major factors were the long-established patterns of discrimination and their virtual exclusion from some of the best-paid sectors of the economy, particularly those sectors in which effective unionization had occurred. Among Chinese American wage earners, over a third (36.7 percent) were in wholesale and retail trade, more than a quarter provided services (26.2 percent), and hardly any (1.2 percent) were engaged in agriculture, fishing, or forestry. Very few Chinese Americans had good-paying blue-collar jobs: Fourteen percent were in manufacturing—large numbers of them underpaid female garment workers—and just 1.9 percent in construction.

To make these data more meaningful they should not be compared to national averages and medians, which are depressed by the inclusion of the South, where standards were low. Instead they should be compared with figures for the West, the region in which most Chinese Americans lived. The easiest comparison to make is with California because the state government's Division of Fair Employment Practices published superb data for 1959-60.[14] The data clearly show that Chinese Americans were better educated than the white majority, although we must understand that the

TABLE 4-3   Educational Attainment in California, 1960: Percent of population, 14 years of age or older

	MALE	FEMALE
Eighth Grade or Less		
Chinese	40.8	38.7
White	27.2	24.2
Completed at Least One Year of High School		
Chinese	59.2	64.3
White	72.8	75.6
Completed at Least One Year of College		
Chinese	29.2	23.2
White	24.1	19.6

Source: California Fair Employment Practices Commission, *Californians of Japanese, Chinese and Filipino Ancestry* (San Francisco, 1965).

white data are somewhat depressed by the inclusion of what the census bureau calls "Spanish surname" data (see Table 4-3).

As shown in the national data, Chinese are both less educated and more highly educated than the state norm. Income data do not produce a similar pattern. The median income was $5,109 for white males and $3,803 for Chinese males. Chinese females earned slightly more than whites, $1,997 as opposed to $1,812, doubtless reflecting larger labor force participation (47 percent of all Chinese women over fourteen and less than 36 percent for white women). If we look at just the income for males twenty-five years of age or older—the persons who earn the most in American society—the disparities are even more striking, as Table 4-4 shows.

Thus, compared with their white counterparts, Chinese American men were 63 percent more likely to be poor, nearly as likely to be lower-middle class, 88 percent less likely to be middle class, and 78 percent less likely to

TABLE 4-4   Annual Income in California of Men 25 Years of Age and Older, 1959

	WHITE	CHINESE
$1–$3,999	29.4%	48.0%
$4,000–$6,999	38.9%	34.8%
$7,000–$9,999	19.6%	10.4%
$10,000+	12.1%	6.8%

Source: California FEPC, *Californians of Japanese, Chinese, Filipino Ancestry* (San Francisco, 1965).

be well-to-do. While it can be argued that the overrepresentation on the lowest rung of the economic ladder reflects the larger number of poorly educated Chinese, the underrepresentation of them in the two higher brackets fails to reflect their educational achievement. On the other hand, the data show clearly that, however they might be disadvantaged vis-à-vis whites, the California Chinese (and Japanese, see Chapters 5 and 6) were achieving middle-class status and income much more rapidly than California Filipinos and other "non-whites," only about 1 percent of whom had incomes of $10,000 or greater.

What the data show is that although increasing numbers of Chinese Americans were finding niches in the larger, as opposed to the ethnic, economy, there were still significant barriers, both real and psychological, to their advancement within that economy. One of the patterns that was readily discernible was that although well-trained Chinese Americans could find suitable employment with relative ease, it was still very difficult for them to gain promotion to supervisory and higher administrative positions. Many were clearly overqualified for the jobs they held, and it was clear that many employers were reluctant to place Chinese Americans in jobs that gave them the power to hire and fire whites. As a corollary to this, it was almost equally clear that some Chinese Americans were reluctant to be placed in such positions. Both phenomena were clearly carry-overs from the more racist past. No rational observer should attempt to deny that substantial progress toward equality has been made since the years before World War II; at the same time there should be no attempt to deny that discrimination and deprivation have continued. Yet, in the years after 1960 the continued existence of discrimination was denied time and again. In addition, the relative success of Chinese and other Asian American groups was used as a kind of rhetorical club to belabor groups whose measurable progress was less outstanding.

Since 1960 the most striking characteristics of the Chinese American population have been its rapid growth and the degree to which much of the Chinese American population would begin to be viewed as a "model minority." In 1960 no one could have predicted that the Chinese American population would increase more than fourfold in the next twenty-five years (see Table 4–5).

These dramatic increases have two primary sources: the Immigration Act of 1965 and the admission of refugees from Southeast Asia, particularly after the fall of Saigon in 1975. (A sizable number of these refugees were of Chinese ethnicity, although most were born in Southeast Asia and had never seen China.) A secondary cause of population growth was the natural increase of the population, whose median age was slightly below that of the general American population. It should be noted that in 1980 the fertility of Chinese American women was significantly below that of whites and most other identifiable groups in the population. Chinese women had 1,020

TABLE 4-5   Chinese American Population, 1960–1985

YEAR	NUMBER	INCREASE PER YEAR (PERCENT)
1960	237,292	5.8
1970	436,062	8.4
1980	812,178	8.6
1985 (est.)	1,079,400	6.6

Source: U.S. Census and Population Reference Bureau.

children per 1,000 women; white women had 1,358. In comparison, Vietnamese, black, and Hispanic women had 1,785, 1,806, and 1,817, respectively (it was clear that these rates were more reflective of class than of ethnicity).

Under the Immigration Act of 1965 the quota system was scrapped, and a complex system of preferences was set up that favored persons with close kin in the United States or who had professional and entrepreneurial skills. The refugees were not as carefully selected—and were to a great degree self-selecting. Since the Chinese in Vietnam and elsewhere in Southeast Asia tended to be entrepreneurial rather than agricultural, large numbers of the Chinese refugees were psychologically prepared to adapt to the economic aspects of American life.

THE "MODEL MINORITY"

By the early 1980s, the American media were noticing the great success of many Asian Americans. In 1982, *Newsweek* headlined a favorable story: "Asian-Americans: A 'Model Minority.'"[15] The catch phrase, "Model Minority," has an interesting history. First coined in 1966 by sociologist William Petersen, who at first applied it only to Japanese Americans, it has become the new stereotype. Like all stereotypes, it has some relationship to reality but is no more indicative of the variety of Chinese American experience than the former "coolie laborer" stereotype was. It is ironic, as Peter I. Rose has put it, that the image of Asians has gone from "pariahs to paragons," and certainly among the current generation of Chinese Americans there are many paragons.[16] For example, in 1983 the grand winner of the Westinghouse Science Talent Search was Paul Ning, a sixteen-year-old Taiwan-born student at the Bronx High School of Science. But even more significant than his achievement was the fact that of forty finalists in Westinghouse's national contest that year, no fewer than twelve—30 percent—were Asian Americans, nine of them immigrants. Nor was spectacular success limited to the young. Two of the first one hundred persons on *Forbes's* 1983 list of the "richest" Americans were Chinese: An Wang, the sixty-three-year-old proprietor of Wang Laboratories, the fifth on the list, was said to be worth $1.6 billion; Kyupin Philip Hwang, the forty-six-year-old head of TeleVideo Systems, logged in at $575 million.[17] Such achievements, plus a very good press, clearly made the Chinese American community more self-confident than it had been, say, in the 1950s. The fact that after 1972 American relations with the People's Republic of China were all but regularized and quite friendly was also a factor leading to greater community self-esteem.

This very self-confidence enabled some community leaders to demand better treatment and redress for wrongs. Early in the 1960s, Chinese American leaders on each coast called for federal assistance for the needy in their communities. Irving S. K. Chin, chairman of the Chinatown Advisory Committee to the Borough President of Manhattan (the mere existence of such a body speaks volumes about social change), told a U.S. Senate committee that Chinese were a "silent minority," who had not previously protested very much because of their problems with English, "a lack of familiarity with the American governmental system," "fear of government," lack of political influence, and a philosophical and cultural reluctance to engage in political activity. Professor Ling-chi Wang, a San Francisco community activist and later chairman of the Asian American Studies Department of the University of California, Berkeley, spoke to the same committee about the "silent" Chinese of San Francisco. Wang advocated manpower training programs, which he said were "long overdue," "much needed," and "relevant." Wang also cited evidence showing that in San Francisco's inner-city Chinatown unemployment was almost double the citywide average, that two thirds of the housing stock were substandard, and that tuberculosis rates were six times the national average. He argued that the major social problems for Chinese Americans were discrimination, educational handicaps, lack of marketable skills, language barriers, citizenship requirements, and culturally biased and irrelevant tests.[18]

How is it possible to square these complaints of poverty and deprivation with reports about "model minorities" and of superior educational achievement? It is possible because there is more than one Chinese America. Chinese Americans often speak of the differences between ABCs and FOBs, that is, between American-born Chinese, and the Fresh-off-the-boat (or plane) immigrant Chinese. The former tend to be college educated, have middle-class occupations, and live outside of the inner-city Chinatowns. Many of the FOBs are poorly educated and deficient in English, live in Chinatowns, and ply the low-wage service trades or sweatshop manufacturing plants typical of inner cities. (Although large numbers of recent Chinese immigrants are poor, there are many that are both middle class and well educated and that have brought a good deal of capital with them. The bifurcated nature of the Chinese American community is indicated quite clearly by some census data. In 1970, to cite just one example, although about a quarter of Chinese American adults were college graduates, another quarter had never completed elementary school.

Although some scholars write as if prejudice and discrimination against Asians were a thing of the past, others have understood the ambivalent nature of the status of Asian Americans in post-1965 America. Bryan Man examined carefully the achievement patterns of Chinese and white men in California and Hawaii in 1960 and 1970. He concluded that race, country of birth, migration experience, and the social structure of American society all had continuing effects. "While some Chinese equal or surpass whites in occupational achievements," he wrote, "it is quite clear that many Chinese achieve less than their white counterparts, all things being equal. This fact, then, calls upon us to seriously question the notion that the Chinese are a 'model minority.'"[19]

By the mid-1980s some of the secret sores of Chinese American society were becoming more visible to the general public, particularly when the problems of inner-city youth erupted into crime and violence. A series of gang shootings in Chinatowns on both coasts—the most gruesome of which involved the mass execution of thirteen Seattle Chinese by young Hong Kong immigrants in a Seattle after-hours gambling establishment—produced a minor wave of stories, television programs, and books about the dangers of the Triad Society, sometimes called the Chinese Mafia. Although Asian American groups remain largely discrete, some leaders, such as Oakland attorney Alan S. Yee, call for a united front:

> even though the Asian-American community has traditional divisions . . . we find that, from the outside, we're all perceived as the same, and, despite an image as "model minorities," we see the search for the scapegoat still there.[20]

Model minority or scapegoat? Obviously neither stereotype is or can be accurate. The more than a million Chinese Americans are a diverse community whose differences are probably increasing more than they are decreasing. Although clearly overrepresented in many areas of achievement in American life, they are also overrepresented among the poor in American society. And even for those who have "made it," there is often, if not always, the nagging reminder of a racist past. Diana Fong put it well on the op ed page of the *New York Times* recently:

> We're still not fully integrated into the mainstream because of our yellow skin and almond eyes. Much has changed in 100 years (since the exclusion act), but we still cannot escape the distinction of race.[21]

NOTES

1. Dorothy Jones, *The Portrayal of China and India on the American Screen, 1896–1955* (Cambridge, Mass.: M.I.T. Press, 1955), p. 36.

2. Harold R. Isaacs, *Images of Asia: American Views of China and India* (New York: Harper, 1972), pp. 71, 155. (Originally published as *Scratches on Our Minds.*)

3. As cited by Isaacs, p. 187.

4. Philip Gleason, "Americans All: World War II and the Shaping of American Identity," *The Review of Politics* 43 (1981): 483–518.

5. Fred W. Riggs, *Pressures on Congress: A Study of the Repeal of Chinese Exclusion* (New York: King's Crown, 1950).

6. Samuel I. Rosenman, ed., *The Public Papers and Addresses of Franklin D. Roosevelt,* 1943 volume (New York: Harper, 1950), pp. 429–430, 548.

7. As quoted in Diane Mei Lin Mark and Ginger Chih, *A Place Called Chinese America* (Dubuque, Iowa: Kendall/Hunt, 1982), p. 96.

8. Isaacs, *Images of Asia,* pp. 123–24.

9. Roger Daniels, "American Refugee Policy in Historical Perspective," in J. C. Jackman and Carla Borden, eds., *The Muses Flee Hitler: Cultural Transfer and Adaptation, 1930–1945* (Washington, D.C.: Smithsonian Institution, 1983), pp. 61–77.

10. Mark and Chih, *Chinese America,* pp. 104–5.

11. As cited in Stanford M. Lyman, "Red Guard on Grant Avenue: The Rise of Youthful Rebellion in Chinatown," in Lyman, *The Asian in North America* (Santa Barbara, Calif.: Clio Press, 1977), p. 198.

12. Mark and Chih, *Chinese America,* p. 104.

13. Maxine Hong Kingston, *The Woman Warrior* (New York: Knopf, 1976).

14. California Department of Industrial Relations, Division of Fair Employment Practices, *Californians of Japanese, Chinese, Filipino Ancestry* (San Francisco: 1965).

15. *Newsweek,* Dec. 6, 1982, pp. 39ff.

16. William Petersen, "Success Story, Japanese American Style," *The New York Times Magazine,* Jan 6, 1966, pp. 20ff.; Peter I. Rose, "Asian Americans: From Pariahs to Paragons," in Nathan Glazer, ed., *Clamor at the Gates: The New American Immigration* (San Francisco: ICS Press, 1985), pp. 181–212.

17. "Confucian Work Ethic: Asian-born Students Head for the Head of the Class," *Time,* Mar. 25, 1983. *Forbes* list as cited by the Cincinnati *Enquirer,* Sept. 30, 1983.

18. Testimony cited in Integrated Education Associates, *Chinese-Americans: School and Community Problems* (Chicago: 1972), pp. 18–28, 12–17.

19. Bryan Dai Yung Man, "Chinese Occupational Achievement Patterns: The Case of a 'Model Minority.'" (Ph.D diss., UCLA, 1978). The quotation is from *Dissertation Abstracts International* 39 (1978): 3172A.

20. Material about the 1980s comes from a variety of sources, including personal observation. Especially useful were two newspaper articles: David Smollar, "Violence, Slurs—U.S. Asians Feel Trade Backlash," *Los Angeles Times,* Sept. 14, 1983, and Robert Lindsay, "The New Asian Immigrants," The *New York Times Magazine,* Sept. 10, 1983, pp. 22ff.

21. Diana Fong, "America's 'Invisible' Chinese" *New York Times,* May 1, 1982.

5

The Japanese:
The Early Years

Although there had been a number of Japanese visitors, students, merchants, and officials in the United States from the middle of the 19th century—and at least one short-lived small Japanese colony at Gold Hill, California, near Sacramento—significant immigration began only toward the
end of the century. The first large group of Japanese migrants to travel
east across the Pacific went to the then-independent kingdom of Hawaii as
indentured laborers; after the United States annexed Hawaii (1898) many
of them re-emigrated to the American West Coast. There, by the late 1880s,
a steady and growing immigration, largely of young men, had begun to create a Japanese American community. In 1900 the census identified almost
25,000 Japanese on the West Coast; by 1920 there were more than 110,000,
almost two thirds of them in California. Although at first this migration
seemed to parallel that of the Chinese—which was halted, as we have seen,
just before that of the Japanese began—the differences between them are
as striking as the similarities.

The similarities, noted by contemporary observers, were that each immigration was predominantly male and that each group worked at physically difficult, low-prestige, and low-paying jobs. The Chinese were em-

ployed in mining, agriculture, and railroad building; the Japanese in agriculture and railroad maintenance. Both groups were composed of peasants. However, whereas the Chinese were almost all from one small district in South China, the Japanese were drawn from rural areas in several parts of Japan and the Ryukyu Islands (Okinawa). In addition, the countries from which they came were in quite different stages of development. China was weak and growing weaker; it had not yet, to any significant degree, begun to take steps toward modernization. Japan had begun the transition toward modernity after the Meiji Revolution (1869) and by the turn of the century was an emerging modern power; increasing numbers of Japanese had been exposed to at least the basics of compulsory education. In this country, the Chinese presence in agriculture, once quite significant, diminished after the 1880s; the Japanese, however, after initially working at many urban occupations, became more heavily involved as agricultural proprietors and tenants than any other 20th-century immigrant group. And, perhaps the most important difference of all, the Japanese had behind them a government that inspired and demanded growing respect, whereas the protests of the weak Chinese government about bad treatment were all but ignored. What the Japanese government most dreaded, in its negotiations about the rights of Japanese nationals in this country, was the enactment of a Japanese exclusion act on the model of the 1882 law barring Chinese. As Hilary Conroy pointed out, the Japanese government, not noted for its concern about human rights, kept an "ever jealous watch against discriminatory treatment abroad" to emigrants from Japan; this concern was chiefly motivated by the desire to protect "her own prestige as a nation."[1]

THE STRUCTURE OF JAPANESE AMERICAN SOCIETY

As we shall see, the influence of the Japanese government was not, in the final analysis, able to offset the combination of American racism and unscrupulous politicians. But—and this was crucially important for the development of the Japanese American community—the pressures of the Japanese government did delay effective exclusion for about two decades, until the barring of the immigration of "aliens ineligible to citizenship" in 1924. In the meantime, the nature of Japanese migration would change from a male-dominated to a female-dominated flow. Thus, by the time immigration was cut off, a firm demographic foundation had been established for a native-born, citizen generation of Japanese, the Nisei,[2] who by 1940 would greatly outnumber their parents, as shown in Tables 5-1 and 5-2.[3]

Thus, the demographic experience of Japanese Americans was quite different from that of Chinese Americans. For the latter, as we have seen, the bachelor society established before passage of the 1882 Exclusion Act prevailed for decades, and the overall population underwent a decline for

TABLE 5-1 Sex Ratio of Japanese in the Contiguous United States, 1900–1940

	CALIFORNIA			OTHER STATES			TOTAL		
	Male	Female	Percent Female	Male	Female	Percent Female	Male	Female	Percent Female
1900	9,598	553	5.4	13,716	405	2.9	23,314	958	3.9
1910	35,116	6,240	15.1	27,954	2,847	9.2	63,070	9,087	12.6
1920	45,414	26,538	36.9	27,239	11,765	30.1	72,653	38,303	34.5
1930	56,440	41,016	42.1	25,331	16,047	38.9	81,771	57,063	41.1
1940	52,550	41,167	43.9	19,417	13,813	41.6	71,967	54,980	43.3

Source: U.S. Census data.

TABLE 5-2 Japanese Citizenship Status in the Contiguous United States, 1920–1940

	TOTAL	ALIEN	NATIVE	PERCENT NATIVE
1920	111,010	81,338	29,672	26.7
1930	138,834	70,477	68,357	49.2
1940	126,947	47,305	79,642	62.7

Source: U.S. Census data.

nearly a half century. Only in the 1950s did Chinese American population reach the levels it had attained in the 1880s. For Japanese Americans there was only a slight dip in the 1930s, and by 1940 nearly two thirds were native-born citizens. Thus, in many ways, by 1940 the acculturation process of the Japanese American community was farther advanced than that of the Chinese Americans, even though significant migration of the latter had begun about half a century earlier.

THE ANTI-JAPANESE MOVEMENT

Because the West Coast had "learned" to discriminate against Asians in the 1860s and 1870s, the anti-Japanese movement arose while the Japanese population was still quite small. There was an abortive anti-Japanese movement in the 1890s, but the effective movement against the immigrants from Japan dates from newspaper agitation in 1905. It became notorious and a matter of diplomatic concern in 1906 as a result of the so-called San Francisco School Board incident,[4] which involved an attempt to force Japanese pupils in San Francisco to attend the long-established segregated school for Chinese. The incident set a pattern that would prevail for nearly twenty years: state, local, or regional discrimination offset in part by federal intervention. President Theodore Roosevelt mediated the San Francisco segregation matter himself; he called San Francisco officials to come to the White House and jaw-boned them to back down. Roosevelt, in return, promised to negotiate with Japan to halt further immigration.

The result of Roosevelt's negotiations was the Gentlemen's Agreement of 1907–1908—actually a series of notes exchanged between the American and Japanese governments—which hinged upon restriction by the Japanese rather than by the American government. Tokyo simply promised not to issue any more passports good for the United States to "laborers." Not fully understanding what would happen—diplomats and legislators have often been ignorant about the facts of life for ordinary people—both governments agreed that Japanese residents in the United States who were established and self-supporting could bring over their wives and other family members.

Thus, although the Gentlemen's Agreement was presented to the public as tantamount to exclusion, it allowed a predominantly female migration for the next sixteen years, which, as we have seen, nearly balanced the Japanese American sex ratio and led to a continuing increase of the Japanese American population. This caused westerners to believe that they had been betrayed by unscrupulous leaders in Washington. Although under American law only the federal government could regulate immigration, state and local governments could, and did, discriminate against Japanese by statute and ordinance. The famous Alien Land Acts of 1913 and 1920 in California and similar statutes in other western states were based on the federal naturalization statutes that made Japanese and other Asians "aliens ineligible to citizenship." Other restrictions were based simply on race (racial segregation would not be declared unconstitutional until 1954). School segregation, despite the 1906 hullabaloo in San Francisco, was not widely practiced,[5] but state law did prohibit the marriage of Asians and whites, restrictive covenants were written into many deeds making it illegal to sell the property to a non-white, movies usually made Asians sit in the balcony or on one side of the theater, and some municipal swimming pools and even beaches were barred to Asians.

The federal government long resisted overt anti-Japanese legislation: In 1917, for example, a restrictive "barred zone" act kept out all Asians except Filipinos, who, as American nationals, could not be kept out, and Japanese. Finally, in 1924, in a deliberately insulting move, Congress denied immigration quotas to any foreigners who were "aliens ineligible to citizenship," which affected only Japanese, although they were not specifically mentioned. This abrogation of the Gentlemen's Agreement was one of the seemingly irreconcilable issues between Japan and the United States in the years before the Japanese attack on Pearl Harbor.

JAPANESE IMMIGRANT ORGANIZATIONS

In the meantime the Japanese American population grew, some prospered, and many of the Nisei, or second-generation children, became increasingly acculturated. The Issei, or immigrant generation, were also exposed to the American world but, in common with most immigrant groups, developed their own organizations. Some of these were influenced by the government of Japan. From the 1890s until the attack on Pearl Harbor—but particularly in the period up to 1924—Tokyo tried very hard to apply various measures of social control to the Japanese immigrants in the United States, largely because it was convinced that Japan's prestige as a nation would be affected by the behavior of its residents abroad.

Crucial to this control were Japanese consular officials and the immigrant organizations they created and nurtured. Evidence of such attempts at control exists as early as 1891. But it was after the Gentlemen's Agreement, which placed certain control responsibilities on the Japanese government, that such control became most important. In 1909 the consulate general in San Francisco formed the Japanese Association of America, the premier institution of the Issei. Theoretically, all Japanese in the United States had to belong to the association; annual membership, through a local or regional association, cost from $1 to $3 a year. To encourage membership, the Japanese government through its consulates gave the associations an official role and made them the intermediaries through which individual Japanese residents had to pass if they wished to retain official connection with the Japanese government. Both Japanese law and the Gentlemen's Agreement required the Japanese consular service to issue certain documents to resident Japanese. The responsibility for these certificates was delegated to the associations, which in turn could collect fees for their issue.

Such certificates required by the Gentlemen's Agreement were related largely to travel abroad, with the right to return and the ability to bring into the country wives, children, parents, and even other relatives. Thus, any Japanese who wished to keep or establish family ties across the Pacific was forced to do so through the appropriate Japanese association. In addition, Japanese law required men of military age who had not fulfilled their military obligations to register yearly, and other certificates were required to register marriages, divorces, births, inheritances, and other vital statistics.

There has been much debate over the true nature of the Japanese associations. Exclusionists, like V. S. McClatchy of the *Bee* newspaper McClatchys, and congressional demagogues, like Representative Martin Dies of Texas, insisted that the associations were part of some kind of sinister Japanese plot to take over America. Apologists for the Japanese, for example, Stanford historian Yamato Ichihashi, claimed that the associations were merely self-help groups analogous to those that flourished among other immigrant groups. Neither was accurate. The associations were semiofficial organs of the Japanese government, but their function was essentially bureaucratic, not sinister. In addition to controlling certificates, the associations encouraged Japanese residents to acculturate and, above all, to send their children to school and have them excel there.

Of all the certificates the associations came to control, the most crucial was the one that gave the right to bring a wife to the United States. From the point of the Japanese government, which tried to abide by the terms of the Gentlemen's Agreement, the major problem was how to determine the socioeconomic status of each Issei male who wished a passport for his wife. Eventually a rule of thumb was established: Anyone who could show liquid assets of $800 or more would be eligible. This was a sizable nest egg. Interviews with surviving Issei indicate that these regulations were often evaded.

One successful ruse involved the pooling of $800 by a group of "bachelors" in what they called "show money" and transferring it from one account to another; in time, the same $800 would provide passports for a number of wives or other relatives.[6]

At the time of the Gentlemen's Agreement and the founding of the Japanese associations, there were perhaps 60,000 Japanese in the entire United States, with about two thirds of them living in California. In the next fifteen years there was a net immigration of some 25,000 Japanese women. These women, some of whom were "picture brides"—married by proxy to immigrant men they would not see until they arrived in the United States— began to have children at what seemed to many Caucasian observers an incredible rate. By the early 1930s, the citizen children of these and other immigrant marriages would outnumber their parents.

JAPANESE AMERICAN ENTERPRISES

Thus, despite a whole series of discriminatory actions and a generally hostile atmosphere, the first generation of Japanese Americans provided a firm demographic base for the future of the community. Part of the reason that it was able to do this was that it created for itself an important economic niche in the agricultural economy of the Far West in general and California in particular.

Although a few Issei immigrants, for example, George Shima (1863–1926), the famed "Potato Baron," came to this country with some capital, most began as laborers, and some remained so all of their lives. Many others, however, soon became proprietors and, from British Columbia to San Diego, began to carve out special niches for themselves. Some, like Shima, ran large-scale, diversified operations, but most were small proprietors concentrating on labor-intensive specialty crops, chiefly fruits, vegetables, and flowers. They also developed essentially ethnic marketing organizations in such centers as Los Angeles and Seattle. By 1919, in California alone, where agriculture occupied about half the Japanese population, Issei farmers controlled over 450,000 acres of farm land, about 1 percent of the state's acreage. But the intensive, high-yield agriculture they practiced brought in more than $67 million, more than 10 percent of the total value of California's crops.

Those who lived in cities primarily worked at service trades and in small businesses, many of which catered either to the ethnic community or as the marketing adjuncts of Japanese American agriculture. Initially, San Francisco and Seattle were the major *nihonmachis*, or Japantowns, but by 1910, Los Angeles began to prevail. By 1940, Los Angeles was clearly the metropolis of Japanese America, with nearly 37,000 persons; Seattle had the second largest Japanese American population, numbering almost 7,000, with another 4,700 in its outlying regions. Although San Francisco ranked third in numbers, with some 5,000, it remained culturally quite important. Its *nihonmachi* was one of the liveliest; it was the headquarters for the major organizations of each generation—the Japanese associations and the Japanese American Citizens League—and it served as a center for the more than 6,000 Japanese in the Bay Area. Only four other cities in the United States had ethnic Japanese communities of 1,000 or more: Sacramento and Stockton in California; Portland, Oregon; and New York City.

THE PREWAR JAPANESE AMERICAN COMMUNITY

By the 1930s the Japanese American community on the West Coast had achieved, economically at least, lower-middle-class status. But there were enough problems faced by the growing Nisei generation that a grant of $40,000 was awarded by the Board of Trustees of the Carnegie Corporation to study the "educational and occupational opportunities offered to American citizens of Oriental races." A book, aptly titled the *Second Generation Japanese Problem,* provided data garnered from interviews with the Nisei during the late 1920s and early 1930s. There was widespread despair and disillusionment. For example, one subject responded, "If, in order to avoid troublesome contact with American workers, we man a whole industry . . . with Japanese . . . the cries of 'yellow peril' . . . are raised . . . if we limit ourselves to . . . only the Japanese community . . . we are accused of being unassimilable and clannish. . . . "[7]

The major issue was race. Americans in the early third of the century simply could not accept Japanese Americans or other Asians as equals. One Japanese American wrote, "So, many of my friends are giving up the fight. 'Why get an education?' they say. 'Why try to do anything at all?' Probably we were meant to be just a servile class."[8]

This was also the period of the Great Depression, a time when job opportunities were limited for all Americans. A few Nisei emigrated to Japan; most stayed in Hawaii and on the West Coast. They developed their own local organizations; there were Japanese American social clubs, athletic leagues, and church groups, where individual Nisei could participate with ethnic peers. There was a high degree of acculturation; most of the groups were modeled on American rather than Japanese or Issei models (i.e., Boy and Girl Scouts, the YMCA and YWCA), but there was very little integration with the dominant community. It was the era of structural separation. Even though Nisei topics of interest were thoroughly American, discussion was limited with members of their own ethnicity. The separation was forced rather than voluntary; even if Nisei desired to enter mainstream groups, opportunities were limited.

But the community was still controlled by the Issei. Most Nisei were economically dependent upon their parents, and there were complaints that the younger generation was becoming American too fast. A relatively large number of Nisei were college and university students, and they were beginning to take on middle-class characteristics. Unlike their parents, they could, as citizens, enter the learned professions—law, medicine, and dentistry, in particular—and they set up their own generational organization, the Japanese American Citizens League (JACL).

The JACL, like many other second-generation organizations, regardless of ethnicity, was hyper-patriotic. Its creed, written in 1940, clearly expressed the hopes, if not the experience, of the second generation:

> I am proud that I am an American citizen of Japanese ancestry, for my very background makes me appreciate more fully the wonderful advantages of this nation. I believe in her institutions, ideas and traditions; I glory in her heritage; I boast of her history; I trust in her future. She has granted me liberties and opportunities such as no individual enjoys in this world today. She has given me an education befitting kings. She has entrusted me with the responsibilities of the franchise. She has permitted me to build a home, to earn a livelihood, to worship, think, speak and act as I please—as a free man equal to every other man.
>
> Although some individuals may discriminate against me, I shall never become bitter or lose faith, for I know that such persons are not representative of the majority of the American people. True I shall do all in my power to discourage such practices, but I shall do it in the American way—above board, in the open, through courts of law, by education, by proving myself to be worthy of equal treatment and consideration. I am firm in my belief that American sportsmanship and attitude of fair play will judge citizenship and patriotism on the basis of action and achievement, and not on the basis of physical characteristics. Because I believe in America, and I trust she believes in me, and because I have received innumerable benefits from her, I pledge myself to do honor to her at all times and all places; to defend her against all enemies, foreign and domestic; to actively assume my duties and obligations as a citizen, cheerfully and without any reservations whatsoever, in the hope that I may become a better American in a greater America.

It should also be noted that the JACL deliberately tried to distance itself from the previous generation. By requiring that all members be citizens, it barred persons born in Japan from membership and, unlike most ethnic organizations, which maintained ties with the country of origin, tried to separate itself completely from Japan and Japanese culture. In the short run at least, the effort of JACL members to separate themselves from their parents and their parents' homeland was a failure. When war came between the United States and Japan, all persons of Japanese ethnicity on the West Coast—regardless of citizenship, age, or sex—were herded unceremoniously into concentration camps, euphemistically called "relocation centers."

EXILE AND INCARCERATION

This wartime exile and incarceration—often called the relocation of the Japanese Americans—was and remains the central event of Japanese American history. It makes that history unique, setting off the Japanese American experience from that of not just other ethnic groups from Asia but from all other immigrant ethnic groups. Because the event has been studied widely, we will provide only a summary here.[9]

At the outbreak of hostilities, the federal authorities responsible for internal security, according to plan, rounded up a few thousand enemy aliens—Japanese, Germans, and Italians—and interned them. Each internee eventually had a hearing as an individual, and as a result of these hearings, some were released. Most of the interned Japanese were community leaders. In addition, the bank accounts and other assets of Japanese nationals were frozen, which meant that the whole community was economically disadvantaged. Almost from the very moment that bombs fell on Pearl Harbor, the federal government began to discriminate against Japanese American citizens. Travel out of the country was barred for German and Italian nationals and all persons of Japanese ancestry. By late December 1941, the armed forces stopped accepting Japanese Americans either as volunteers or as draftees, even though the Selective Service Act barred racial discrimination. There was a great deal of agitation from the old anti-Japanese forces, from a number of influential persons in the media (including the widely respected columnist Walter Lippmann), and from many senators and representatives. Finally, after a formal recommendation from Secretary of War Henry L. Stimson, President Roosevelt, on February 19, 1942, issued Executive Order 9066, which, as a matter of "military necessity," authorized the army to exclude "any or all persons" from as yet unspecified "military areas." That military area turned out to be the entire state of California, most of Washington and Oregon, and part of Arizona. The persons moved were all Japanese.

As a result, the entire Japanese American population of the affected area—men, woman, and children, alien and citizen alike—were herded, under military auspices, first to Assembly Centers, usually close to where they lived, and eventually to one of ten Relocation Centers, run by a newly created civilian agency, the War Relocation Authority.

There has been much controversy regarding the nature of the relocation centers. On more than one occasion during the war President Roosevelt, who authorized their creation, referred to them bluntly as "concentration camps," as did U.S. Supreme Court Justice Owen J. Roberts. However, the uncovering of the incredible dimensions of the Nazi Holocaust in Europe made the term "concentration camp" synonomous with "death camp" or "extermination camp." Thus, many who were involved in the relatively humane incarceration of the Japanese Americans, such as Dillon S. Myer, the Department of Agriculture bureaucrat who ran the War Relocation Authority so "well" that a grateful government made him Commissioner of Indian Affairs, vehemently reject the notion that the places where Japanese Americans were kept should be called concentration camps.[10]

But, whatever one calls them, the camps created to house the Japanese American population were places persons were sent to and confined in with neither charge nor trial, simply on the basis of their ancestry and their place of residence. Age, sex, and citizenship meant nothing. The camps were surrounded by barbed wire and were patrolled by armed soldiers, who in several instances shot and killed persons whom they were guarding. Unlike the camps of the Nazis, or those of the Soviet Gulag Archipelago, or those in the killing fields of Cambodia, the American camps cannot be called death camps. Many more persons were born in them than died there. Yet, they were, indeed, concentration camps, as the term has been used since it was introduced by the British during the Boer War at the turn of the century.

It is important to note that not all Japanese Americans were incarcerated. The Japanese Americans who lived east of the proscribed area—or were able to move there before the Army ordered them "frozen" in the early spring of 1942—were left in nervous liberty. There were about 10,000 such persons. In addition, the more than 150,000 Japanese Americans who lived in Hawaii—then a territory—were largely left alone. Martial law was established in Hawaii, but even though Hawaii had actually been a theater of war and its Japanese Americans represented about one-third of the islands' total population, the military authorities there did not deem it necessary to intern them. It was even pointed out to Washington that their continued labor was vital to the successful conduct of the war. This—and not the foolish vaporings of media strategists, politicians, and chairborne generals—was true "military necessity."

BEGINNINGS OF REDRESS

That the mass incarceration of the West Coast Japanese not only was morally wrong but actually retarded rather than advanced the American war effort has long been recognized by scholars. As early as 1948 the United States government admitted that there was some injustice in the procedure by enacting the Japanese American Claims Act, which allowed some of the victims of the relocation and incarceration to collect damages for property lost—but not for wrongful imprisonment. In 1976, partially in recognition of the bicentennial of American independence, President Gerald R. Ford repealed FDR's executive order by proclamation and declared that:

We know now what we should have known then—not only was the evacuation wrong, but Japanese-Americans were and are loyal Americans. . . . I call upon the American people to affirm with me this American Promise—that we have learned from the tragedy of that long-ago experience forever to treasure liberty and justice for each individual American, and resolve that this kind of action shall never be repeated.[11]

Finally, in 1980, the Congress created the Commission on Wartime Relocation and Internment of Civilians (CWRIC) to investigate the whole process and make whatever recommendations seemed appropriate. In 1983, after a long and detailed investigation, the CWRIC found that a "grave injustice" had been done to the Japanese American people and recommended, among other things, that Congress formally apologize and appropriate enough money to pay $20,000 in damages to each survivor of the relocation experience. At this writing (mid-1987) legislation effecting the commission's recommendations has been introduced into each house of Congress but has not been acted upon.

During the war, the whole procedure was given the color of law by the American judicial system, which has traditionally bowed to the executive and legislative branches during wars and national emergencies. Three cases, known collectively as the Japanese American cases, actually were decided by the Supreme Court in 1943 and 1944. In effect, the court endorsed what the government had done, but it did rule in December 1944, when the war was clearly won, that Japanese Americans who were American citizens and still being held behind barbed wire were free to go anywhere—including the West Coast—that other citizens could go unless there were individual charges against them. It should be noted that the high court was not unanimous in sanctioning the relocation: In 1944 three of the nine justices argued that the whole relocation procedure, as it was applied to American citizens, violated the Constitution. The judge who most vigorously attacked the majority was Justice Frank Murphy, who, in dissenting from what he called a "legalization of racism," argued that:

All residents of this nation are kin in some way by blood and culture to a foreign land. Yet they are primarily and necessarily a part of this new and distinct civilization of the United States. They must accordingly be treated at all times as the heirs of the American experiment and as entitled to all the rights and freedoms guaranteed by the Constitution.[12]

In 1982 former Supreme Court Justice Arthur J. Goldberg, then a member of the CWRIC, remarked that Justice Murphy's 1944 dissent would surely be a majority, if not a unanimous, opinion were the case to be heard by a contemporary court. But in 1944, Murphy was virtually alone. Although many Americans regretted what one official called the "unavoidable injustices" involved in the relocation, the overwhelming majority supported putting their fellow citizens of Japanese ancestry in concentration camps and, if wartime public opinion polls are to be believed, would have supported much harsher measures. Large numbers—an absolute majority in some polls—wanted all Japanese Americans sent "back" to Japan after the war, even though most of them—native-born citizens—had never been there!

During World War II, the lives of almost all Japanese Americans were turned upside down. By the closing days of the war more than half of those who had been in the wartime camps had left them for work and residence east of the coastal mountain ranges, for college, or for military service. In 1942 and 1943 some Japanese Americans had been allowed to volunteer for military service, and in 1944 the draft was reinstituted for Japanese American young men, even those still behind barbed wire! The wartime military service of some 25,000 Japanese Americans, including a hundred or so members of the Women's Army Corps, was largely either in segregated combat units in Europe—the famed 100th Battalion and the 442nd Regimental Combat Team—or in particularly dangerous military intelligence work with front-line units in the Pacific. The well-orchestrated publicity that the former group received—including a postwar White House ceremony at which President Harry S. Truman awarded the survivors the Presidential Unit Citation for bravery—was an important element in the relatively rapid rehabilitation of the reputation of the Japanese Americans. As we shall show in the next chapter, within two decades this one-time pariah group was being hailed as a "model minority."

But for thousands of Japanese Americans, this rehabilitation came too late. Their lives had been ruined, their property lost or badly damaged by neglect, vandalism, and theft, their self-esteem shattered. Some 5,000 persons of both generations, hopelessly embittered by the treachery of American democracy that had promised so much and delivered so little, chose to emigrate or repatriate to Japan after the war. Others, particularly older people, were never able to resume their shattered lives. Several hundred Japanese Americans, insisting that their incarceration was a violation of American principles, resisted the draft and were tried, convicted, and sent to federal penitentiaries. The image of a resilient, spunky Japanese American population rolling up its sleeves and successfully pursuing upward social and economic mobility after the war has been a popular one that the public and conservative ideologues like S. I. Hayakawa, Thomas Sowell, and William Petersen like to dwell on and exploit. After all, as William Dean Howells pointed out a century ago, what the American public really wants is a tragedy with a happy ending. For many, if not most Japanese Americans, there has been a relatively happy ending, although as with most happy endings, there were many unreckoned costs.

But for tens of thousands of Japanese Americans the relocation was a tragedy without a subsequent triumph. Only in the early 1980s, when the public hearings of the Commission on the Wartime Relocation and Internment of Civilians enabled hundreds of the survivors of America's concentration camps to come forth and tell their stories publicly, was it possible to imagine how deep the scars of the wartime experience were and how much pain they were still capable of inflicting. Unlike most wartime suffering, the agony of the Japanese Americans was inflicted by their own government. What happened to them remains, happily, a unique experience. But it is an experience that must trouble all Americans as it demonstrates so very clearly how fragile our constitutional protections can be in a time of crisis.

NOTES

1. Hilary Conroy, *The Japanese Frontier in Hawaii, 1869–1898* (Berkeley and Los Angeles: University of California Press, 1953), p. 140.
2. Japanese immigrants in the New World have used forms of the words for numbers to distinguish between generations. Thus, the first generation are called "issei" (ichi = one); the second generation, "nisei"; the third, "sansei"; the fourth, "yonsei"; and the fifth, "gosei." Nisei who were sent to Japan for education are called "kibei."
3. Because there are minor discrepancies in the 1920 census data for Japanese, the figures in these two tables, taken from different places in the fourteenth census, do not agree. For example, at different places native-born Japanese are enumerated at 29,506 and 29,672.
4. Donald T. Hata, Jr., *"Undesirables": Early Immigrants and the Anti-Japanese Movement in San Francisco, 1892–1893* (New York: Arno Press, 1978), and Roger Daniels, *The Politics of Prejudice: The Anti-Japanese Movement in California and the Struggle for Japanese Exclusion* (Berkeley and Los Angeles: University of California Press, 1962).
5. Irving G. Hendrick, *Public Policy Toward the Education of Non-White Minority Group Children in California, 1949–1970,* (Riverside, Calif.: University of California Press, 1975), and Charles M. Wollenberg, *All Deliberate Speed: Segregation and Exclusion in California Schools,* 1855–1979 (Berkeley and Los Angeles: University of California Press, 1977).
6. Roger Daniels, "The Japanese," in John Higham, ed., *Ethnic Leadership in America* (Baltimore: Johns Hopkins University Press, 1978), pp. 36–63, and Yuji Ichioka, "Japanese Associations and the Japanese Government: A Special Relationship, 1909–1926," *Pacific Historical Review* 45 (1977): 409–37.
7. Edward K. Strong, *The Second Generation Japanese Problem* (Stanford, Calif.: Stanford University Press, 1934), p. 2.
8. Ibid., p. 12.
9. Roger Daniels, *Concentration Camps, North America: Japanese in the United States and Canada During World War II* (Malabar, Fla.: Krieger, 1981).
10. Richard Drinnon, *Keeper of Concentration Camps* (Berkeley and Los Angeles: University of California Press, 1986). Drinnon sees Myer as the prototype of the dull, faceless, spineless bureaucrat who is promoted because of his willingness to serve. The term "the banality of evil" comes to mind.
11. President's Proclamation No. 4417 of Feb. 19, 1976, 41 "An American Promise," *Fed. Reg.* 35 (Feb. 20, 1976).
12. *Korematsu v. U.S.,* 323 *US* 214 (Dec. 18, 1944).

6

The Japanese
After World War II

The end of World War II and the closing of the concentration camps signified the end of an era, not of happy times, but of the worst aspects of discrimination, prejudice, and segregation. The Issei, many of whom lost their life savings, were still without citizenship and had to start life anew in an unknown, but presumed hostile environment. A few thousand Japanese Americans had opted for repatriation or expatriation to Japan; many others had settled in the Midwest, the Rocky Mountain West, and on the East Coast. But the majority were to return to the familiar environs of California and other West Coast states.

THE ISSEI

The period starting with the immigration in the late 1890s and continuing through the concentration camp period can be rightfully termed the Issei era, although there was some loosening of the power and control of the older generation by the time of the attack on Pearl Harbor. It was the Issei who forged the community, started family life, and laid the groundwork for the future generations. But they operated under severe handicaps. Like most immigrant groups they were faced with an unfamiliar culture and lacked the formal education and skills necessary for upward mobility. Further, they faced a hostile environment: They could not become citizens, could not own land, and were relegated to positions largely outside of the American mainstream. Many saw themselves as a sacrificial generation; they could not be successful, but their children might be.

There are a variety of ways of assessing the lives of the Issei. In common with most late-19th and early-20th-century immigrants, very few Issei integrated and became a part of the mainstream. Cultural barriers were too great. Even when institutional barriers were let down, the Issei preferred to interact primarily with fellow ethnics and families, thereby setting up an ethnic community and the basis for later participation in a pluralistic society. Therefore, if their goals included acculturation, integration, and assimilation, then most would admit that they did not come close to participating in the American mainstream. If their goals were couched in terms of a pluralistic adaptation—the development of independent, self-sufficient communities and the retention of many of the old, cultural ways—then there would be indications of success. If success were to be measured in terms of the lack of social problem behavior—crime, delinquency, mental illness, and poverty—then the group would have to be evaluated as successful. But if the assessment were to rely on the development of highly creative individuals, the number of such individuals would be very small. But taken in the context of the America that they faced, racist, hostile, and discriminatory, the Issei were a remarkable generation.

As the rapidly diminishing number of Issei survivors look back on their lives, they find some satisfaction in the lives of their children, many of whom have been outwardly more successful than they and thus, in their view, worthy of their sacrifices. They also have lived through the erasure of many of the racist barriers that plagued their lives—citizenship, land ownership, voting, and freer choices in housing. Relationships between the United States and their mother country have also improved; Issei admit that even in their wildest dreams they would not have foreseen these changes, especially while sitting in the concentration camps of World War II.

The Issei are a rapidly disappearing generation. Survivors are generally in their eighties and nineties; some have even lived past the century mark. Children remain important to them, but there is a fear of depending too much on them. Many Issei are forced to live with family members; others live in senior citizens' housing, such as the Little Tokyo Towers in Los Angeles (which has a long waiting list). Some are not so fortunate and have to live out their years in isolated apartments; most have lived away from the mainstream so long that integrated settings and acculturation have come too late.

Their values and life-styles are reminiscent of a Japan that may have never been—family responsibility, the importance of rituals, duty and obligation, a concern about what other people think, a strong group and family orientation, modesty, knowing one's place in society, and maintaining a low posture. Issei are often shocked to find that in their trips to Japan or in their contacts with Japanese newcomers that the "new" Japanese are as difficult to understand as the Sansei and Yonsei (third and fourth) generations here in America.

THE NISEI

The period during and after World War II and the next several decades was the Nisei period. The concentration camps forced some of the Nisei to assume leadership positions, sometimes prematurely, since many were barely out of their teens. Most of the Issei community leaders were rounded up by the FBI in the weeks after Pearl Harbor. Later, in the camps, it was a deliberate policy of the War Relocation Authority to shift responsibility to the American-citizen Nisei. The Nisei were therefore exposed to a variety of new life experiences, both in the camps and in the outside world, which gave them a broader view of the American society. Some had been in the armed forces and seen the world; others had left the camps for life in cities like New York, Chicago, Minneapolis, Denver, and Cleveland. Unlike their job experiences in prewar California, they found a wider range of occupational opportunities. Factory jobs were available, as well as positions more appropriate to their level of education and training. Some decided to live permanently in their new environments, but the majority, like their Issei parents, chose to return to the West Coast.

The Sansei, or third generation, were primarily dependent children in this era. Choices were not yet theirs to make. Instead, their role was to follow the lead of their parents. Thus, the picture after World War II included three generations: one aging, another as young adults, and the third as children, too young to make choices.

What the Nisei brought with them were experiences and feelings learned in environments different from li͡e in prewar California and the West. For those who stayed in the camps, exposure was to norms, attitudes, and behaviors appropriate to life in a closed environment. Standing in line, dependence on the government, control from the outside, and living day by day were key learnings; a saving grace for most evacuees was the relatively short duration of the incarceration. Therefore, the internalization of camp norms was apparently not deep enough to become a style of life for most. However, being forcibly placed behind barbed wire was an experience that could never be forgotten.

When people are taken out of their natural homes and placed in artificial settings (i.e., prisons, camps), their ability to readapt upon release will be dependent on what they have learned in the closed environment. A few camp experiences were positive. Positions usually reserved for dominant group members in the outside world were open to Nisei for the first time. Nisei teenagers became high school leaders, athletic heroes, and class officers. Nisei could become firemen or policemen, and lower administrative positions were open to them (higher positions were filled by appointed Caucasian personnel). One competed with other Japanese Americans in camp, so race was not a determining factor.

However, most camp norms were inappropriate for life in the outside world. Hard work, putting in long hours, loyalty, and responsibility were difficult norms to uphold under camp conditions. Acculturation to camp life included relaxed views of the use of government property (pilfering of lumber and other government supplies was common), the modification of parent-child roles, and a unique language. Phrases such as "waste time," "boochie" (being Japanese), and "monku, monku" (always complaining) became a part of a vocabulary that quickly disappeared when the camps were closed. Perhaps the most damaging acquired characteristic was the cynicism that developed regarding such concepts as democracy, American citizenship, and equality.

Japanese Americans who resettled met a variety of Americans from different cultures. Life east of the forbidden zone was different; there was discrimination and prejudice, but it was not as intense as on the West Coast. This lack of intensity was probably due to the existence of other pariah groups; blacks, Jews, Mexican Americans, and poor whites deflected some of the hostility away from the Japanese Americans and other Asians. Those who served in the armed services also had new experiences; the outcome for these people tended to be a higher level of expectation.

But changes within the ethnic group made up only a part of the equation. The critical changes were in the dominant society. There was an increased liberalization of attitudes and behavior toward Asians. Immigration and naturalization laws were changed; legal discrimination in housing gradually disappeared; antimiscegenation legislation was overturned in California in 1948 and nationally by the Supreme Court in 1967. Occupations previously closed to Asians, such as public school teaching, began to open. Hence, the picture of Nisei college graduates working at fruit stands was no longer common. College degrees, which were long a part of Nisei expectations, began to mean something, and career choices could be planned with a reasonable expectation of success.

An influential factor affecting the Nisei, and eventually, all Asian Americans, was the entrance of Hawaii as the fiftieth state of the union in 1959. Hawaii was the first state to elect public officials of Japanese ancestry. The United States Senate today includes Daniel K. Inouye and Spark Matsunaga, both of whom are sons of Issei immigrants and served in the military during World War II.

For the majority of Nisei, the period following World War II through the 1960s was one of trying to recover from the losses of the concentration camp period. It meant extra work, overtime, and dependence on multiple family incomes and multiple jobs. Gardening was one popular field; professionals and businessmen mowed lawns on a part-time basis to accumulate the capital needed to buy homes, to start their own enterprises, and to finance the education of their children, the Sansei. Many Nisei wives also worked, some in the clerical fields where they became very much in demand, others in whatever jobs that could be found, including housework. A special occupation, that of determining the sex of chickens, also used the talents of some Nisei.[1] The G.I. Bill and programs addressing first equal opportunity and later affirmative action were aids in their upward mobility.

Barriers in the social and recreational arenas were more difficult to overcome. Although segregation in movie theaters and public swimming pools was a thing of the past, most prestigious social clubs were closed to Japanese Americans, as were country clubs, fraternities, sororities, and other private organizations. De facto housing discrimination only began to be breached in the 1960s.[2] But the arena of higher education was largely open, and streams of Nisei could be found at colleges and universities. Most of them chose "safe" majors and aimed toward professional fields—medicine, pharmacy, dentistry, accounting, or education—where employment patterns were thought to be less discriminatory. The fear of racism could never be completely erased.

There was a reemergence of Nisei athletic and social organizations; the structure of the Japanese community in the 1950s and 1960s appeared to be similar to prewar times. But there were several differences. Whereas there was almost no choice but to belong to ethnic groups in the 1930s, the decades following World War II saw the diminishing of discrimination. Also, compared to the 1930s, Nisei social functions began to take on a much more middle-class quality. Whereas earlier conventions took place in unpretentious ethnic sites, the postwar Nisei began to look for first-class hotels and resorts in the mainstream community. This change has continued up to the present, and many old-timers complain about the additional costs of attending ethnic get-togethers. The most recent JACL convention (1986), for example, was held in Chicago's Hyatt Regency.

Most Nisei are facing the world today as mature and aging adults. Topics of discussion include retirement, health issues, and how to understand the new generations. The Nisei are primarily a "low profile" group; most are unknown, aside from such successful politicians as Representatives Norman Y. Mineta and Robert T. Matsui of California, Patsy T. Mink, the head of Americans for Democratic Action, and the previously mentioned senators from Hawaii. Fields often used by other minorities, such as athletics and show business, have not had significant Nisei participation, although actor Noriyuki "Pat" Morita has gained wide recognition, particularly through his roles in the *Karate Kid* movies and the television series "Ohara." The greatest Nisei contributions have been in everyday activities, often associated with the middle class: working hard, saving, raising children, and demonstrating good citizenship. Issei are surprised that the aging Nisei generation—in the 1980s they were in the sixty- to seventy-year-old age range—have become very much like them. Whereas at one time the Nisei were castigated for irresponsible behavior—they were becoming American too fast—they now reflect some of the old Issei values. Perhaps age is a variable that has some universal qualities.

In their own lives there have been dramatic changes: a "problem minority" in the 1930s; life in the concentration camps in the 1940s; reestablishment in the 1950s; political progress in the 1960s; and recognition as the "model minority" in the 1970s. Or as Ogawa says, "from Japs to Japanese."[3] Perhaps as more Nisei enter their retirement years in the 1980s, they will be in a good position to comment on some of the critical changes in American society which they have lived through.

THE SANSEI

The Sansei era, or third generation, can be arbitrarily assigned to the 1970s on, although by that time the generational references were beginning to lose their meaning. The relatively clear-cut generational differences that once characterized the Japanese American community have been eroded by new immigrants (Issei), the mixture of fourth- and fifth-generation Japanese Americans, and the influx of Japanese businessmen (most here for a temporary stay), students and the ubiquitous Japanese tourist. A broader term, Nikkei (Japanese people), has become more popular, since it refers to Japanese Americans as a whole, rather than to specific generations.

The Sansei and the Yonsei, or fourth generation, are the most "American" of any Japanese group; many of them have never faced overt discrimination, and some have never had close ethnic ties or ethnic friends. They flock to colleges and universities, eager for good jobs, especially in medicine, engineering, and law. Like many of their mainstream peers, they question the life-style and values of their parents but are the primary beneficiaries of the material success of the previous generation. Family life may now include as many as four generations: Issei great-grandparents, Nisei grandparents, Sansei parents, and Yonsei children, although the number of Issei survivors diminishes with each passing year. Most of the old Japanese ways are also passing with the Issei; new input, new technology, and "modern American values" appear more comfortable for each new generation.

One question raised by many Sansei that is difficult for many Nisei to answer relates to their behavior during the wartime evacuation. Why was there so little organized protest? What about litigation? Why did they go so meekly? For generations who grew up during the turbulent campus protests of the 1960s and 1970s, these questions are natural. And for the Nisei, the answers are also time related. They grew up in an era when dissent and overt protests by minority groups were rare. Further, the unequal power relationships, the wartime atmosphere, and the inexperienced leadership precluded any organized action. But because these issues were seldom discussed in the homes—many Sansei students complain that verbal exchange, especially of personal matters, has not been a part of their family style—questions of this nature come as a surprise. Japanese American homes appear harmonious to outsiders, especially since areas of potential conflict are often carefully avoided.

Although there are more opportunities to interact with the mainstream community, many Sansei still prefer ethnic organizations. For example, although more fraternities and sororities now accept Asians, all-Asian fraternities and sororities also continue to flourish. The atmosphere and the activities are identical, except that one group features all Asian faces.

One of the more surprising survivors in the tide toward the mainstream is the continued existence of the Japanese athletic leagues. In the past the Nisei athletic teams (the most popular sport was basketball) served a definite need—social and recreational opportunities were limited—but by the time of the Sansei, ample opportunities were available outside of the ethnic community. Acculturation and integration have occurred, but in some areas, for example, Los Angeles, Sansei basketball and volleyball leagues continue. It is interesting to note that ethnic norms often come into play; for example, players who "hot dog," shoot a lot and go for individual glory, are often controlled by their more team-oriented peers, who do not pass to them.[4]

Other ethnic activities also continue. The Nisei Week celebration in Los Angeles, which could probably be more accurately retitled as Nisei participation diminishes, has its counterparts in Hawaii and in San Francisco and other cities. One mainstream tradition, queen contests, are an integral part of these festivities—who will be the Nisei Week Queen, or Miss Cherry Blossom? But this bit of Americana raises some interesting questions. The contestants by now are Sansei and Yonsei, but with the rise of interracial marriage, the question is, Should they be "full-blooded" Japanese? What about those who are of mixed parentage? And with the rise of feminism, should there be such contests at all?

The new generations reflect the growing openness of American society. The ethnic community and family offer supportive frameworks, but opportunities, especially in terms of employment, are primarily in the dominant community. Gone are the Japanese gardeners, the "mom and pop" grocery stores, and other service occupations; perhaps other newer immigrant groups have taken them over. Sansei, like most other Americans, usually do not take over the trades of their parents, especially if they are low-status positions. And even if some so desire, the major occupations of many of their Nisei parents are in the professions, where education, training, and credentials take precedence over nepotism.

Sansei are more apt to reflect the ambience of their surrounding communities, rather than a strictly ethnic one. A Japanese American growing up in St. Louis will be more Missourian than Japanese, just as Sansei from Los Angeles, Honolulu, and New York will reflect the culture of these cities. The testimonies of individual Sansei make this point clearly.

One Sansei grew up in Gardena, a suburb of Los Angeles, which is often referred to as the Japanese American city. With a population made up of about a quarter Japanese, Gardena has Japanese councilmen, a Japanese pay cable TV station, and numerous ethnic stores. She tells a story of growing up which reflects a strong ethnic culture. This Sansei grew up in a bilingual, bicultural background and was surrounded by Japanese Americans throughout her high school years. She dated only other Sansei, and she was part of the "in group" in high school—scholarship society, class officer, cheerleading. Culture shock for her was enrolling at UCLA, where there were so many non-Japanese.[5]

Conversely, another Sansei grew up in the only Japanese American family in a suburb of San Diego. Her only contact with other Japanese was through the ethnic church, but her primary contacts, especially her close friends, were Caucasians. For her, culture shock was the large number of Asian Americans at UCLA.[6] It is interesting to note that she now has a Sansei boyfriend, although her behavior and her expectations appear much more "American" than "Japanese American."

A survey of students currently attending colleges and universities in the Los Angeles area shows a number of interesting findings.[7] Although the bulk of respondents represented the Sansei generation, there were even responses from fifth- and sixth-generation Japanese Americans. Respondents still believed in such values as hard work, good education, family and community solidarity, and perseverance—values passed down from their Issei and Nisei heritage. Most of them represented a Yuppie outlook, but it should be noted that they also held part-time jobs while attending school. The majority came from materially affluent backgrounds and enjoyed good relationships with their parents. They felt most comfortable with other Asians and belonged to Asian organizations such as the Community Youth Council, the Nisei Athletic Union, the Orange County Sports Association, and the Crescent Bay Optimists. In spite of these continuing ethnic ties, they overwhelmingly believed in interracial dating and marriage. Therefore, there appears to be a continuity between the Japanese generations on certain values, but the belief in interracial marriage adds to the possible acceleration of assimilation as the future of the Sansei and subsequent generations.

Summary data, taken from the 1980 census, provides a current broad picture of the Japanese American.[8] Of the 716,331 Japanese, 46 percent were males and 54 percent were females. Their median age was 33.6 years. Family size was 3.26. The great majority, 92 percent, lived in urban areas. Japanese Americans were unevenly distributed across the country—37.5 percent lived in California and 33.5 percent in Hawaii. In a variety of measures—income, high school graduates, life expectancy, those living under conditions of poverty and on public assistance—the Japanese were doing better than the whites. Approximately 72 percent of the group were born in the United States. Of the employed males, the two most common occupational categories were "technical, sales, and administrative support," with 32 percent, and "managerial and professional specialty" occupations, with 29 percent. The most popular female occupations were "technical sales," with 46 percent, and administrative support occupations, including clerical, with 32 percent, and "managerial and professional specialty," with 23 percent.

But there remains one common factor that still shapes Japanese American experiences. It is that of visibility; no matter how acculturated or talented a Sansei may be, the physical features identify him or her as an ethnic. Show business provides an example of this dilemma. For Japanese and other Asian Americans, acting positions remain primarily as stereotypes. Roles for Japanese actors include the gardener, cook, the camera-carrying tourist, the enemy soldier—always with an accent. Female roles are a sexy geisha or a compliant, submissive, "confused-about-America" character. The desired body type and physical image in America remains that of a Caucasian; it may take time and the continued introduction of new immigrants before the image of an American includes other models.

There are signs that the variable of visibility may be changing. Both Norman Mineta of San Jose and Robert Matsui of Sacramento have been elected and reelected to the U.S. Congress in areas where the number of Asian American voters is negligible. Sansei are entering occupations and fields that were once considered closed, such as advertising, the performing arts, journalism, and broadcasting. They are also taking over the leadership positions in such ethnic organizations as the Japanese American Citizens League (JACL); the current national director, Ron Wakabayashi, is Sansei. Nisei leaders sometimes appear just as reluctant as the old Issei used to be in giving up positions of power and authority; the accusation that the new generation wants things too quickly and easily, without "paying their dues," has a familiar ring.

For example, an interview by a Sansei reporter with Dan Aoki, a World War II veteran and reputed "hatchet man" of the Governor Burns Democratic political machine of Hawaii, gives a flavor of one Nisei's attitude toward the Sansei.[9] Aoki complains that the Sansei take everything for granted. He grew up when children of immigrants were "poisoned" by the idea that haoles (whites) were superior and when the highest position for

Nisei college students was bank teller or clerk. The World War II experiences transformed naive plantation kids, including himself, into belligerent ex-soldiers, fighting for their rightful place in Hawaiian society. His message was that the younger generations did not understand the struggles of the older, and that things that came too easily were never fully appreciated.

Many Sansei hear the same story from their Nisei parents, just as Nisei remember hearing a similar story from their Issei parents.

The most appropriate generalization concerning the Sansei deals with their heterogeneity. There are those who shop along Rodeo Drive in Beverly Hills, concerned primarily with brand names, status, and upward mobility; there are activists and militants who have little use for material possessions; some serve in the armed forces; others participate in almost every endeavor open to Americans everywhere. But the majority choose the so-called safer professions, where visibility is not as important as the quality of their education and credentials.

Most Sansei have acculturated; there is a high degree of integration in terms of housing, education, and occupations. A great deal of marital assimilation is taking place (see Chapter 13). But there is also the retention of pluralistic structures, especially in areas with large Japanese (and other Asian) populations, such as Honolulu and Los Angeles. The major difference between the old ethnic community and the newer ones is that of voluntarism. In the old days segregation was forced; in the current era there are choices. Perhaps this difference is an apt commentary on the changes that Japanese Americans have lived through.

NOTES

1. See Patricia Ward Biederman, "Separating the Chicks: A Baffling Job," Los Angeles *Times*, Nov. 29, 1985, p. 1. Chick sexing has been a skill that has been dominated by Japanese Americans.
2. Harry H. L. Kitano, "Housing of Japanese Americans in the San Francisco Bay Area," in Nathan Glazer and Davis McEntire, eds., *Studies in Housing and Minority Groups* (Berkeley: University of California Press, 1960), pp. 178–97.
3. Dennis Ogawa, *From Japs to Japanese* (Berkeley: McCutchan Publishing Company, 1971).
4. Discussions with a Sansei Ph.D. candidate in history at UCLA. There is a "jock" mentality among some Sansei: World affairs and politics are unimportant; their primary interest is how many points they scored and whether their teams are winning in the local athletic leagues. Then there are many others intensely involved in community change, in searching for an identity and their role in American society. The wide spread is similar to the diversity seen in the larger Los Angeles community.
5. Joy Taguma, "What Gardena Means to Me" (term paper, UCLA, 1985).
6. Karen Amano, "Interracial Marriage: A Comparative Analysis of the Views of Asian Americans" (independent study, UCLA, 1985).
7. Linda Takahashi, "Studying the Sansei Generation" (independent study, UCLA, 1985).
8. Robert W. Gardner, Bryant Robey, and Peter C. Smith, "Asian Americans: Growth, Change and Diversity," *Population Bulletin* 40, no. 4 (Oct. 1985): 1–44.
9. Roland Kotani, "Dan Aoki: 1918–1986," *Hawaii Herald*, July 4, 1986, p. 1.

7

The Filipinos

The history of Filipinos in the United States is, in one way, different from that of all other Asian ethnic groups in the United States: their history was, initially, a direct and unforeseen result of American imperialism. Because of this, Filipino Americans enjoyed, for a time, a unique status among Asian immigrants. They were not "aliens" but enjoyed a "privileged" status as American nationals. In other ways, the early history of 20th-century Filipino immigrants bears a resemblance to that of other Asian migrations.

BACKGROUND

The earliest Filipinos were students; then, largely in the 1920s and early 1930s, came farm laborers; finally, after 1965, came what some writers have called the "third wave" of Filipino immigrants—educated, upwardly mobile professionals and would-be entrepreneurs, similar to those coming from India. We now know that long before the American conquest of the Philippines in 1898 there were handfuls of Filipinos settled in the United States, almost all of them having come via Mexico as a result of Spanish imperialism. As early as the 18th century there was a tiny group of such immigrants in and around New Orleans, and there may well have been other Filipinos

in what later became the United States.[1] But there was no connection between these pioneers and 20th-century Filipino migrants.

The Spanish-American War of 1898, a series of disconnected skir-
mishes on land and sea over a period of ninety days, was called by one
contemporary a "splendid little war." At the cost of 389 combat dead, the
United States humbled once-mighty Spain, drove her from the New World,
and, in the process, gained a protectorate over Cuba and took possession
of Puerto Rico, Guam, and the Philippine Islands. In addition, in the wave
of martial patriotism that flooded the United States, Congress agreed to
annex Hawaii, which it had refused to do earlier.

But the relatively bloodless Spanish-American War was followed by
the bloodier and much longer Philippine-American War, which the American government called the Filipino Insurrection. This was an early and unsuccessful example of a third-world anticolonial war, what some would call
a war of national liberation. A segment of the Filipino people, who under
the leadership of Emilio Aguinaldo (1869–1964) had been resisting Spanish
rule, proclaimed themselves independent after the United States defeated
Spain, but the Americans refused to recognize their government and insisted that the Filipinos were not ready to rule themselves.

To establish American sovereignty firmly, an army of 100,000 was
shipped to the islands, and in the guerrilla war that followed both the Americans and their opponents resorted to the kinds of atrocities that irregular
warfare usually breeds. The Filipino "insurrection" was officially ended in
1902, although some fighting continued in the southern Philippines for several years. Altogether 4,243 American soldiers were killed "pacifying" the
islands and many times that number of Filipinos, both guerrillas and civilians. After the fighting was over, the first American civilian governor of the
Philippines, William Howard Taft, began nearly half a century of avowedly
benevolent despotism by proclaiming his concern for the welfare of the
people of the Philippines, whom he described as our "little brown brothers." United States leaders soon realized that the Philippines could not be
defended in case of war, so the Filipinos were promised independence by
1945. World War II unavoidably delayed that timetable, but the United
States did grant the Philippines independence in 1946. (The United States
still maintains military bases there, chiefly naval facilities on Manila Bay
and the northern Luzon air complex at Clark Field, which, after the fall of
Vietnam, became the most significant U.S. outpost in Southeast Asia.)

The more than 7,000 Philippine Islands lie off the shores of Southeast
Asia and today have a population of some fifty million persons. The islands
were visited by the Portuguese explorer Fernando Magellan in his circumnavigation of the globe in 1521. Later in the sixteenth century, Spain took
possession of the Philippines. Most of the Filipinos, Malaysian people ethnically, had been converted to Roman Catholicism long before the Philippine-
American War, although a considerable population in the southern Philip-

pines, particularly on Mindanao, had been converted to Islam. Although there are many languages spoken in the Philippines—all of them of the Malayo-Polynesian group and enough alike that most are mutually understandable—just three indigenous languages are spoken by about 85 percent of the population: Visayan, a language of the central Philippines, is spoken by about 44 percent; Tagalog (now Pilipino and since 1946 the official language), a language of central Luzon, is spoken by about 25 percent; and Ilocano, a language of northern Luzon, is spoken by about 16 percent. In addition, both Spain and the United States imposed their own languages; thus the educated elites have spoken Spanish or English. Virtually all of those who have immigrated to the United States have been Roman Catholics, and a majority have been Ilocano speakers.

THE PENSIONADOS

The first Filipino immigrants to the United States were students, the *pensionados,* who were chosen, financed, and sponsored by the U.S. government. This program, which lasted from 1903 to 1910, provided several hundred students with practical training. In 1907, for example, 183 students were reported at forty-seven American educational institutions, largely in the Midwest. The two largest enrollments were at the University of Illinois (13%) and Purdue (11%). Education attracted forty-four students; civil engineering, thirty-two; agriculture, twenty-three; mechanical engineering, nineteen; and medicine, seventeen.[2] Thousands of Filipino young men, usually underfinanced, continued to come to the United States to study. One early scholar of the Filipino American experience, Benicio T. Catapusan, himself a student who earned a Ph.D. in sociology at the University of Southern California in 1940, estimated that between 1910 and 1938 some 14,000 Filipinos had enrolled in American educational institutions. Most, for one reason or another, were never able to complete their studies, but the bulk of those who did—from institutions such as the University of California, Columbia, Cornell, Harvard, Northwestern, Stanford, the University of Washington, and Yale—returned to the Philippines to occupy important positions in government and business.[3] The majority of those who stayed in the United States usually plied the manual labor occupations that employed most Filipino Americans in those years.

One of the survivors of that experience recently told an interviewer in Portland, Oregon:

> When I finished high school in the Philippines I intended to study agriculture at Oregon State University. I went and looked at the campus. Then the depression came. It was hard for me to find a job. I found a job in the fraternity house, waiting tables for room and board. I was not able to continue my stud-

ies. When the depression was over, I thought I was too old. I said I would rather work. At that time we were not able—even with how educated we were—the only jobs to do were odd jobs: cooks, janitors, waiters, busboys, and farm work, but there were no white collar jobs.[4]

A surprising number of Filipino intellectuals lived and worked in America, the most notable of whom was Carlos Bulosan (1911–1956), who spent the last twenty-six years of his life here. Bulosan and others came to the United States filled with democratic ideals they had learned in American-run schools and with an unrealistic vision of what their life in the United States would be like. Thus, their reaction was often bitter. As Bulosan wrote to a friend:

Do you know what a Filipino feels in America? ... He is the loneliest thing on earth. There is much to be appreciated ... beauty, wealth, power, grandeur. But is he part of these luxuries? He looks, poor man, through the fingers of his eyes. He is enchanted, damnably to his race, his heritage. He is betrayed, my friend.[5]

THE SECOND WAVE

But, as with most other immigrants, it was economic rather than intellectual aspiration that motivated most Filipinos who came. The Manila *Times* described it very well in 1929:

The migrating Filipino sees no opportunity for him in the Philippines. Advertise in a Manila paper and offer a job (at below a living wage) and you will get a thousand applicants. Make the same offer in any provincial town, and the response will be twice as great, comparatively. Is it any wonder, then, that the lure of pay four to ten times as great, in Hawaii or the United States, draws the Filipino like a magnet? Plus the certainty he feels that he will get a job?[6]

The first important magnet was Hawaii, where, after the Gentlemen's Agreement of 1907–1908 made it impossible to continue to recruit male Japanese laborers, the Hawaiian Sugar Planter's Association (HSPA) began to recruit laborers in the Philippines. Between 1909 and 1934, according to the careful work of Mary Dorita Clifford, the HSPA arranged for 119,470 Filipinos to come to work in their sugar fields and mills. Of these, 86.6 percent were men, 7.5 percent women, and 5.9 percent children. Most of those who came were under three-year contracts. Upon expiration of the contracts, some continued to work in Hawaii, others went back to the Philippines, and still others went on to the West Coast of the United States.[7] Table 7-1 shows the number and incidence of Filipinos in Hawaii's population.

The migration of Filipino laborers to the American mainland, either

TABLE 7-1   Filipinos in Hawaii, 1910–1980

YEAR	NUMBER	PERCENT OF POPULATION
1910	2,361	1.23
1920	21,031	8.22
1930	63,052	17.17
1940	52,569	12.42
1950	61,062	12.22
1960	69,070	10.91
1970	95,354	12.41
1980	109,203	13.08

Source: U.S. Census.

from Hawaii or directly from the Philippines, is primarily a product of the post–World War I years (see Table 7–2).

Filipino laborers occupy exactly the same niche in California agriculture as their Asian predecessors had, except that by the end of the 1930s significant numbers of them were working for Asian American agricultural entrepreneurs, most of whom were of Japanese ethnicity. As both the Hawaiian and California data show, the pre–World War II Filipino migration was overwhelmingly male (94 percent in 1930).

Unlike earlier Asian immigrants, Filipinos actively sought white female companionship, and this overt sexuality enraged much white opinion. California newspapers focused on commercial dance halls, some of which catered exclusively to Filipino men, where, at ten cents a dance of only momentary duration, an agricultural worker could spend a week's wages in an hour or two. One group of headlines in the *Los Angeles Times* read:

Taxi Dance Girls Start Filipinos on Wrong Foot
Lonely Islanders' Quest for Woman Companionship Brings Problems of Grave National Moment
Mercenary Women Influence Brown Man's Ego
Minds Made Ripe for Work of Red Organizers[8]

TABLE 7-2   Filipino American Population, 1910–1950

	CONTINENTAL UNITED STATES	CALIFORNIA	PERCENT IN CALIFORNIA	MALES IN CALIFORNIA	FEMALES IN CALIFORNIA
1910	406	5	1.2	—	—
1920	5,603	2,674	47.7	—	—
1930	45,208	30,470	67.4	28,625	1,845
1940	45,876	31,408	68.5	—	—
1950	61,645	40,424	65.8	30,819	9,605

Source: U.S. Census.

Although the focus of nativist attention was on these transitory com-mercial sexual relationships—and several of the anti-Filipino riots began in and around dance halls—a significant number of more lasting interracial relationships took place. Some involved marriage, and Californians discov-ered, to their horror, that the existing miscegenation statutes only forbade marriages between white persons and Negroes, mulattoes, and Mongolians. Although California Attorney General U. S. Webb, a racist of long standing, conveniently ruled that Filipinos were Mongolians, he was reversed by the courts. Thus, in 1933, California amended the statute to include "members of the Malay race," and within four years Filipino-white marriages were also forbidden in Oregon, Nevada, and Washington.[9]

We know very little about these interracial marriages in general, but Barbara Posadas in a sensitive study has examined a number of Filipino-white marriages in and around Chicago in the pre–World War II years. Al-most all of these were marriages between Filipino men and the daughters of Eastern European immigrants; they were the foundation of a small but stable Filipino American community in Chicago, some of whose breadwin-ners were Pullman porters.[10] There were clearly more such marriages in the Far West, but no one has published findings about them.

In addition to agriculture and menial service jobs, such as dishwash-ing, Filipino workers also played a significant role in Alaska's fish canneries. Most cannery workers were recruited in Seattle, which became the major non-California center of Filipino American population. One cannery worker wrote in his diary for June 1924:

> Worked in the ship unloading salmon cans, at $.75 an hour. It was my first time in America to work. Worked exactly ten hours. Donning the overall for the first time in my life, handling the wheelbarrow, and carrying salmon boxes, was a thrill and an unforgettable experience.... Was laughing at the easy job and easy money. $7.50 for working 10 hours. In the Philippines it takes a month for a policeman to earn that. Such is the better prospect of life in this beautiful country.[11]

This worker and others soon discovered that if wages were higher, so were living costs. They also learned that canning runs last only for the summer months. Their involvement in the Alaska canning industry—by 1930 they outnumbered all other ethnic groups combined by about two to one—brought many Filipino Americans into contact with the trade union move-ment. More than any other Asian American group of this era, they became involved in both union activities and radical politics. This, however, did not stop the American Federation of Labor (AFL) from agitating for their exclusion. Starting in 1928, national AFL conventions passed a series of resolutions such as the following:

> Whereas, the desire for cheap labor has acted like a cancer ... destroying American ideals and preventing the development of a nation based on racial unity; and
>
> Whereas ... this desire has exploited the Negro, the Chinese, the Japanese, the Hindus, as in turn each has been regulated and excluded; and
>
> Whereas, the Malays of the Philippines were in 1924 omitted from the general policy excluding all who cannot become citizens; and
>
> Whereas, there are a sufficient number of Filipinos ready and willing to come to the United States to create a race problem equal to that already here ... we urge exclusion of Filipinos also.[12]

Although labor took the lead in opposing Filipino immigration, even before the Great Depression of the 1930s stemmed the migration, a broadly-based anti-Filipino movement developed in California and elsewhere on the Pacific coast. Beginning in 1929 there were anti-Filipino riots in Watsonville and other small central California cities. Civic organizations, such as the Los Angeles and Northern Monterey County Chambers of Commerce, deplored their presence. In 1930 one California judge declared from the bench that Filipinos were but ten years removed from the breechcloth. Another, after the depression had set in, insisted that "it is a dreadful thing when these Filipinos, scarcely more than savages, come to San Francisco, work for practically nothing and obtain the society of white girls. Because the Filipinos work for nothing, decent white boys cannot get jobs."[13]

In many ways the anti-Filipino agitation resembled that of previous anti-Asian movements. C. M. Goethe, a Sacramento businessman associated with the nativist Joint Immigration Committee, ignoring the absence of women in the Filipino migration, argued that ten million American blacks were descended from "an original slave nucleus of 750,000" and insisted that "Filipinos do not hesitate to have nine children ... [which means] 729 great-grandchildren as against the white parents' twenty-seven."[14] But, as suggested earlier, the fact that the Philippines were an American possession and Filipinos were American nationals made the majority of Congress unwilling to exclude them along with all other Asians, as a bill first introduced in 1928 proposed to do. After six years of discussion and debate and one presidential veto, Filipino immigration was tied to independence for the Philippines. The Tydings-McDuffie Act of 1934 successfully combined the two issues. The Philippines were promised independence in 1945, and, effective almost immediately, Filipinos were given an annual quota of fifty immigrants, half of the previous minimum. This was at least a small defeat for exclusionists such as Senator Hiram W. Johnson, who had wanted total exclusion.[15] Nonetheless, Filipinos remained "aliens ineligible for citizenship." To demonstrate further that Filipinos were unwanted, Congress in 1935 passed resolutions providing free passage on army transports for Filipinos desiring to return home. Although the resolution spoke of "humanitarian" considerations, its Senate sponsorship by Hiram Johnson indicated the true motives of most of its supporters. As it turned out, only 2,190 Filipinos took advantage of the offer.

For the rest of the 1930s, Filipinos, like other noncitizens, saw their relative economic status undermined. A fairly large number, 7,869 in 1930, were employed in the American merchant marine. In 1936, Congress enacted legislation mandating that 90 percent of each ship's crew be American citizens, which eliminated most Filipino jobs. Ironically, Filipinos were still allowed to serve in the U.S. Navy, where they were restricted to menial employment as mess stewards. Although the United States Civil Service Commission allowed Filipinos, as nationals, to take examinations for federal jobs, this was of little use to Filipino Americans who were uneducated (in Chicago there was a small group employed in the post office). Most states had licensing laws that required all kinds of activities—from doctors to plumbers to barbers and hairdressers—to be licensed and often insisted that all licensees be citizens. During the worst of the depression, Filipinos were barred from federal relief, until in 1937 Federal Relief Administrator Harry L. Hopkins made them eligible, but on a nonpreferential basis.

Between 1934 and the end of World War II no significant migration from the Philippines occurred, and the heavily male Filipino population aged and declined. The onset of wartime prosperity and the removal of Japanese Americans from West Coast agriculture created economic opportunities for Filipino Americans, and the overglamorized media portrayals of all Filipinos as loyal friends of American and enemies of Japan, made them, along with Chinese Americans, at least "assistant heroes" in the great Pacific war. In 1946, as a reward for loyalty, Congress made Filipinos eligible for citizenship, and President Truman boosted the quota for the Philippines to a "normal" 100 annually.

THE THIRD WAVE

However, as was true with other groups of immigrants from Asia, nonquota immigrants—usually close relatives of United States citizens—far outnumbered quota immigrants. For the thirteen years of the McCarran-Walter Act, 1953–1965, when a quota of 100 was in effect and would have yielded a total of 1,300 immigrants, the Immigration and Naturalization Service recorded 32,201 Filipino immigrants. In addition, even larger numbers of nonimmigrants—tourists, business people, students—were admitted, and many of these became permanent additions to the American population. In 1963, for example, 3,618 Filipino immigrant entrants were outnumbered by the arrival of 13,860 nonimmigrants. Thus, in the twenty years after World War II, many more Filipinos entered the United States than in the previous half century. The scrapping of the quota system in 1965 transformed immigration from the Philippines, and in all of the years since then the Philippines

TABLE 7-3   Filipinos in the United States, 1960–1985

	TOTAL	MALE	FEMALE	PERCENT FEMALE
1960	181,614	114,179	67,435	37.1
1970	336,731	183,175	153,556	45.6
1980	774,652	374,191	400,461	51.7
1985 (est.)	1,051,600	—	—	—

Source: U.S. Census and Population Reference Bureau.

have been one of the chief suppliers of immigrants to the United States. Table 7–3 illustrates that growth and includes Filipinos on the mainland and in the Hawaiian Islands.

The post-1965 immigration has not only changed dramatically the size of the Filipino American population, it has radically changed its composition. Perhaps two-thirds of the immigrants since 1965 have been of the professional classes, particularly health professionals. Filipino American nurses are clearly the most conspicuous single group of employed Filipinos, and, in part because of them, a greater percentage of Filipino American women were in the labor force in 1980 than were any other group of Asian American women. Filipino Americans had about as much education as white Americans and slightly less than East Asian Americans. But they were strikingly better educated than Filipinos who stayed in the Philippines. In 1980 just over a quarter of all Filipinos aged 25 to 29 in the islands were high school graduates; of those in the United States who were recent immigrants, the figure was almost 85 percent. The median income of full-time Filipino American workers in 1979 was $13,690, well below that of most other Asian American groups and about halfway between the wages of white American workers on the one hand and black and Hispanic workers on the other. But, partly because of the greater employment of Filipino American women, only 6.2 percent of their households were in poverty, a rate below every other group (including whites) except for Japanese Americans. Another reason was that recently arrived Filipino American households were larger than those of other ethnic groups. In 1980 such households contained, on average, 5.4 persons, 60 percent of whom were *not* nuclear family members. By comparison, all Filipino American households averaged only 3.6 persons, only a sixth of whom were not, as the census puts it, "householder, spouse or children." Such larger household units are and have been typical of recent immigrants. Filipino Americans are highly concentrated in California and Hawaii, where in 1980 almost two-thirds of them—62.7 percent—lived. Of Asian American groups, only Japanese Americans were more concentrated in those two states, with 71 percent of them living there.

In common with most immigrant groups, it is the diversity of the Filipinos that is most striking. There are the first-generation old-timers, primarily males who emigrated in the 1920s. These survivors can often be found living in dingy hotel rooms in California valley towns—Stockton is one favorite—or in urban centers such as Los Angeles, San Francisco, and Honolulu. Many had lived their lives as itinerant fruit pickers; Filipino labor gangs were known for their efficiency in the fields and their strong work ethic. There was little acculturation and integration among them, except for the few who "outmarried" and started family life.

The American-born second generation shared many of the problems that children of other Asian immigrants faced. There was a lack of social acceptance, low income, and a negative self-image. In contrast to some of the other Asian groups, there was little encouragement to obtain higher education. Even those who wanted to go to college frequently found the financial burdens an obstacle. Further, they knew little about the roots of their culture and yet could not gain full acceptance into the mainstream. Questions of an identity and some understanding of their role in America became major preoccupations during the civil rights struggles of the 1970s. It is also interesting to note that when Asian Americans were deemed ineligible for affirmative action consideration by the University of California system in the 1980s, protests were mounted, and the Filipinos were then included in such programs.

The post–World War II veteran made up another important element in the community. Many arrived in their adult years; most arrived with impressive-sounding diplomas that did not qualify them for much in the new country. They had served with the Filipino Scouts during World War II or as mess stewards in the U.S. Navy; they had lived under armed forces discipline and shared a mixture of high patriotism and a naive view of life in America. Although life in the United States was marginal—poor housing, low-status jobs, and minimal income—it was deemed better than what they could have expected in the Philippines. Acculturation and participation in the American mainstream were minimal. Many continued to retain close ties with the Philippines and to live within their own cultural network.

The newly arrived make up the bulk of the current Filipino population. As with the other fast-growing Asian groups, their numbers are the result of the 1965 immigration legislation. Reasons behind their immigration are familiar—unstable economic and political conditions in the home country, family reunification, and the expectation of better economic and educational opportunities in the new country. Many come with advanced training—medical degrees are common—and some are able to continue their careers. Many others, however, find difficulty in obtaining jobs commensurate with their past background. Filipino lawyers may find work as clerks; teachers as secretaries; dentists as dental aides; and engineers as mechanics. Still, a low-paying job in America often pays more than a higher-status job in the home country.[16]

Munoz's study of the adaptation of the Filipinos contrasted the different life-styles and the subsequent transformation in the new country.[17] Whereas a more leisurely pace would have been appropriate in the Philippines, they learn that the American style calls for work with a vengeance. Moonlighting becomes a new way of life; the goal of making money and retiring in the Philippines has become popular.

The new immigrants face a variety of problems, including education, finances, unemployment, child guidance, and the elderly. Culture shock, racism, credentialing, and licensing are other issues.[18] Perhaps the major problem of the Filipinos has been their lack of cohesion. There are island differences, different languages, ideological rifts, and subgroup cultures that separate the community. It appears difficult to form an overall Filipino organization because of the strength of local groups and their competing loyalties. Filipino organizations tend to multiply, rather than to unify.[19]

Azores studied the current generation of Filipino high school seniors and found that a very high percentage had aspirations for a college education.[20] However, many of them lacked the grades. Azores suggested three possible reasons for this dilemma:

1. Filipino students have unrealistic expectations.
2. High aspirations may not be linked to personal commitment.
3. Students may feel that there are characteristics other than grades that define a good student.

Her findings contradict a commonly held belief that many Filipino Americans do not aspire toward higher education.

Min compared Filipinos and Koreans in terms of their orientation toward small business.[21] Koreans turned to small business because of language difficulties and other disadvantages in the labor market, whereas Filipinos, who were less disadvantaged in language and were more familiar with American practices, were able to bypass the small business model. Koreans also had the availability of family and other kinship networks for the intensive labor often required in small business; there were also such factors as the industrialization of South Korea and import-export ties. In contrast, the English-speaking Filipinos, especially those with degrees in medicine and nursing, can find employment relatively easily outside of the ethnic community.

Nevertheless, when looking at the group as a whole, Filipinos suffer from economic inequality. Cabezas, Shinagawa, and Kawaguchi analyzed the status of Filipino Americans in California.[22] Using the 1980 census, they found that Filipinos remain in a subordinated position in relation to other Asians and the white majority, whether "sailors or professionals, educated or less educated, skilled or unskilled." They are often clustered in the secondary labor market, where the pay is low and mobility is limited.

A few Filipino Americans have been political exiles in recent years, largely exiles from the dictatorship of Ferdinand E. Marcos, who ruled the Philippines from 1965 to 1986. Most prominent of these exiles were Benigno S. Aquino and his wife, Corazon. Benigno returned to the Philippines to lead the opposition to Marcos but was assassinated, with apparent government complicity, as he arrived at the Manila airport on August 21, 1983. His wife then took up the reform cause and daringly challenged the dictator. Although she was "counted out" in an election, she was so clearly the winner that Marcos and his wife, Imelda, were forced to flee and are themselves, at this writing, living in exile outside Honolulu.

Despite political reforms and a popular government under "Cory" Aquino, the same lack of economic opportunity for educated persons that led hundreds of thousands of Filipinos to emigrate in past years continues to prevail. Assuming our immigration laws are not changed, experts believe that Filipinos will continue to come to the United States in large numbers. One projection by Leon F. Bouvier and Anthony Agresta has guesstimated that by the year 2000, Filipinos will be the largest Asian American group, with just over two million persons, nearly double the 1985 figure. However, we should note that all previous projections have been wrong. No one, for example, predicted in 1970 that Filipino American population would nearly triple by 1985.

In any event, the aging veterans of the earliest immigration, *pinoys* as they call themselves, are rapidly passing from the scene, as are the Issei generation of Japanese, the pioneers of the Korean immigration, and the Sikh farm workers and rebels. The current Filipino immigrants and their descendants will surely play a different role in the United States. This role will be middle class, professional, and urban for some. Others, unless there is a drastic change in the economy, will remain trapped in the secondary labor market and experience continued inequality.

NOTES

1. Marina E. Espina, *Readings on Filipinos in Louisiana* (privately printed, ca. 1982).
2. H. Brett Melendy, *Asians in America: Filipinos, Koreans and East Indians* (Boston; Twayne, 1977), contains the best historical account. The most recent sociological work is Antonio J. A. Pido, *The Pilipinos in America* (New York; Center for Migration Studies, 1986).
3. Benecio T. Catapusan, "The Social Adjustment of Filipinos in the United States" (Ph.D. diss., University of Southern California, 1940).
4. As cited in Tricia Knoll, *Becoming Americans* (Portland, Ore. Coast to Coast Books, 1982), p. 100.
5. Carlos Bulosan, "Selected Letters of Carlos Bulosan," *Amerasia Journal* 6 (1979): 143. For the most recent work on Bulosan, see Susan Evangelista, *Carlos Bulosan and His Poetry: A Biography and Anthology* (Seattle: University of Washington Press, 1985).
6. Bruno Lasker, *Filipino Immigration to the Continental United States and Hawaii* (Chicago: University of Chicago Press, 1931), p. 233.
7. Mary Dorita Clifford, "The Hawaiian Sugar Planter Association and Filipino Exclusion,"

in J. M. Saniel, ed., *The Filipino Exclusion Movement, 1927–1935* (Quezon City, Philippines: University of the Philippines, 1967), pp. 11–29.

8. *Los Angeles Times,* Feb. 2, 1930, p. 1.

9. Melendy, *Asians in America,* p. 53.

10. Barbara M. Posadas, "Crossed Boundaries in Interracial Chicago: Pilipino American Families since 1925," *Amerasia Journal* 8 (1981): 31–52. See also her "The Hierarchy of Color . . . Filipino Immigrants, the Pullman Company and the Brotherhood of Sleeping Car Porters," *Labor History* 23 (1982): 349–73.

11. Diary, Victorio A. Velasco Collection, University of Washington Archives, Seattle.

12. American Federation of Labor, *Proceedings,* 1928 (Washington, D.C.: 1928).

13. San Francisco *Chronicle,* Jan. 22, 1936. See also Howard A. DeWitt, "The Watsonville Anti-Filipino Riot of 1930: A Case Study of the Great Depression and Ethnic Conflict in California," *Southern California Quarterly* 61 (1979): 291–302.

14. C. M. Goethe, "Filipino Immigration Viewed as a Peril," *Current History,* January 1934, p. 354.

15. For details see Robert A. Divine, *American Immigration Policy, 1924–1952,* (New Haven, Conn.: Yale University Press, 1957), pp. 68–76.

16. Fred Cordova, "The Filipino American: There's Always an Identity Crisis," in Stanley Sue and Nathaniel Wagner, eds., *Asian Americans* (Palo Alto, Calif.: Science and Behavior Books, 1973), pp. 136–39.

17. Alfred N. Munoz. *The Filipinos in the United States* (Los Angeles: Mountainview Publishers).

18. Royal F. Morales, *Makibaba* (Los Angeles: Mountainview Publishers, 1974).

19. H. Brett Melendy, "Filipinos," in Stephan Thernstrom et al., eds. *The Harvard Encyclopedia of American Ethnic Groups* (Cambridge, Mass.: Harvard University Press, 1980), pp. 354–62.

20. Tania Azores, "Educational Attainment and Upward Mobility: Prospects for Filipino Americans," *Amerasia Journal* 13, no. 1 (1986–87): 39–52.

21. Pyong Gap Min, "Filipino and Korean Immigrants in Small Business: A Comparative Analysis," *Amerasia Journal* 13, no. 1 (1986–87): 53–71.

22. Amado Cabezas, Larry H. Shinagawa, and Gary Kawaguchi, "New Inquiries into the Socioeconomic Status of Pilipino Americans in California," *Amerasia Journal* 13, no. 1 (1986–87): 1–21.

8

Asian Indians

The history of people from India in the United States may most readily be divided into two parts. A first and relatively small number—perhaps 10,000 persons or so—came mostly around the turn of the century, when India was a unified colony of Great Britain. A second, much larger increment of persons have come since India and Pakistan became independent in 1947.[1] As of 1985, there were more than half a million persons in the United States of Indian birth or ancestry, as well as a few thousand from both Pakistan and Bangladesh.

BACKGROUND

Although there were a few Indian seamen reported in New England in the late eighteenth century and tiny communities of Indian merchants were established in the eastern United States from the mid-nineteenth century on, statistically significant migration of Indians began just after 1900. Like most other Asian immigrants at that time, they came on trans-Pacific ships, usually via Hong Kong, since there was no direct passenger service between India and the West Coast. Although the first sizable group of Indian immigrants—a few hundred—came to the Pacific Northwest after landing at Vancouver, British Columbia, California became the goal of most of the early Indian immigrants.

India is a huge country with dozens of distinct and diverse ethnic groups, but, as was the case with immigrants from China, most early Indian immigrants came from just one region, the Punjab, a prosperous fertile region of North India. The Punjab, unlike most of the areas from which other Asians immigrated, is not a coastal region. Because of the advanced railroad network, one of the few positive achievements of the British rule in India, Punjabi immigrants could get to seaports quickly, cheaply, and safely.

The overwhelming majority of these Indians were Sikhs, although some Hindus and a few Muslims immigrated as well. Sikhism, which developed in the Punjab early in the sixteenth century, was an attempt to reconcile Muslim and Hindu in a region that was then and still is multiethnic. By the eighteenth century the Sikhs had become implacable enemies of the Muslims and had become a largely military caste in which all members took the name Singh (Lion). At that time the still-current practices that give the Sikhs high visibility were adopted: the wearing of turbans, the wearing of a dagger and an iron bracelet at all times, and never cutting the hair or beard. Modern Sikh life is dominated by the Akali Dal (Army of God) movement, which demands the creation of a Sikh state in the Punjab.

ON THE WEST COAST

The early Sikh migrants to California, perhaps 5,000 strong, first were employed in lumbering and railroad work but soon turned to agriculture, first as laborers and later as proprietors and tenants. In two areas of the state, the Imperial Valley in the south and the Sacramento Valley in the north, they became a numerically significant minority. They experienced the same kinds of legal and extralegal discriminations as did other Asians. The alien land laws, for example, were used against them. While a few racist Californians saw the East Indians, as they were usually called, as superior to other Asians, others saw them as "the least desirable race of immigrants thus far admitted to the United States." Immigration records showed some 5,800 East Indian immigrants entering between 1901 and 1911, only 109 of them female.

Despite the very small number of women, large numbers of the Asian Indian migrants appear to have been married. One Immigration Commission survey—the only one we have for this period—questioned 474 laborers working on the West Coast. Slightly more than half said that they were married but in every instance reported that the wife was "abroad." This was a pattern common to all Asian working men on this continent, a condition sociologists have called "mutilated marriage." Large numbers of these men planned to be sojourners, that is, work here for a time, save some money, and send it home to buy land. According to H. A. Millis, the first scholar to study East Indians in America, two thousand dollars was the goal of many. Since agricultural laborers could expect to save, at best, between fifteen and twenty-five dollars a month, and since, even assuming continuous employment, it would take from seven to eleven years to amass such a sum, most sojourners were bound to be frustrated. Yet, savings did occur, and money was remitted to India. The Marysville, California, post office, for example, in an area in which many Indians worked, reported that in one eight-month period ending in mid-1908, $34,000 in postal remittances were sent to India. How many immigrants sent money home? No one knows. The Immigration Commission interviewed seventy-nine millhands in Washington and California in early 1909. Thirty-one of them—about 40 percent—said that in the previous year they had sent a total of $4,320 to India, an average of nearly $140 for each of those who sent, but only about $55 for the whole group.[2]

MANGOO RAM (1886–1980)

Many of those who were not Sikhs, were, like the Sikhs, Punjabis. It is very difficult to imagine what life was like for these toilers, rural proletarians in California's factories in the field, but we do know, thanks to Mark Juergensmeyer, a great deal about one of them, a man named Mangoo Ram, who was born a Hindu on January 14, 1886, in the Punjab. His father had left the traditional Chamar caste occupation of tanning hides and had become a hide merchant. First taught in his village, Mangoo Ram later attended a number of district schools. As the only scheduled caste student in most of his schools, he had to sit in the back of the classroom or sometimes in a separate room listening through an open door. When he attended high school, he had to stay outside of the building and listen through an open window.

Mangoo Ram left school in 1905, married, and worked for his father for three years. In 1909 in the Punjab, as Juergensmeyer puts it, "America was in the air." Scores of upper-caste farmers from Mangoo Ram's part of the Punjab had gone there. It was arranged for him to go, too. There was a tight network. The labor contractor for whom Mangoo Ram first worked in the orchards of central California was the brother of a local landlord in the Punjab. Part of Mangoo Ram's passage was paid by the contractor who took it, and interest, out of the young man's wages. This was quite similar to the credit-ticket system pioneered by the Chinese in the mid-nineteenth century. In California, Mangoo Ram picked fruit in orchards up and down the central valley and worked in a sugar mill.

Mangoo Ram's life was very much like other sojourners until 1913, when he became someone special. In that year he joined the revolutionary

Gadar movement in San Francisco, and from then until his death in 1980 at age 94 he was a figure in Indian history. For his activities during World War I as what we would now call a freedom fighter—the British called him a terrorist—he was sentenced to death. He escaped from prison, and, after a sojourn in the Philippines, made his way back to the Punjab only in 1925. There he helped form the Ad Dharm movement of untouchables in 1926.

Unlike most of the early Indian immigrants, Mangoo Ram was not an anonymous individual. As Juergensmeyer indicates, his sixteen years abroad helped transform him, as, of course, did his education. While abroad he was treated as an individual, not as a Chamar. The hostility to all East Indians in America tended to blur differences within the immigrant community; in addition, as Ram himself puts it, within the Gadar movement "we were treated as equals."[3]

GADAR MOVEMENT

The tragic and quixotic story of the Gadar movement, often referred to by American historians as the Hindu Conspiracy, needs to be considered briefly here. While Gadar was special and violent in its aims and involved only a small minority of the Indian immigrants in America, almost all of them were, in one way or another, involved in or at least sympathetic to the Indian freedom movement. Gadar, which may be translated as "revolution" or "mutiny," was nothing less than an attempt to overthrow the Raj from a base in San Francisco. It was founded in San Francisco in 1911 by Har Dayal, a brilliant young Indian scholar who had resigned a British government scholarship at Oxford University to undertake revolutionary activity in the United States. He was a radical who had been an officer of the syndicalist Industrial Workers of the World. Gadar was primarily an organization of young intellectuals and students. These Indian students—by 1913 there were thirty-seven at the University of California at Berkeley alone—formed the backbone of the freedom organization here, although later this role was taken over by merchants and established farmers and ranchers.

With the outbreak of World War I, the Gadarites, who used both romantic and socialist rhetoric, citing Mazzini and Marx, began to receive financial support from the German government. Almost from the beginning, the movement had been penetrated by British moles and agents provocateurs; thus, in the final analysis, the conspiracy here had no chance even to strike a blow, much less topple, the Raj. The San Francisco Gadarites managed to charter two vessels in California and tried to get them loaded with arms purchased in Mexico, intending to sail to India to start an armed revolt, another mutiny. In addition, perhaps as many as 400 Asian Indians left North America and, by various routes, returned to India to foment revolution. Almost all were apprehended; many were executed. One vessel, without arms aboard, got as far as Java.

There were also less radical groups of Asian Indians working for freedom here in those years. One such peaceful organization, formed in New York in 1918, was the India Home Rule League. For the next three decades—until Indian independence was achieved—one or more patriotic organizations existed in the Indo-American community. It must be remembered that in those days the United States was not thought of as a bastion of suppressive regimes throughout the world and that only the United States had an established revolutionary tradition. Many Asian revolutionaries of that era, including Sun Yat-sen and two of the leading Asian members of the Communist International, Japan's Sen Katayama and India's M. N. Roy, spent some time in the United States either as agitators or settlers.[4]

THE STRUGGLE FOR CITIZENSHIP

The war all but stopped Indian immigration, and in 1917 the American Congress, as part of an immigration act whose most heralded feature was a largely ineffective literacy test, excluded almost all Asians and all East Indians by means of a so-called barred zone, expressed in degrees of latitude and longitude. That exclusion was not total; skilled professionals, ministers, religious teachers, students, and travelers for pleasure were largely exempt from its provisions. In any event, from 1914 to 1946 there was no sizable immigration of East Indians.

As we have seen, the U.S. naturalization statutes had made Asians "aliens ineligible for citizenship." In the *Ozawa* case of 1922, the court had ruled unanimously that "white persons" in the 1870 statute meant a person of the Caucasian race. In 1923 a case brought by Bhagat Singh Thind came before the court. Thind, a Sikh who had been granted citizenship by a federal court in Oregon, was denied citizenship by the Supreme Court even though, as a Caucasian, he passed the test set up by *Ozawa.* The court, speaking through Justice George Sutherland, now held that the word "white" in the 1870 statute meant "white" in the "understanding of the common man." Whatever we may think of the result, it is clear that in *Thind* the court was adhering to the intent of Congress.

The *Thind* decision meant that Indian farmers were still subject to the provisions of alien land laws in California and other western states. As one Indian immigrant, who nevertheless became a very successful California rancher, remembered it years later:

> It was made quite evident that people from Asia—the Japanese, Chinese and Hindus—were not wanted.... A friend of mine, a property owner in the

Imperial County, helped me by holding my lease contracts in his name.... I had also leased some property in my wife's name since she was an American citizen. However some landowners didn't like to take a chance on leasing land even to an Asiatic's wife for fear of violating the Alien Land Act.[5]

Thus, for a variety of reasons, the Asian Indian population of California—and of the United States—declined precipitously from its pre–World War I high of perhaps 10,000. The census, notoriously inaccurate for minority populations generally, could find only 1,873 persons born in India in California in 1930 and 1,476 in 1940. Since hardly any of the agricultural laborers and entrepreneurs who dominated this small population had come with wives, the majority of those who stayed were "bachelors." Yet, as Bruce La Brack and Karen Leonard have demonstrated, a significant number of these California agriculturalists did get married, and these small communities demonstrate patterns of acculturation worth noting.

La Brack and Leonard have tracked and reconstituted almost 400 Asian Indian families in California before 1946, mostly in the Imperial and Sacramento valleys. Of these marriages only nine—fewer than 2.5 percent—seem to have been with Asian Indian women. The overwhelming majority, some 80 percent, were with Hispanic women, most of whom were from Mexican and Mexican American migratory worker families. Frequently the Hispanic marriage partners had picked cotton or had done other work on the men's farms. Such a bride often moved into an established male household consisting of her husband and several Punjabi immigrants. Surviving wives often speak of the men's "single-minded concentration" on putting their resources into farming. Often immigrant—and perhaps bigamous—husbands were simultaneously sending remittances to a family in India. There was a tendency for sisters to marry partners, so many households contained related women.

Not surprisingly, these marriages were conflict ridden. In Imperial County, for example, at least a fifth of them ended in formal divorce, with husbands and wives filing in roughly equal proportions. The men's petitions stress neglect of duty, refusal to cook and clean for the husband's friends, verbal disobedience, too much visiting of mothers and sisters, shopping in town, using make-up, and dancing with other men. The women complained that their husbands drank, beat them, committed adultery, and demanded unreasonable services. Leonard also investigated 220 marriages of children resulting from Asian Indian–Mexican marriages; only eleven of them involved two "Mexican-Hindu" partners.[6]

It is necessary to contrast these Asian Indian–Mexican American marriages with the kinds of marriage patterns that tended to develop in other contemporaneous American immigrant communities. Very large numbers of these latter immigrants lived in ethnic enclaves; although men greatly outnumbered women in these enclaves, there were usually enough women that a majority—often a very large majority—of marriages were intra-ethnic. Among most other immigrants from Asia, but particularly among those from Japan, enough women were able to immigrate, and a pattern of intra-ethnic marriage prevailed in those communities as well. The only other group of Asian immigrants of this era for whom a pattern of extra-ethnic marriage has been reported is the Filipinos. As noted in the previous chapter, Barbara Posadas described with great sensitivity the marriages of Chicago Filipino immigrants with first- and second-generation daughters of Eastern European immigrants.[7]

IN THE EAST AND MIDWEST

Smaller Asian Indian communities were developing in New York and other eastern and midwestern cities. Most of the few hundred members of these communities were merchants and middle-class professionals; ethnically most were Hindu, with a sprinkling of Sikhs and Muslims. Almost all were involved, in one way or another, in the struggle for freedom in India. They organized a surprisingly large number of organizations, which were generally peaceful and legal. The most spectacularly successful was the India League of America, whose leading figure was J. J. Singh, a Sikh merchant with a talent for public relations and lobbying. Singh was able to exploit two very different streams of sympathy for India that existed in the minds of many Americans and were wholly unrelated to immigration. One stream was religious and cultural, the other political.

Although it is traditional to begin discussions of American percep-tions of Hinduism with the Swami Vivekananda's dramatic appearance at the World's Parliament of Religions held in conjunction with the Chicago World's Fair of 1893, Carl Jackson has recently shown that the roots of sym-pathy can be traced back, however tenuously, to the seventeenth century. And, it is important to note, that sympathy was a two-way current. If Emer-son, and through him Thoreau, were influenced by Eastern thought—how-ever misperceived—Thoreau, in particular, was a strong influence on Gandhi, who, in turn, provided much of the inspiration for Dr. Martin Luther King's philosophy of nonviolent change.[8]

Vivekananda and a small group of successors, the most important of whom was the Swami Yogananada, who first came in 1920, established small but influential Western outposts of Hindu religious thought in America through organizations like the former's Vedanta Society and the latter's Self-Realization Fellowship. Unlike the contemporary Hare Krishna move-ment, membership in these societies did not involve public begging or other "outlandish" behavior. Most of their members, who probably numbered in the low thousands, were drawn from middle- and upper-middle-class Protestants. In addition, many secular movers and shakers from India also visited the United States, although a much-discussed visit by Gandhi never materialized. Of particular importance were the several visits by the Bengali poet and Nobel Laureate Rabindranath Tagore, who first came here in 1916. On a later visit he had some celebrated difficulties with American immigration officials, who treated him as if he were attempting to come in as a laborer. Tagore was an important influence on many moderate Indian reformers here, as marked by the establishment of Tagore Societies on both coasts.[9]

The political sympathy was largely an outgrowth of the American tradition of anticolonialism and was often abetted by strong anti-British feelings on the part of American ethnocultural groups, particularly Irish and German Americans. During the years between the two world wars many American "progressives" adopted an isolationist stance and used anticolonial rhetoric as one argument against an Anglo-American alliance. But some internationalists were anticolonialists, too. As William Roger Louis has demonstrated, few issues so divided Franklin D. Roosevelt and Winston Churchill as the future of India.[10]

Singh and other pro-Indian lobbyists utilized both these streams of sympathy. The Sikh import merchant had been born into an elite family in Rawalpindi in 1897 and came to the United States in 1926. In a perhaps overadmiring profile of him in the *New Yorker* in 1951, Robert Shaplen wrote:

> Sirdar Jagjit Singh, the president of the India League of America, a privately sponsored organization that seeks to interpret India to, and to further Indian causes in, this country, is, at fifty-three, a handsome six-foot Sikh who by means of persistent salesmanship, urbane manners, and undeviating enthusiasm, has established himself as the principal link between numberless Americans and the vast mysterious Eastern subcontinent where he was born.[11]

By the time Shaplen wrote, Singh had already engineered his greatest triumph, the passage through Congress of the Act of July 2, 1946, which gave the right of naturalization and a small immigration quota to "persons of races indigenous to India." This act followed by less than three years the repeal of Chinese exclusion (see Chapter 4) and was accompanied by a similar dispensation for Filipinos, but not for other Asians, who remained until 1952 "aliens ineligible for citizenship."

THE 1946 ACT

Had not the 1946 act—and even more importantly the 1952 and 1965 acts—drastically changed the patterns of immigration from Asia, the "circuitous assimilation" of Asian Indian immigrants and their children would probably have continued. But the renewed postwar immigration rejuvenated established communities. La Brack has carefully documented these changes for the northern Sacramento Valley. There, a population of 400 aging Punjabi Sikhs in 1950 swelled, by immigration of persons of both sexes and by natural increase, to more than 6,200 by 1981.[12]

Obviously, the 1946 law did not, as some of its opponents had predicted, result in a "flood" of immigrants from India. The immigration data show that fewer than 7,000 "East Indians" entered the United States in the seventeen years between 1948 and 1965. Almost 6,000 were nonquota immigrants, mostly close relatives of persons who were or became American citizens. Since the Asian Indian population base was so small in the United States, the rights of naturalization and immigration did not have the numerical impact as did the granting of similar rights to Japanese Americans in 1952. With its much larger population base that community attracted, as we have seen, more than 40,000 new immigrants between 1952 and 1960.

The most spectacular individual Asian Indian beneficiary of the 1946 act was Dalip Singh Saund. Born in 1899 just outside Amritsar, the holy Sikh city in the Punjab, into a family headed by an illiterate but well-to-do contractor, Saund graduated with a degree in mathematics from Punjab University. Shocked by the Amritsar massacre (1919) in which British troops fired repeatedly into a crowd of peaceful protestors, killing hundreds and wounding thousands, and attracted by what he had read about America, Saund resisted his parents' wishes that he enter government service and came to the United States, via England, in 1920. He entered the University of California—living, rent free, in a "clubhouse" just off the Berkeley campus that had been established and maintained for Indian students by the Sikh Temple of Stockton, California. Saund eventually earned three degrees: an M.A. and a Ph.D. in mathematics and, more practically, an M.S. in agricultural science, specializing in food preservation. He was offered professorships by two Indian universities, but he decided to make America his home.

Despite his education, Saund soon concluded that "the only way that Indians in California could make a living" was to join with compatriots who were successful in farming. Thus, he settled in California's Imperial Valley, working first as a foreman on a cotton ranch operated by Indian friends—surely the only agricultural straw boss ever with a Ph.D. in math!—and then became a rancher and a businessman. He was determined to acculturate—he had begun shaving and stopped wearing a turban shortly after he came here—and in 1928 he married a woman from an upper-middle-class Czech-American family. Well established in the farming center of Westmoreland, he and his wife became involved in a whole panoply of civic activities, including the twin causes of Indian independence and citizenship for Asian Indians in the United States.

Shortly after he was able to become a citizen, Saund was elected to a local judgeship, and in 1956 he was elected to Congress as a Democrat in a race that attracted national attention not only because of Saund's origin but also because his opponent was a famous aviator, Jacqueline Cochran Odum. Taking office in January 1957, Saund became the first Asian American congressperson, and the only one, so far, to have been born in Asia. (The only other naturalized Asian American to serve in Congress, the one-term California Senator S. I. Hayakawa, was born in Canada.) Saund's election caused a small sensation and was exploited by the United States Information Agency, which soon sent him on a tour of Asia as evidence of the growth of ethnic democracy in the United States. He was twice reelected, but was defeated in 1962 after a stroke confined him to a hospital bed.[13]

THE STRUCTURE OF THE ASIAN INDIAN COMMUNITY

The great changes in the Asian Indian community have come since 1965. Rather than reinforce old communities or increase the status of members of the immigrant elite, that migration has created a new community, one that has few connections in ethnicity, in class, in occupation, or in location with the majority of its early 20th-century predecessors. These new immigrants have *not* been predominantly Sikhs, have *not* entered agriculture, and are *not* concentrated in the Far West.

By 1970 there were perhaps 75,000 Asian Indians in the United States, of whom fewer than a third represented the older communities and their natural expansion. At the first scholarly conferences examining the new Asian Indian immigration, held in Chicago in 1976, it was predicted that the 1980 census might show as many as 250,000 persons of Indian origin.[14] That census—the first specifically to ask about Indian nationality and ethnicity and the first to denominate them "Asian Indians"—in fact found nearly 390,000. An estimate for late 1985 put the new total at just over 525,000, representing a growth of 700 percent in fifteen years, or an average of nearly 47 percent per year for the period. To put the figures for the 1980s into perspective, about every tenth Asian American was either an immigrant from India or the offspring of such a person.[15]

Statistically, these Asian Indians present a profile somewhat different from that of Asian Americans generally. In 1980, while nearly 60 percent of Asian Americans lived in the Far West, only 19 percent of Asian Indians did. Part of this disparity is because there is no significant Asian Indian community in Hawaii, but it is also because Asian Indians are more evenly distributed throughout the nation. A third of Asian Indians live in the Northeast, and almost a quarter each live in the South and Midwest. In age, Asian Indians are quite close to the national median—30.1 years as opposed to the national 30.0—whereas all other Asian American groups, except Japanese Americans, are younger (from Chinese at 29.6 years to Vietnamese at

21.5 years). In terms of sex ratio, the once predominantly male Asian Indian migration has been largely balanced, and there were 107.2 males per 100 females in 1980.

Asian Indian women, like almost all other Asian American women, have demonstrated significantly lower fertility than American women generally. Age-standardized rates for Asian Indian women, for example, showed 1,224 children per 1,000 women aged 15 to 44, as opposed to 1,358 for white women, a national figure of 1,429, and black and Hispanic figures of 1,806 and 1,817, respectively. What these data reflect, as far as Asian Indian women are concerned, is class rather than ethnicity, education rather than national origin. The overwhelming number of Asian Indian women of childbearing age were foreign born.

The 1980 census indicated that of adult Asian Indians in this country, a startling 52 percent were college graduates, compared to 35 percent of all Asian Americans age 25 and older. The figure for the comparable white group was less than a third of the Asian Indian (17 percent). More than 93 percent of Asian Indian males aged 25 to 29 and 87.9 percent of similarly aged females were high school graduates. Comparable figures for whites were 87.0 and 87.2; for blacks, 73.8 and 76.4; and for Hispanics, 58.4 and 59.2. In 1980, 44.5 percent of all Asian Indians aged 20–24 were enrolled in school. The comparable figure for whites was 23.9 percent; for similarly aged Chinese and Japanese Americans the percentages were an astounding 48.0 and 59.8 percent.

An occupational profile of the Asian Indian population shows that 47 percent of foreign-born workers in the group were managers, professionals, and executives, as opposed to about half that—24 percent—for the white population. Even though many of these were not particularly well compensated proprietors, the median income of full-time Asian Indian workers was reported as $18,079 in 1979, higher than the figure for whites or for any other Asian American group. The next most prosperous individuals, Japanese Americans, earned $2,000 less. Asian Indian family income, however, while ahead of that of whites, was close to the Asian American norm and lower than that for Japanese Americans, because a significantly smaller percentage of Asian Indian women were in the labor force. For the group that the census calls "female family householders," only 58.2 percent of Asian Indian women were in the labor force as opposed to 72.5 percent of such Japanese American women.

At the other end of the economic spectrum, Asian Indian families were very unlikely to receive public assistance; only 4.5 percent of these families received assistance in 1979. Only they among recent Asian immigrant groups had a figure below that for whites, which was 5.9 percent. Public assistance was received by 6.2 percent of Korean families, 6.6 percent of Chinese families, 10 percent of Filipino families, and 28.1 percent of Vietnamese families. (The last figure was higher than that for Hispanics,

15.9 percent, and blacks, 22.3 percent.) Incomplete data indicate that welfare dependence for immigrant groups goes down sharply with extended
residence in the United States.

Data on Asian Indian families below the federal poverty line indicate
this quite clearly. For all Asian Indian families with foreign-born wage
earners (the vast majority of all Asian Indian families), only 5 percent were
below the poverty line, a figure lower than that for the foreign born of any
other Asian American group. For those who emigrated before 1970, the
Asian Indian poverty rate was 2.2 percent of all families; for those who
came between 1970 and 1975, the figure was 3.2 percent; and for those
arriving between 1975 and 1980, the poverty rate was 10.7 percent.

Asian Indian families seem remarkably stable. In 1980, for example,
92.7 percent of all Asian Indian children under eighteen years of age lived
in a two-parent household, a figure higher than that for any other Asian
American group and significantly higher than that for white Americans,
which was 82.9 percent. Asian Indian households tended to be small—2.9
persons on average—but, not surprisingly, households of recent immigrants
were larger. In 1980, Asian Indian households composed of post-1975 immigrants had an average of 3.5 persons. Forty-five percent of the persons in
these households were not members of one nuclear family; for all Asian
Indian households such persons amounted to only 9 percent of the members.

Nathan Glazer has characterized the Asian Indian population as being
"marked off by a high level of education, by concentration in the professions, by a strong commitment to maintaining family connections, both
here in the United States and between the United States and India."[16] Professor Parmatma Saran, on the basis of a 1977–78 survey of 345 Asian Indian residents in the New York metropolitan area, has written, perhaps too
sweepingly, about the Asian Indian experience in the United States. However, since New York had the largest single concentration of Asian Indians—68,000 persons (17.5 percent in 1980), with another 31,000 (7.9 percent) in New Jersey—that region is certainly not unrepresentative of the
whole.

In Saran's sample, 73 percent of the men in the labor force could be
classified as technical or professional. Among Asian Indian women in his
sample, the profile was similarly high; nearly half—47 percent—were professional and technical.[17] The overwhelming majority of these people are
recent immigrants who received all or most of their training in India, and
thus they are part of what is often called the brain drain. What this brain
drain reflects is the fact that many underdeveloped countries, as part of
their modernization, are training more professionals than can be employed
profitably in those countries. A study in the early 1970s indicated that
nearly 10 percent of doctors trained in India were practicing abroad,
mainly in the United States and Great Britain.[18] (Large numbers today are

also employed in the oil-rich states of the Persian Gulf.) Those with a Marx-ist bent fulminate about a "gift of labor to the imperialist countries,"[19] and those with a free-market bias talk about individuals making choices based on their perceptions of economic opportunity. What is all too often ignored is that settler societies—the United States, Canada, Argentina, Brazil, Aus-tralia, New Zealand, and South Africa—have from their inception drained talent and enterprise from the countries that nurtured them.[20] To cite an important but little noted example, the extraordinary number of college graduates—largely from Cambridge—who helped settle New England in the early seventeenth century made persons with university educations more prevalent in the colony than in the metropolis.[21]

More recent students of patterns of Indian migration to New York have suggested that the flow in the 1980s has been of persons less well trained. One of the more obvious phenomena in New York is the degree to which Asian Indians have begun to predominate in the newsstand industry. Many, if not most, of the thousands of kiosks in New York subways are owned and staffed by Asian Indians. Those who put in ten-hour, twelve-hour, and sometimes longer days below ground in the subway stands are often recently arrived and less-educated relatives of better-educated persons who came earlier and put their savings into profitable enterprises.[22]

On a national basis—where there are no systematic studies—one of the most startling occupational niches that Asian Indians have come to oc-cupy has been hotel and motel operation, particularly the latter. One news-paper story recently estimated that two fifths of all the motels in the Inter-state 75 association—Interstate 75 runs between Detroit and Atlanta—are owned and operated by Asian Indians, often as a part of national franchises. Again, in many instances, these operations are often owned by persons whose relatives run them. A very large percentage of the motels are run by one ethnic group, the Gujarati (persons from the northern Indian state of Gujarat), many of whom share the surname Patel. One joke prevalent in southern California talks about "hotel, motel, Patel." Other businesses in which Indians tend to cluster are restaurants and small clothing operations (the so-called sari shops), some of which cater to the ethnic community and some of which appeal to the fashion-conscious in the general community.

National occupational data, while not as impressive as that in Saran's New York sample, still show a profile of occupational achievement. Accord-ing to the 1980 census nearly half—47 percent—of all foreign-born Asian Indian workers were in the category of "managers, professionals, execu-tives," nearly twice the rate for white Americans (24 percent) and signifi-cantly higher than that of any other segment of an Asian American group. (The next highest such segment was 33 percent for native-born Chinese Americans; foreign-born Chinese came in at 30 percent.)

This elite socioeconomic profile must not be thought of as an ethnic characteristic. India is the home of some of the most heart–wrenching poverty, and Indian immigrants to Great Britain have a very different profile. One needs to compare Saran's New York sample with Arthur Helweg's Punjabi Jats in the small British city of Gravesend. The "vast majority" of the approximately 7,000 Asian Indians there in 1978 were in unskilled jobs. That also probably applied to most of the approximately 900,000 Asian Indians who then lived in the United Kingdom.[23]

THE FUTURE

The future of the Asian Indian community in the United States is probably a bright one. Two recent movies, *Gandhi* and *A Passage to India,* and the television series "The Jewel in the Crown" have created interest in India, but in an India that no longer exists. Despite what one writer called "a rage for the Raj," most Americans are unaware of the Asian Indians in their midst. Their broad geographical distribution and the absence of ethnic neighborhoods have kept their social visibility low. One recent demographic projection suggests that in the year 2000 there will be more than a million Asian Indians, which would represent a thirteenfold increase from 1970. Whether that prediction comes true depends on, among other things, what changes are made in American immigration law between now and then. Any substantial change in the preference system would undoubtedly affect that projection significantly.

What is clear and indisputable is that the Asian Indian community is putting down roots. In Cincinnati, for example, some 400 largely well-to-do, middle-class Indian families have pledged to raise $700,000 in three years to build a temple that will serve as a community center as well as a place for religious observances. In Artesia, a suburb of Los Angeles, there is a four-block stretch that some residents now call Little India.[24] Enterprising Indian merchants have given a different flavor to this small, middle-class community, with stores selling Indian sweets, clothing, groceries, and jewelry. Only Jackson Heights in Queens and Chicago's Devon Street have more ethnic Indian stores and restaurants, according to a spokesperson at the Indian Embassy in Washington.

Many of the merchants are the brothers, sisters, and other relatives of the professionals who moved here earlier. Not as well educated and lacking the professional qualifications, they have moved into the small-business sector, just as other Asians in previous eras made similar moves. They do not mind working long hours and are ardent advocates of the free enterprise system. Some established merchants have complained about the growing competition—Indian stores are said to be taking away customers from the regular businesses—but others ask who would rent the stores if the Indians were not there?

Despite these and other evidences of a continuing tie to India and to

Indian culture, there were strong evidences of a growing acculturation. Many, including a number of Asian Indian community leaders, have argued that Indians here have been particularly reluctant to make what seems to many to be the crucial break with their past and become American citizens. The one sophisticated study that we have suggests exactly the opposite. Elliott Barkan has recently examined American naturalization patterns between 1951 and 1978. His results show that not only have Asians in general been more likely to become citizens than most other resident aliens who arrived during those years, but also that Asian Indians were more likely to do so than were members of other major Asian ethnic groups. Barkan calculated for the period from 1969 to 1978 the percentage of aliens who were naturalized during the fifth to eighth year of their permanent residence in the United States. Dividing all such persons into a simple Asian/ non-Asian dichotomy, he reported that almost 65 percent of Asians became naturalized as opposed to only 45 percent of non-Asians. The same data, when broken down into five main Asian ethnic groups, showed Indians with by far the highest naturalization rate, more than 80 percent. The next highest rate is that of the Filipinos, just over 60 percent.[25]

It must be pointed out that such rates do not just represent a transfer of loyalties. As we have seen, current immigration law provides a strong incentive to acquire citizenship for those wishing to practice chain migration, as both Asian Indians and Filipinos are currently doing. However, whatever the reasons, Asian Indian immigrants to the United States seem to have been extraordinarily eager to become American citizens. There is no reason not to believe that their patterns of acculturation will be similar to those of other modern ethnic groups, although their unique religious heritage may provide some new variations.

NOTES

1. For general historical surveys of Asian Indians, see Gary R. Hess, "The Forgotten Asian Americans: The East Indian Community in the United States," *Pacific Historical Review* 43 (1974): 576–96; H. Brett Melendy, *Asians in America: Filipinos, Koreans and East Indians* (Boston: Twayne, 1977); and S. Chandrasekhar, ed., *From India to America* (La Jolla, Calif.: Population Institute, 1982). An important book by Joan M. Jensen, *Passage from India*, on the early history of Indian immigrants will be published by Yale University Press in 1988.

2. United States Immigration Commission, *Reports of the Immigration Commission*, part 25, *Japanese and Other Immigrant Races in the Pacific Coast and Rocky Mountain States*, vol. I, *Japanese and East Indians* (Washington, D.C.: Government Printing Office, 1911).

3. Mark Juergensmeyer, *Religion as Social Vision: The Movement Against Untouchability in the 20th Century Punjab* (Berkeley and Los Angeles: University of California Press, 1982), pp. 30–31, 383–89.

4. The literature on Gadar is extensive. I have used chiefly L. P. Mather, *Indian Revolutionary Movement in the United States of America* (Delhi: S. Chand, 1970); Arun Comer Bose, *Indian Revolutionaires Abroad, 1905–1922* (Patna, India: Bhavati Bhawan, 1971); Emily C. Brown, *Har Dayal: Hindu Revolutionary and Rationalist* (Tucson: University of Arizona Press, 1975);

Don Dignan, *The Indian Revolutionary Problem in British Diplomacy, 1914–1919* (New Delhi: Allied Publishers, 1983); and Joan M. Jensen, "The 'Hindu conspiracy': A Reassessment," *Pacific Historical Review* 48 (1979): 65–83.

5. D. S. Saund, *Congressman from India* (New York: E. P. Dutton, 1960).

6. Bruce La Brack and Karen Leonard, "Conflict and Compatibility in Punjabi-Mexican Immigrant Marriages in Rural California, 1915–1965." *Journal of Marriage and the Family* 46 (1984): 527–37.

7. Barbara Posadas, "Crossed Boundaries in Interracial Chicago: Philipino American Families since 1925," *Amerasia Journal* 8, no. 2 (1981): 31–52.

8. Carl T. Jackson, *The Oriental Religions and American Thought: A Socio-Historical Study* (Westport, Conn.: Greenwood, 1981).

9. Wendell Thomas, *Hinduism Invades America* (Boston: Beacon Press, 1930).

10. William Roger Louis, *Imperialism at Bay: The United States and the Decolonization of the British Empire, 1941–1945* (New York: Oxford University Press, 1978).

11. Robert Shaplen, "One-Man Lobby," *The New Yorker*, March 24, 1951, pp. 35–55. See also R. Narayanan, "Indian Immigration and the India League of America," *Indian Journal of American Studies* 2, no. 1 (1972): 1–30.

12. Bruce La Brack, "The Sikhs of Northern California: A Socio-Historical Study," (Ph.D. diss., Syracuse University, 1980), and "Immigration Law and the Revitalization Process: The Case of the California Sikhs," *Population Review* 25 (1982): 59–66.

13. Saund, *Congressman from India*.

14. Hekmet Elkhanialy and Ralph W. Nicholas, eds., *Immigrants from the Indian Subcontinent in the U.S.A.* (Chicago: India League of America, 1976).

15. Robert W. Gardner, Bryant Robey, and Peter C. Smith, *Asian Americans: Growth, Change and Diversity* (Washington, D.C.: Population Reference Bureau, 1985). This invaluable booklet is the source for all further unattributed population data.

16. Nathan Glazer, Foreword, in P. Saran and E. Eames eds., *The New Ethnics: Asian Indians in the United States* (New York: Praeger, 1976), pp. vi–viii.

17. Parmatma Saran, *The Asian Indian Experience in the United States* (Cambridge, Mass.: Schenkman, 1983).

18. Rosemary Stevens and Joan Vermeulen, *Foreign Trained Physicians and American Medicine* (Washington, D.C.: Government Printing Office, 1972).

19. Hilbourne A. Watson, "Migration and Political Economy of Underdevelopment: Notes on the Commonwealth Caribbean Situation," as cited in Saran, *The Asian Indian Experience*, p. 23.

20. John Higham, "Immigration," in C. Vann Woodward, ed., *The Comparative Approach to History* (New York: Free Press, 1968).

21. Samuel E. Morison, *The Puritan Pronaos* (Cambridge, Mass.: Harvard University Press, 1936).

22. From a discussion by Johanna Lessinger at the conference "India in America: The Immigrant Experience," held at the Asia Society, New York, April 17, 1986. (On April 23, 1987 two brothers, Bhawnesh and Supresh Kapoor, Asian Indian immigrants who were the principal owners of a firm that paid $2 million annually for newsstands in New York subways and Long Island Railroad stations, pleaded guilty to evading $325,000 in sales tax revenues. *New York Times*, Apr. 24, 1987).

23. Arthur Wesley Helweg, *Sikhs in England: The Development of a Migrant Community* (Delhi: Oxford University Press, 1979).

24. "Indian Immigrants Gain Here," *Los Angeles Times*, May 19, 1987.

25. Elliott R. Barkan, "Whom Shall We Integrate? A Comparative Analysis of the Immigration Act (1951–1978)," *Journal of American Ethnic History* 3 (1983): 29–57.

9

The Koreans

The Koreans are among the fastest-growing ethnic groups in the United States. In 1970 there were an estimated 70,000 residents; by 1980 the census recorded 357,393, and the Population Reference Bureau estimated 542,400 in 1985. The growth is almost entirely due to immigration; thus, this population is primarily a two-generation group—that is, immigrants and their children. However, unlike the early Chinese, Japanese, and Filipinos, who came largely as individuals, Korean immigrants often arrived in family groups. Thus, even though all of the individuals were born in Korea, the family composition may include infants, adolescents, and young adults, along with the father and mother. As a consequence, intergenerational differences in terms of acculturation, identity, language facility, and coming to grips with the dominant culture have an immediacy that was delayed for the older Asian groups. Parents, on arrival in the United States, send their children to American schools and are faced with the question of differences between their traditional ways and the norms of the new culture. The Chinese and the Japanese old-timers faced these issues at a later time in their American experience. As we saw, the first generation of Chinese was largely without children in America, and the early Japanese pattern was the single, male immigrant, calling for a wife from the old country after several years in the

United States, followed by the birth of American-born children. Thus, for the Koreans generational terms often have not been meaningful.

An individual who was born in Korea but emigrated to the United States at a very young age may be for all intents and purposes similar to the second generation of other ethnic groups. It is not unusual to see the following structure in the current Korean community: father and mother, born in Korea, following traditional, old country patterns; elder daughter, arriving with a Korean high school diploma, being more Korean than American; second daughter, finishing high school in America and having more American ways than Korean ways; and the younger son, having gone through his entire schooling in the United States, being almost thoroughly American in culture. But it should be emphasized that acculturation is seldom totally linear or predictable; we have seen parents selectively adopt certain very American ways, with the almost completely Americanized youngster holding onto some old-country values. The mixture, referred to as culture conflict, often causes a considerable amount of difficulty within families.

Korean immigration to America has consisted of three waves, although only the current migration is large enough to warrant such a description. There were Korean political exiles in the United States as early as 1885,[1] but the first significant trickle was to Hawaii (1903–1905). The second movement came after the Korean War (1950–1953), and the third, current migration resulted from the 1965 Immigration Act. Each of the groups is different in its demographic characteristics, the conditions surrounding its migration, and the kind of America that it entered. Therefore, it is anticipated that the three groups' adaptation and their experiences in America will be different.

BACKGROUND

Modern Korean history has been shaped by the influence of three powerful neighbors—China, Japan, and Russia—and by the strategic location of Korea between these nations. These three countries struggled over which should have the most influence over Korea; China dominated Korea as a tributary state until 1868, when Meiji Japan began to contest China's influence. The defeat of China in the Sino-Japanese War (1894–1895) saw Japan replace China. The aggressive Japanese policies led Korea to a search for other foreign powers who could serve to limit Japanese aggression, and this search led to relationships with Russia and the United States.

American diplomatic relations with Korea started in 1882 with the Korea-American Treaty at Chemulpo (now Inchon). This treaty of "amity and commerce" called for free traffic between the two nations, including the permission for Koreans to reside, to rent, and to purchase land in America and reciprocal rights for Americans in Korea. Very few Koreans took the opportunity to come to the United States during this period.

THE FIRST WAVE

Internal and international events soon led to the initial immigration of Koreans to Hawaii. In 1894 the Tonghak Rebellion, basically an antimodern revolt similar to the Boxer Rebellion, failed because of lack of unity and discipline. The rebellion served as a catalyst for the Sino-Japanese War, which was fought on the Korean peninsula. China's defeat gave Korea political independence but also gave Japan great influence over the country. From 1895 to 1905, Russia and Japan struggled over who should "protect" Korea. The Russo-Japanese War (1904–1905) saw the defeat of Russia, and through the Treaty of Portsmouth (1905), Russia recognized Japanese predominance in Korea, which Japan annexed in 1910.[2]

Hyung-chan Kim sees the 1882 treaty with the United States allowing entry and the effect of the wars as the main conditions leading to initial Korean immigration.[3] It should be recalled that at one time Korea was known as the "hermit kingdom" because of the reluctance of its people to travel out of their country. However, the wars uprooted a large number of Koreans, forcing many to move to port cities in search of hard-to-find employment, and the treaty with the United States offered potential opportunities in a new land. Many Koreans also emigrated to Japan, Manchuria (China), and Asiatic Russia.

The Hawaiian Islands were a natural locus for the immigrants. Hawaiian sugar planters were desirous of replacing Chinese and Japanese laborers, especially the Japanese because they had become militant in their demand for better treatment. Patterson, however, notes that the first proposal to import Korean labor was denied and that it was only in 1903, seven years later, that the first laborer arrived in Hawaii.[4] Up to 1905, 7,266 Koreans arrived in Hawaii, with another 1,033 immigrating to Mexico. Most of these regarded themselves as sojourners who would one day return to Korea. The immediate trigger leading to the immigration was severe famine, but there were also other factors, such as an epidemic of cholera, heavy taxes, and government corruption.[5]

Although the first Korean immigrants to Hawaii were primarily from the lower classes, very few were peasants. The Korean peasant was very conservative; maintaining Confucian tradition and staying on the land were high priorities, so the peasant viewed immigration as thoughtless and even immoral.[6] The Korean immigrants came to Hawaii with a weak national identity, but a new life in a strange land and traumatic events back in their home country, which was in the process of being taken over by Japan, led many to adopt a strong nationalism.

The migrants were neither integrated nor assimilated. Plantation life was characterized by racial and ethnic segregation, hard work, low wages, and minimal contact with other groups. Interaction was further limited by language and cultural differences and by a sojourner's orientation. There was no pressing need to think about entering the mainstream, or of cooperating with other groups. However, when Korea was formally taken over by Japan in 1910, there was no independent country to which they could return. The Japanese also prevented Koreans from leaving Korea, so their numbers in Hawaii remained static.

One consequence was that emotional attachment to Korea became very strong. The immigrants started Korean language schools in 1905, and the children were taught Korean values, customs, history, and geography. They also founded churches and patriotic societies, including military training centers to support Korean independence movements and the end of Japanese rule. It was a "government-in-exile" model: emphasis was given to military training and to retaining old-country ways until such time that they could return to liberate their country from foreign domination.

It might be expected that a small group, cut off from its country of origin and unable either to go back or be replenished by new immigration, would soon disappear as a distinctive entity. But, as Japanese immigrants and other contemporary immigrants from Europe did, the Koreans resorted to "importing" wives from Korea—picture brides— so there was family life for some and the beginning of an American-born generation. But the number of Koreans was very small; in 1930 they constituted only 1.8 percent (6,461) of the entire Hawaiian population of 347,799.[7] Yet Adams reported that only 104 Korean males married out of the group in the period from 1912 to 1924.[8] High rates of exogamy were to occur only generations later.

The adaptation of the descendants of the early Korean immigrants to Hawaii provides some interesting data. Factors such as small numbers, the lack of a cohesive community after the demise of the independence movements, acculturation, and the "pull" of the Hawaiian melting pot have had an effect. Harvey and Chung report that, in addition to the above factors, Koreans placed a high value on becoming American, on obtaining an education, and on entering the professions.[9] As a consequence, the children and grandchildren of the initial immigrant group have one of the highest inter-ethnic marriage rates in Hawaii. Between 1960 and 1968, 80 percent of the Koreans married non-Koreans, compared to 40 percent outmarriage rates for Hawaii's other ethnic groups during the same period. It was noted that the Korean women generally chose Caucasian grooms, while the Korean males generally chose Japanese brides. Outmarriage rates for 1970 and 1980 were even higher, reportedly 90 percent.[10]

But the rapid move toward acculturation and becoming a part of the Hawaiian mainstream has not been without its cost. High rates of separation and divorce, psychological problems, and other dysfunctional symptoms have been reported. The immigrant experiences of the Koreans in Hawaii between 1903 and 1965 can be summarized as follows: political preoccupation, the role of Christianity and the Christian churches, importation of brides, birth of a second generation, ethnic dormancy, rapid acculturation, and rising rates of outmarriage.[11]

A smaller group of Koreans migrated to the mainland; the 1930 census showed fewer than 2,000, most in California. Their situation was truly ironic. Exiles from their own country, which had been seized by Japan, they tried to organize in America to free Korea. Yet, when they were discriminated against here, it was the hated Japanese government that represented them. Two incidents illustrate this tension. Yang reports that in 1913 a group of Korean laborers was attacked in Hemet Valley, California, by a white mob that had mistaken them for Japanese workers. The Japanese consul general in Los Angeles stepped in to protect the Koreans and asked for compensation on behalf of its "nationals," an offer that was rejected by the Koreans because they questioned the validity of the Japanese government.[12]

The assassination of Durham W. Stevens in San Francisco in 1908 further illustrated the feelings of Koreans about their relationship with Japan.[13] Stevens, a Caucasian American who had been appointed by the Japanese government as adviser to the Foreign Affairs Department of Korea, made a number of statements that were printed in the San Francisco *Chronicle.* His points were (1) that Koreans had been exploited and corrupted by their own officials, (2) that they were illiterate and backward, (3) that if not for Japanese protection they would be under Russian domination, and (4) that, under the present Japanese resident-general, they were happy and enjoyed life in every aspect.

The Koreans in San Francisco were outraged over these remarks. Stevens was shot to death by a Korean patriot, Chang In-hwan, who was convicted, sentenced to serve twenty-five years in prison, and released in 1919. He died in 1930, and in 1975 his corpse was flown to Seoul, where he was reinterred as a patriot in the National Cemetery.

There was also a small, but important number of Korean students and political exiles who emigrated to the United States as early as 1885. Many of them were from the upper classes and were admitted without passports because the American government sympathized with the plight of anti-Japanese Koreans who could not go back to their homes without fear of persecution. Under current terminology, they would be classified as refugees.

The most well known of these exiles was Syngman Rhee (1875–1965).[14] A converted Christian who had been imprisoned for political activities in Korea from 1897 to 1904, Rhee came to the United States after his release to plead, in vain, that President Theodore Roosevelt use his good offices to protect Korea, as had been promised in the 1882 Treaty of Chemulpo. He attended and graduated from George Washington University and received an M.A. from Harvard (1908) and a Ph.D. in international relations from Princeton (1910). Rhee went back to Korea briefly as a YMCA organizer but returned to the United States in 1912. (He did not visit Korea again until after its liberation in 1945.) He became principal of a Korean school in Honolulu and in 1919 was selected by exiles there as the first president of what they called the provisional government of Korea. After the defeat of Japan (1945) and the gaining of Korean independence—split between the North and the South—Rhee was elected the first president of the Republic of Korea (South Korea) in 1948. He had influential American supporters, such as General Douglas MacArthur and other U.S. military authorities, who saw in Rhee a staunch conservative and militant anticommunist. But Rhee's rule was wracked with problems; he was forced into exile again in 1960 and died five years later in Hawaii. He remains a patriot and a statesman to some, a failed hero to others. Choy, in evaluating the first president writes, "Rhee's police state fell because of official corruption, favoritism, political oppression and fraudulent elections. All of these practiced in the name of patriotism and in the guise of anti-communism."[15]

THE SECOND WAVE

The second group of Koreans—arriving between 1951 and 1964—was a heterogeneous one, consisting of wives of American servicemen (the Korean War took place in 1950–1953), war orphans, and students.

The number of war brides who arrived between 1950 and 1975 was 28,205, yet few studies are available on this generally "invisible minority." They integrated and assimilated before they acculturated, and since most followed their husbands, they could be found throughout the United States. Many can be found clustered around army bases; one author remembers being greeted by a group of Korean wives at the isolated army base at Fort Huachuca, Arizona.

Bok-Lim Kim, in one of the few studies, evaluated the adjustment of Korean wives of American servicemen and noted some of their problems.[16] They suffered from culture shock, lack of education, isolation, problems of communication, and general alienation. There were high divorce rates. Kim notes that there were some happy marriages, but that there were also cases of physical abuse, suicide, and attempted suicide. The females were marginal, both to the dominant community and to the Korean community, and the high rates of social problems were attributed to their marginal positions.

Korean war orphans remain even less known than the wives of American servicemen. Hurh and Kim, citing various sources, indicate that in 1950,

24,945 children were institutionalized in Korean orphanages.[17] Of these, 6,293 were adopted in the United States, mostly through the Holt Adoption Agency, between 1955 and 1966. Roughly 46 percent had white fathers, 13 percent had black fathers, and the rest were full Koreans.

Dong S. Kim conducted a nationwide study of adopted Korean adolescents.[18] In general, they were placed in white, middle-class, Protestant families in rural areas and small urban communities. Religious and humanitarian reasons were given as primary motives for adoption, and family relations were deemed as supportive. The children were reported to have healthy self-concepts, and the adoptions were generally considered successful.

However, in a later report, the problem of racial differences was observed.[19] Although all of their surroundings and inputs were typically American, their physical characteristics set them aside from the mainstream. The adoptees were seen as Asian, yet they were almost totally cut off from their native contacts and culture. The implications of this dual identity with minimal ethnic support may be a cause of future problems.

The last group included in the second wave is that of a relatively large number of Korean students who came to the United States between 1945 and 1965. An estimated 5,000 are in the country today, yet almost nothing is known about them. Such questions as how many went back, how many changed their resident status, and what were their marriage and adaptation patterns remain as topics for future research.

THE THIRD WAVE

The third wave of Korean immigration was a result of the Immigration and Naturalization Act of 1965, and the migration still continues. For the first time in American immigration history, Asian nations have achieved a parity, or better, with European countries. For example, in 1965 the three countries outside of the western hemisphere with the most immigrants were the United Kingdom, Germany, and Italy; in 1975 the three most highly ranked such countries were the Philippines, Korea, and China. The Korean share of the United States total immigration rose from 0.7 percent in 1969, to 3.8 percent in 1973, to 6.2 percent in 1985.

However, it should be noted that the number of Koreans living in other parts of the world is much higher. An estimated 1,255,000 Korean residents were living in Manchuria in 1961. Approximately 600,000 are residents of Japan, and a large, but unknown, number are living in Soviet Asia. The estimated 542,000 in the United States in 1985 ranks it third or fourth as a home for persons of Korean ethnicity.[20]

The current immigration is mostly of families and thus includes a large proportion of women and children. It is a highly educated group, and like most contemporary immigrants its members are highly urbanized. This group is arriving at a time when ethnic and racial groups are asserting their identities and when there has been a shift in the American ethos away from monolithic assimilation and toward ethnic and cultural pluralism.

It is difficult to assess their current adaptation because of the lack of research data and the recency of their arrival. As Bok-Lim Kim says, it is too early to tell in detail what the pattern of adjustment of the Koreans will be, although there are several trends.[21] Some features include (1) expectations of economic success in the majority culture, (2) retention of aspects of the Korean culture, (3) rapid flight to more "desirable" housing in the suburbs, and (4) the development of ethnic business districts. Other expectations include permanent residence, a good education for their children, and the acquisition of American citizenship.

Major barriers toward participation in the mainstream include lack of familiarity with American society and the language handicap. In this the Koreans are not unique, as all immigrants have had to deal with these differences. In summary, the present-day immigrant is confronting a multitude of issues: cultural and linguistic differences, parent-child stresses, changes in roles, conflicts in norms and values, achieving a healthy identity in a predominantly white society, and the varied levels of acceptance by both the majority and other minorities already living here.

OCCUPATIONAL ADJUSTMENT

Occupational adjustment for the new immigrant generally means downward mobility (very few are able to gain jobs of equal status to those that they held at home), segregation from the mainstream (the small businesses are often in Koreatowns or other minority areas), and general isolation from the white community. Many are in the small-business sector, which means working long hours, weekends, and holidays. There is a constant struggle to lower labor costs in order to survive, and the struggle can lead to poor work conditions and to the overuse of family, extended family, and other relatives.[22]

Many of the small-business enterprises are run by immigrants with considerable educational or professional backgrounds, but difficulties with English have forced them to take a different path. They may start by taking menial jobs, scrimping and saving enough to buy a gas station, liquor store, convenience market, or laundromat. Stores that sell wigs and the "mama and papa grocery" are also popular. According to a survey by the Korean Chamber of Commerce of Southern California in 1984, there were about 7,000 Korean-owned businesses in Los Angeles County.[23]

Although the Korean business community in Los Angeles is located in an area that is at least 50 percent Hispanic and only 12 percent Korean, it serves as the hub of the ethnic community. Here the Koreans—newcomers, elderly, old-timers, and the young—can find ethnic food and ethnic stores; can run into old friends and meet new ones; and, perhaps the most refreshing practice of all, can do so without having to understand English.

However, there are growing concerns about the unrestrained growth of Koreatowns. Zoning regulations, the need to attract non-Korean clientele, ethnic segregation, the proliferation of shopping centers, and inadequate parking have had an effect on Korean business. One Korean leader commented on the need to funnel the energy and vitality of his group toward a better planned and orderly development. Perhaps, as the immigrants obtain citizenship and participate in the political process, a more sophisticated Koreatown may develop.[24]

Hurh and Kim report that the majority of Koreans employed in non-small-business occupations worked in segregated work places under unfavorable conditions.[25] Past skills and education may not be as important as how immigrants are integrated into the work place and may be indicative of the split-labor market duality facing many non-white immigrants. By split-labor conditions, we differentiate between employment that has adequate pay and chances for upward mobility and jobs that are lower paying and are basically dead-end positions.[26] Minorities are often caught in the latter position.

Perhaps the greatest change for the newcomers is the ease of female and youth employment. Families, who when in Korea would never think of wives and children working, now find that such positions, even though low paying, are readily available. In some instances, wives find employment more easily than husbands, and children more easily than adults. The effect on family dynamics can be stressful. The temptation to make money is difficult to restrain; problems of child care, of latchkey children, and of becoming sheer "economic persons" appear to be emerging.

RELIGION

One of the special characteristics of the Korean immigration has been the role of the Christian churches. Catholicism was introduced into Korea through China as early as 1784 but was banned soon after; the ruling class considered the new religion dangerous since it challenged the Confucian system of loyalties and ancestor worship that lay at the foundation of its rule.[27]

American religious influence began in 1884 when the Presbyterian Board of Missions sent a representative to Korea. During the Sino-Japanese

War (1894–95), missionaries gave their time and effort to alleviate the suffering of people caught in the conflict. Their unselfish devotion endeared them to many, and a number of Koreans adopted the Christian faith.

Adopting Christianity was also a means of identifying with and gaining foreign protection. Later it was also associated with a growing nationalism and an anti-Japanese position. Even today, political resistance in Korea is often associated with the church communities.

American missionaries were influential in persuading the first group of immigrants to go to Hawaii. The proportion of the early immigrants to Hawaii who were Christians or who later converted to the faith was large. Kim estimates that there were thirty-nine churches and 2,800 Christians between 1903 and 1918, when the total Hawaiian Korean population was about 8,000.[28] He hypothesizes several reasons for the strength of the church. It provided a group tie that was lacking in the community; the adherence to Christianity was a means of gaining sympathy from the white community; the church served as a social outlet; and there were group pressures to belong.

The churches also played several other roles for the first group of immigrants to Hawaii. They were active in the Korean independence movement and were also important in maintaining cultural traditions. They sponsored language schools, taught Korean history, and served as recreational and social centers. They were pluralistic structures; membership was almost exclusively Korean, even though the religious practices were drawn from Western Christianity.

The Christian churches continue to play an active role in the present-day Korean community. In southern California the number of Korean churches has increased from eleven in 1965 to 215 in 1979. The results of a survey indicated that 10 percent of the Korean American Christians there belonged to the Catholic Church, and the rest belonged to several Protestant denominations. The Presbyterians were by far the most numerous, while the number of Buddhists was too small to be analyzed.[29]

Many of the reasons for the continued strength of the Christian churches in the Korean community have not changed. They provide for many needs—religious involvement, an identity, and a resource for newly arrived immigrants. In addition, they provide a place for meeting people and a sanctuary for obtaining peace of mind and self-improvement. But there have also been some negatives—too much gossip, self-interest, schisms, and conflict, as well as the constant solicitation for money.[30]

The Korean churches are central to the Korean community. It will be interesting to follow their development as acculturation and new opportunities arise. Will they remain separated from the dominant community, or will there be integration, especially as housing and other patterns of the ethnic community change?

The experiences of the Japanese Christian churches in America may be informative. The Japanese churches began as exclusively ethnic entities; services were given in Japanese to all-Issei congregations. English-speaking services were introduced as the American-born generations began their participation, but the church remained ethnic, though bilingual. At first, almost all ministers were Caucasians, but now ethnic Japanese predominate.

Questions of the viability of the Japanese ethnic church are now being heard, with issues of integration and pluralism as focal points of discussion. But Japanese immigration patterns have not included a constant replenishment from the old country. Thus, the pattern for the Korean community may be different.

It will also be important to follow the mobility of the ministry of the ethnic churches. Will they be permitted to gain power and to enter the decision-making bodies of the host churches, or will they remain as auxiliaries, outside of the mainstream?

FAMILY AND KINSHIP TIES

Much of Korean immigration has included family, extended family, and other kinship ties. It is not unusual for former elementary schoolchildren in Korea to be reunited with schoolmates several decades later in Los Angeles, just as aunts, uncles, nephews, and nieces form extended family units in the new country.

The Koreans come from a traditional culture, where tasks and roles were clearly divided. Wives were expected to stay at home and to bear the major responsibility for household tasks, while the husband served as the major breadwinner. The husband was the final authority and had the power to enforce his decisions. Children were expected to be obedient and to defer to parental wishes.

Hurh and Kim studied family role expectations in Korean American families and found that even though many wives worked, the great majority of both wives and husbands adhered to the other traditional role patterns brought over from the old country.[31] A substantial proportion of husbands did not perform household tasks, even when their wives were employed. Explanations for the persistence of the traditional division of household tasks included past strong socialization to male-female roles, the relative isolation of most Koreans from American influences, the continued strong influences of traditional families, the long work hours of Korean husbands, and financial pressures. The authors concluded that given the present-day life realities for most Korean families, the traditional role of males and females has not been drastically altered. However, as we will point out in a later chapter, when analyzing interracial marriages, one common response of Korean females, as well as other Asian females, was that they did not wish to marry males who expected them to behave in a "traditional" female pattern. Rather, they expected more egalitarian roles and had to look outside of the Asian community for such partners.

The most visible changes in family life center around children. The younger the immigrant child is, the more strongly he or she is likely to be influenced by the American culture. Going to an American school leads to acculturation, especially if the child attends an integrated school, where his or her ethnic group remains a numerical minority. Such was and has been the case of Korean children in America.

Bok-Lim Kim studied the adjustment of Korean school children to American schools in Chicago and Los Angeles.[32] There was a surprising amount of similarity between the two sites. The children reported a variety of difficulties in school, including reading, spelling, and mathematics, but almost 20 percent indicated that American schools were easy. Some children had encountered racial discrimination, which in part came from their inability to handle the English language. They showed a relatively strong identification with facets of the Korean culture; a liking for Korean food and a desire to visit the ancestral homeland were common.

Acculturation, especially if rapid, can lead to conflict with parents. Dress and hairstyles, music, dancing, movies, and other seemingly superficial aspects of a culture can lead to misunderstandings, the raising of voices, and a gulf between parent and child. Issues involving differences in values, a clash of norms, and changing family roles remain as deeper problems.

A study by the United Way in Los Angeles addressed some of the problems and social service needs of the Korean community.[33] It noted that Western-based value systems, stressing individuality, autonomy, and competition, were in conflict with the old Korean ways of family centeredness, interdependence, and harmony. Underemployment and intergenerational problems were also causes of concern.

The most pressing problem was language. Other common concerns were unemployment, health, services for youth, and the lack of adequate social services to meet the needs of a newly arrived immigrant group.

GEOGRAPHIC ADAPTATION

The majority of Korean Americans have settled in urban areas such as Chicago, New York City, and especially Los Angeles. They are, after the Asian Indians, the most scattered Asian group in terms of geographic distribution. Part of the spread is related to job opportunities; for example, at academic meetings it is not surprising to run into Korean colleagues who are teaching in Iowa, Virginia, Georgia, and other states with very small Asian populations. Many of them are Korean born, and thus the first-generation questions of acceptance, of isolation, of ethnic concerns, and of the socialization of their children have yet to be studied. The conventional wisdom is that

Koreans living outside of popular ethnic settlements will acculturate and integrate at a faster rate than those with many ethnic neighbors.

Seipel studied the social integration patterns of Koreans in upstate New York.[34] He noted that although they belonged to the Korean church and other ethnic organizations, they also belonged to a large number of non-ethnic organizations. Most of these outside organizations were job related; Koreans were absent from civic, political, and labor organizations. Most significantly, none of the respondents held membership in organizations that represented leadership and power. Therefore, Seipel concluded that although there is an impressive participation by Koreans in both ethnic and non-ethnic organizations, the data can be misleading since they are affiliated with marginal organizations in terms of community influence.

In New York City and, to a lesser degree, in Philadelphia and other Eastern cities, Koreans have become visible as grocery store owners and fruit stand operators. Many of their small-business enterprises are located in predominantly black communities and, given differences in background and culture, it comes as no surprise that tensions and conflicts exist. It is not unusual to see the problems of such enterprises in the news; the idea of "foreigners" opening their businesses in a black ghetto is no doubt deemed newsworthy, whereas black business in a black ghetto, whether successful or not, gets no mention. The hope is that relationships will become better as both groups begin to interact and understand each other.

SUMMARY

The three waves of Korean immigrants entered into America with differences in motivation, population, and resources, and the reception they received from the American society was just as different. The first wave was numerically small and consisted of mostly single males, brought to work on Hawaiian plantations. They lived segregated existences, enforced by the American-Hawaiian oligarchy; they developed their own organizations, especially the Christian church. Although there were expectations of returning to their homeland, they found that once the Japanese had taken over their country they had nowhere to go. Much of their time, money, and energy was geared toward the day when they could reconquer their homeland. They lived segregated lives, with a minimum of acculturation and integration into the American-Hawaiian society. They importation of picture brides meant the start of family life for some.

Their children and the following generations paint a more familiar American immigrant picture. They moved away from the plantation, and many were not interested in freeing Korea—more pressing goals were acculturation, education, and job mobility. The boundaries between Hawaii's various ethnic and racial groups were open; therefore, without the social control and enforcement of a strong ethnic community, acculturation, integration, and intermarriage took place.

It is interesting to meet some of the descendants of the first wave. One of our acquaintances, a Los Angeles lawyer and a graduate of a prestigious mainland university, has a Korean surname and an Anglo first name. He can trace his background to the early arrivals. He is married to a Japanese American woman from Hawaii, and, much to the astonishment of Koreans making up the third wave, he has little knowledge of the Korean language and culture. Although his story is a rather typical American story—immigration, acculturation, integration, and assimilation—it comes as a surprise to some because it happened to an Asian person rather than to a European one.

Little evidence is available about the second wave. They came as individuals—brides and students—so their experiences were much more on an individual basis. Stories of tragedies abound, especially of failed war-bride marriages; however, we seldom hear about those unions that turned out successfully. Their children, mostly of mixed ancestry, have not come to public attention, so it can be presumed that they have quietly moved into the American system. Expected outcomes would include acculturation, integration, and assimilation.

The third wave is the largest, and the migration continues. Although it is too early to make a final judgment, Hurh and Kim postulate an "adhesive adjustment."[35] The term refers to the immigrants' strong sense of attachment to the Korean culture, but there is also an adherence to some of the ways of the new culture. Bok-Lim Kim also makes a similar assessment, using a bilingual, bicultural model.[36] She indicates that Korean parents have no intention of discarding the Korean language and their cultural ways, yet at the same time they have a strong and positive orientation toward the majority culture. They want their children to learn English, to excel in school, and to become a part of the American mainstream. The existence of these two cultural ways can lead to a healthy biculturality; however, it can also lead to marginality, conflict, and alienation.

The most optimistic sign is the America that the third wave has entered. They come at a time when immigration laws do not single out Asians as undesirables; when there is an emphasis on family reunification, and when the government supports "equal opportunity," "affirmative action," and small business loans. Legal discrimination has disappeared; the rights of minorities and the popularity of ethnic pluralism have meant a solid base from which to interact with the mainstream. Although they have run into some hostility from other ethnic minorities, it may well be that the third-wave Koreans will be the Asian group that will make the transition from their own culture to the American way in the least amount of time.

An apt summary comes from an essay written by a young Korean: "Being Korean in a white majority may be difficult, but it is clear that many of the younger generation of Korean Americans will find a way to survive, to grow and to overcome."[37]

NOTES

1. Hilary Conroy, The *Japanese Seizure of Korea, 1868–1910* (Philadelphia: University of Pennsylvania Press, 1960), p. 174.

2. Hyung-chan Kim, "Korean Community Organizations in America: Their Characteristics and Problems," in H. Kim, ed., *The Korean Diaspora* (Santa Barbara, Calif.: Clio Press, 1970), pp. 65–83.

3. Ibid.

4. Wayne Patterson, "The First Attempt to Obtain Korean Laborers for Hawaii," in ibid., pp. 9–32.

5. Yo-jun Yun, "Early History of Korean Immigration to America," in ibid., pp. 33–46.

6. Ibid.

7. Won Moo Hurh and Kwang Chung Kim, *Korean Immigrants in America* (Cranbury, N.J.: Fairleigh Dickinson University Press, 1984).

8. Romanzo Adams, *Interracial Marriage in Hawaii* (New York: Macmillan, 1937).

9. Young S. Kim Harvey and Soon-hyung Chung, "The Koreans," in John McDermott et al. eds., *Peoples and Cultures of Hawaii,* (Honolulu: University of Hawaii Press, 1980), pp. 135–54.

10. Harry H. L. Kitano, Wai-tsang Yeung, Lynn Chai, and Herb Hatanaka, "Asian American Interracial Marriage," *Journal of Marriage and the Family* 46 (1984): 179–90.

11. Harvey and Chung, "The Koreans."

12. Eun-sik Yang, "Korean Community, 1903–1970: Identity to Economic Prosperity" (Paper presented at the Korean Community Conference, Koryo Research Institute, Los Angeles, Mar. 10, 1979).

13. Won-yong Kim, *Koreans in America* (Seoul: Po Chin Chai Printing Co., 1971), and Bong-youn Choy, *Koreans in America* (Chicago: Nelson-Hall, 1979).

14. Choy, *Koreans in America,* pp. 182–89.

15. Ibid., p. 184.

16. Bok-Lim Kim, *The Korean American Child at School and at Home* (Washington, D. C.: Government Printing Office, 1980).

17. Hurh and Kim, *Korean Immigrants in America,* pp. 182–89.

18. Dong Soo Kim, "How They Fared in American Homes: A Follow-up Study of Adoped Korean Children," *Children Today* 6 (1977): 2–6, 31.

19. Dong Soo Kim and Sookja P. Kim, "A Banana Identity: Asian American Adult Adoptees in America" (Paper presented at the annual meeting of the Council on Social Work Education, Washington, D.C., Feb. 17, 1985).

20. Hyung-chan Kim, "Korean Community."

21. Bok-Lim Kim, *Korean American Child.*

22. Kwang Chung Kim and Won Moo Hurh, "Social and Occupational Assimilation of Korean Immigrant Workers in the United States," *California Sociologist* 3 (1980): 125–42.

23. David Holley, "Koreatown Suffering Growing Pains," Los Angeles *Times,* December 8, 1985.

24. Ibid.

25. Hurh and Kim, *Korean Immigrants in America.*

26. Edna Bonacich, "A Theory of Ethnic Antagonism: The Split Labor Market," *American Sociological Review* 37 (1972): 547–59.

27. Hyung-chan Kim, "The History and Role of the Church in the Korean Community," in Kim, ed., *The Korean Diaspora,* pp. 47–63.

28. Ibid.

29. Hurh and Kim, *Korean Immigrants in America.*

30. Ibid.

31. Ibid.

32. Bok-Lim Kim, *Korean American Child.*

33. Koreatown Profile Committee, *1984 Koreatown Profile Study Report* (Los Angeles: United Way, 1984).

34. Michael Myong Seipel, "Social Integration Patterns of Korean Americans in Predominantly White Communities" (Paper presented at the annual meeting of the Council on Social Work Education, Washington, D.C., Feb. 17, 1985).

35. Hurh and Kim, *Korean Immigrants in America.*

36. Bok-Lim Kim, *Korean American Child.*

37. Jack Slater. "Courage to Overcome Obstacles Revealed by Young Essayists," Korea *Times,* English section, Dec. 6, 1984, p. 1.

10

The Pacific Islanders

The idea that people would willingly leave sandy beaches, clear skies, warm weather, and the "romantic life-style" of tropical isles like Samoa for over-crowded freeways, poor housing, and urban living is difficult to believe. Yet such a migration is now taking place. It has meant that for some of the small island communities, a greater number of persons now live on the mainland than remain in their former homes. Perhaps paradise, as depicted in Holly-wood movies, is not sufficient to sustain life, or, more likely, the island image reflects a stereotype not a reality. Economic incentives, reunification of the family, and a better life for children sound rather mundane when describing migrants from tropical isles, but these reasons appear as power-ful for them as for others who have immigrated to America. Relevant ques-tions center on the same variables that are asked about any immigrant group: Who are they, why did they come, how were they received, and what are their adaptive patterns in the United States?

Prior to 1980, Pacific Islanders did not appear as specific groups in the United States Census. The 1980 census divided the Pacific Islander pop-ulation into Polynesian, Micronesian, and Melanesian (see Table 10–1). The most numerous are the native Hawaiians, who make up 85 percent of the Pacific Islander population, followed by the Samoans, Guamanians, and Tongans. This chapter will cover the Samoans, Guamanians, and Hawaiians,

TABLE 10-1   Pacific Islander Population in the United States, 1980

Polynesians	220,278
Hawaiian	172,346
Samoan	39,520
Tongan	6,226
All other	2,186
Micronesians	35,508
Guamanian	30,695
All other	4,813
Melanesians	3,311
Fijian	2,834
All other	477
Pacific Islander	
not reported	469
Total	259,566

Source: Bureau of the Census, 1980 Census of Population, Asian and Pacific Islander Population, Supplementary Report, PC 80-S1-12, p. 4.

although the generalizations may also be pertinent to other Pacific Islanders.

SAMOANS

The Samoan Islands are located in the South Pacific, approximately 2,300 miles southwest of Honolulu and 1,600 miles northeast of New Zealand. There are nine major islands, with high rainfall, high humidity, and a tropical climate. The islands are divided into two political entities, American Samoa and Western Samoa. The population of American Samoa increased from 5,679 in 1900 to 27,159 by 1970. Western Samoa also saw a dramatic increase in population during the same period, from 32,815 to 131,379. However, large-scale emigration during the last several decades has slowed the population growth.[1]

Samoan legends indicate that its people originated on the islands, but social scientists believe that Samoa was populated by Asians who came over the ocean in canoes. They lived in isolation until 1816, when Christian missionaries arrived via Tonga and Tahiti. Because the chiefs accepted the Christian faith, the islanders also became Christians. The missionaries were soon followed by traders from Great Britain, Germany, and the United States. The influx of the foreigners dramatically changed the native ways of life.

Prior to foreign intervention, Samoans lived under *faasamoa,* a term that denotes their customs, culture, values, and traditions.[2] The people living on the various islands shared the same language and culture, with the family as the central unit. The family name and reputation were important; respect for brothers, sisters, and older persons was built into the structure. Thus, *faasamoa* gave the people a sense of cohesiveness, pride, and identity.

The social structure was hierarchical. Central to the social system was the family, with the children at the bottom, the parents above the children, and the chief at the top. In the village, the family was below the village council of chiefs; at the district level, the district council was made up of certain chiefs from each village. The stratification, which continued up to the national level, was called the *Matai* system, which acted as the basic governing unit. The system of governance was effective in keeping unity among the islands for thousands of years prior to the arrival of the foreigners.

Great Britain, Germany, and the United States were the primary contenders for influence over the islands. In 1899, Western Samoa became a colony of Germany; after World War I it came under the mandate of the League of Nations and was administered by New Zealand. In 1962 it became independent. The United States acquired its part of Samoa in 1899, used it as a naval base for the next five decades, and still maintains sovereignty.

The intrusion of the colonial powers forced changes in the Samoan way of life. The division of the islands, the introduction of Western education, individualism, wage labor, and a cash economy meant that the Samoans could no longer live under their traditional models. The foreign powers stripped the local governance structures of their ability to exercise authority and control: the Samoan way was replaced by colonial administrators.

The effects of westernization on a small population, living in a restricted space, were dramatic. The native way of life became an anachronism; the world powers divided the islands, with different powers exerting their spheres of influence. Acculturation meant becoming more American in American Samoa, more English in Western Samoa. It is this background that leads Milford to indicate that whatever the reasons given for leaving the islands, the primary impetus was provided by Western colonialism and imperialism.

Migration

The first modern migration from Samoa occurred in the 1920s, when Samoan members of the Mormon church were brought to Hawaii to help build the Hawaiian Mormon Temple at Laie, about 35 miles from Honolulu.[3] This first group of immigrants was guided by a primarily religious orientation and most stayed on in Laie, in contrast to subsequent groups who were more concerned with economic issues and tended to move on to Honolulu and other areas where there were better economic opportunities.

Pierce, in contrasting some of the differences between the native Hawaiians and the Samoans who made up the bulk of the population at Laie, noted that the Samoans were much more business oriented than the Hawaiian population.[4] He attributed these differences to prior contact; the Samoans had developed a business sense, including a desire to acquire goods in a manner that had eluded the Hawaiians. He also noted that the Samoans were never apologetic about their culture, whereas the Hawaiians often made derogatory remarks about their own way of life.

The second significant migration occurred after the U.S. Navy transferred administration of American Samoa to the Department of the Interior in 1950. Many Samoans followed the U.S. Navy to Hawaii and then to the mainland. Others migrated to the United States in search of better jobs or a better education and to join relatives. Western Samoans, as members of an independent nation, have to go through regular immigration procedures; Samoans from the American territory are able to travel to the United States without passports or visas.

Adaptation

Most of the Samoans have settled in Honolulu, San Francisco, Los Angeles, San Diego, and Seattle. In sites other than Hawaii, they face a vastly different physical as well as a cultural climate. As one Samoan told us, she never felt that she was a member of a minority group in Hawaii, but in Los Angeles she definitely recognizes that she is a minority.[5] In the Samoan islands, where distances are short and where one is surrounded by family and kin, skin color and language are not marks of difference, and there is an easy familiarity. Age is treated with respect, and family needs have the highest priority.

But in America, the primarily first-generation populations of Samoans are "invisible" and generally ignored by the dominant community. Because of their small numbers and the relative insignificance of their home islands in international affairs, they possess little political power. An additional handicap is that they are often "lumped in" with other Asian groups, often more successful than they. They suffer disadvantages based on language barriers, lack of educational and occupational skills, and low income.

Most live in family and extended family units and expect to have other kin join them in a chain migration. Although they are a first-generation community, there are many young children. Their median age of 16.8 years is well below the American median of 28.8 years. Their sex ratio is about evenly divided, and they tend to marry within the group.[6]

Like all Americans, Samoans rank finding a job and securing housing among their highest priorities. Since most are unskilled laborers, wages are minimal. One solution to the problems caused by low wages is exchange of goods and services among kinfolk; this is also reinforced by their past ways.

Thus the family and kinship network serve as important resources, and there is a partial maintenance of the Samoan way, tempered by the realities of living in urban America.[7]

The Samoan adaptation reflects a bicultural life-style. At work a Samoan man might dress and act like his fellow Americans, but at home he will take off his shoes, put on a *lava lava* (a long wraparound skirt), sit on the floor, and converse in Samoan. He may wait for the adolescents in the household to prepare the evening meal and expect his school-aged children to take care of the younger members. Household decorations may reflect an island ambience.[8] It will be interesting to see how long this life-style will be retained as a younger, more acculturated group achieves adulthood.

The demographic picture of the Samoans indicates that *faasamoa* may be affected by the large number of young children in the Samoan community. While the first-generation adults are participating in community life in the old-country, Samoan style—oratory, exchange of gifts, and Samoan chatter—younger children are moved to the outer circle. Whereas in Samoa the children might hear and participate from their outside positions, in urban America they are more likely to retreat to another room to watch their favorite television programs.[9] Parents are also likely to encourage their children to speak English and to practice the behavioral patterns that will allow them to get ahead in the new culture. But, as one Samoan told us, Samoans still emphasize higher education less than other Asian Americans, especially the Chinese and Japanese. Given the choice of getting a job and putting food on the table or spending the next four years in college, a Samoan high school graduate is likely to choose the former.[10] Younger adults are likely to find that the old culture is less relevant and a hindrance toward their participation in the new society. Perhaps it will be up to future generations to appreciate the ways of the ancestral culture.

One of the special facets of the Samoans that differentiates them from the other Asians is their athletic ability, coupled with large body size. They have become prominent in football, both at the college and professional level, and it is not uncommon to hear sports broadcasters struggling over a name like Tuiasasopo. One potential problem is that athletic role models may become too attractive—only a small proportion can make it into professional sports.

GUAMANIANS

In many ways, the problems and the adaptations of the Guamanians, Tongans, and other Pacific Islanders are similar to those faced by the Samoans. Perhaps the absence of a Margaret Mead made the rest of the islanders lesser known than the Samoans, which may have been a mixed blessing.

Guam, Saipan, Tinian, and Rota, are territories of the United States and constitute the commonwealth of the Northern Marianas. The native people are the Chamorros. The islands are located about 1,500 miles east of Manila, 1,500 miles south of Tokyo, and 6,000 miles west of Los Angeles.

Guam was "discovered" by Magellan on his famous circumnavigation in 1521 and was under Spanish rule until Spain lost the Spanish-American War of 1898. It then became a United States possession. Spanish rule was characterized by a missionary zeal and attempts to totally change the life of the natives. But the Chamorros did not submit with docility; there were revolts and other forms of strong resistance. As a consequence, there was a virtual elimination of the natives by the Spanish rulers. Early accounts placed their number at over 50,000, but by the first recorded census in 1710, only 3,539 had survived. Eventually, the natives, composed primarily of females—most of the males had been eliminated—mixed with Filipino and Mexican exiles, as well as later arrivals such as Anglos and Japanese. Thus, the modern Guamanian is likely to be the product of a multiracial background.

Migration

Guamanian immigration was aided by the 1950 Organic Act, which conferred American citizenship upon the inhabitants of Guam. It has been a two-way migration—Guamanians have been coming and going in both directions—so precise figures of their numbers are difficult to ascertain. There are a number of reasons for the migration. One is related to military service; as early as 1938, young men volunteered for the Navy and ended their careers, years later, in West Coast cities such as San Francisco, San Diego, Seattle, and Los Angeles. Another group immigrated to attend American schools since there was a need for trained people to help in the administration of the islands. Prospective teachers, nurses, doctors, and lawyers left to be trained on the mainland, and many did not return. Then there were those who were dissatisfied with island life; they saw a dearth of educational and vocational opportunities, as well as inadequate public services, medical facilities, and job opportunities. Other reasons behind the immigration were overpopulation and several destructive storms in 1962 and 1976.

The immigrants had dreams of America that were similar to the images held by immigrants ever since its discovery. It was the land of opportunity, of milk and honey, and of peace and tranquillity. A more practical reason was to join old friends and relatives.

The year 1970 was an important one for Guam, for the first indigenous governor was elected in that year. Prior to that time, Guam had experienced a series of colonial administrations: the Spanish, the Americans, the Japanese, and once again the Americans. The island was also opened to immigration. Previously it was under the "protection" of the U.S. military, and few immigrants were allowed to come in. The opening up of the island meant increased foreign competition, especially from Filipinos, Taiwanese, and Koreans. Natives often lost their jobs to the newcomers.[11]

Chamorro values include a strong family, ancestor worship (despite a Catholic tradition), a fishing and farming life-style, and the authority of the mother in the home. The mother is the primary decision maker; the families are closely knit, with parents, unmarried and married children, and aunts and uncles often in close proximity. Child rearing is viewed as a family responsibility. Munoz cites an example of the role of one strong mother.[12] A couple, married for twenty-eight years and living in California, continues to seek the permission of the wife's mother if they wish to go out. If the mother says no, the couple will stay at home.

Adaptation

Guamanian problems are similar to the problems faced by other islander groups. They are unsophisticated in the business and technological world. Whereas groups such as the Chinese, Japanese, Koreans, and Vietnamese have opened restaurants, grocery stores, and liquor stores, few Guamanians can be found in small business. There are almost none in the professions; common jobs are in the unskilled and semiskilled sector as custodians, cooks, and clerks.

Guamanians come from a culture with rich oral, rather than written, traditions. Children born in the United States and those who left Guam before the age of twelve have difficulty with the native language; therefore, there is a fear that much of the Guamanian heritage will fade away.

Older folks suffer from isolation; they rarely integrate. They know more about political activities and occurrences in the home islands than in their present residences on the West Coast. Other problems include low pay, inadequate education, and difficulty in supporting large families. They do not understand their neighborhoods or the larger political system. There are problems of where to turn for help, whether in terms of personal, business, or social services. Their former island networks, perhaps effective in their previous lives, are less relevant. As Munoz indicates, although the Chamorros had been exposed to American influences since the turn of the century, their needs and priorities were deemed less important than the defense requirements of the United States.[13] As a consequence, they became dependent on America—paternalistic models, no matter how benign, often do that—which left them unprepared for independent living once they gained their freedom.

THE HAWAIIANS

Of all of the Pacific Islander groups, the Hawaiian represents either the most successful or the least successful adaptation, depending on one's orientation. If the criteria for success includes racial amalgamation and inter-racial mixing, then Hawaiians would certainly be ranked as very successful. There are almost no "pure" Hawaiians left, although their disappearance cannot be attributed solely to racial amalgamation. However, if success is measured by pluralistic models—the ability of a group to retain its auton-omy and culture and to remain racially "pure"—then the natives of Hawaii would certainly be classified as unsuccessful.

Background

Hawaii was believed to have been colonized by Polynesian voyagers, mostly from the Marquesas Islands and Tahiti, over 1,500 years ago. When Captain James Cook, the famous English explorer, came upon the islands in 1778, they had a thriving, highly stratified culture, with over 300,000 in-habitants. There was a class of chieftains (Aliis) at the top; an elite group of specialists (Kahunas) active in the arts, crafts, medicine, and religion at the next tier; and the commoners, who made up the majority of the population, at the bottom.[14]

The past of Hawaii has been marked with conflict. "Tribal" warfare and eventual bloody reunification of the islands under the control of Ka-mehameha I left them unprepared for the "foreign" invasion.

"Foreign" Invasion

By the time the first New England Congregationalist missionaries ar-rived in 1820, one year after the death of Kamehameha, Hawaii had already undergone a change from the "idyllic isle" discovered by Cook several dec-ades before. For example, Cook emphasized the strength, intelligence, and cleanliness of the natives, who farmed, fished, and enjoyed athletic games and dances. But by the 1820s commentators complained about the laziness, apathy, and bad health of the Hawaiians; thus, the destruction of the native culture was already well under way.[15]

The hospitality of the islanders—Hawaii was a place for happy refresh-ment after a long voyage—and the importance of trade were the key factors in their demise. Hawaiian chiefs rushed to trade with the haoles (non-Hawaiians) for fancy clothes, ornaments, and weapons, and in their greed they claimed rights to fishing grounds and fruit trees and often worked the commoners to death. Agricultural resources that were formerly consumed by the people were put up for sale to the visitors; the insatiable tastes of the chiefs for foreign goods resulted in heavier taxes. Hawaiian boys went sail-ing on the big ships; derelict haole seamen roamed the ports, encouraging commerce in alcohol and sex. There was also the introduction of the "white man's diseases" from European sailors and traders—syphilis, gonorrhea, colds, pneumonia, smallpox, and cholera, with which the Hawaiian genetic system had had no experience. Powerful-looking, robust Hawaiians could succumb as easily to measles as to cholera.[16] There was widespread drunkenness, and in extreme cases Hawaiians lost the will to live. From a relatively stable population of about 300,000 in 1778—before the coming of the white men—the natives were reduced to a population of about 35,000 in 1890. As Fuchs says, within thirty years of Cook's arrival, indifference and apathy became a part of the Hawaiian way of life, to be replaced years later by overwhelming despair. The old social ties had disappeared, and group respect had been demolished.

The Christian missionaries, largely from New England, also sped the process of social change by attacking the roots of the Hawaiian way of life. The native language, dress, dances, and art were downgraded, and the entire sociopolitical system of the islanders was constantly forced to change. But at least initially the missionaries were moved by spiritual goals, whereas sailors and merchants came for lust and profit.

The Great Mahele

The Hawaiians were introduced to Western culture in the form of explosives, iron implements, a money economy, and Christianity. The single event that most dramatically changed the social system was the Great Mahele of 1848, which permitted the purchase of land by private persons.[17] Through a series of complicated manipulations, much of the land, formerly under the king and chiefs, ended up in the hands of a few white oligarchs.

After the Great Mahele, the growing of sugar and other enterprises grew at a rapid pace, and the demand for cheap labor changed the demography of the islands. The native Hawaiians did not make good laborers: Why should any man work from dawn to dusk, week after week, performing backbreaking labor for someone else when the fish are plentiful in the sea and the coconuts drop from the tree? One visitor, commenting on Hawaiian labor, noted that "if the overseer leaves for a moment, down they squat . . . and the longest-winded fellow commences upon a yarn . . . that keeps the others upon a broad grin . . . as soon as he comes in sight, [they] seize their spades and commence laboring with an assiduity that baffles description, and perhaps all the while not strain a muscle."[18] The importation of cheap labor thus became a high priority for the plantation owners. Chinese, Japanese, Korean, and Filipino laborers were imported from Asia; lesser numbers were also brought over from many European areas, most notably Portugal and the Cape Verde Islands.

Haole Oligarchy

Beginning in the early 1840s, American residents in Hawaii, although a tiny minority, played an enormous role in Hawaiian politics. From 1842 to 1854, for example, an American, J. P. Judd, served as prime minister to Kamehameha III. By the end of the century, Americans dominated the Hawaiian economy as well. The United States made a series of commercial treaties with Hawaii, and in 1887 received the exclusive right to establish a naval base at Pearl Harbor. The coming to power of a nationalist and traditionalist queen, Liliuokalani, threatened the control of the American elite. In 1893 she was overthrown in a coup that was aided by U.S. naval forces. A provisional government headed by Sanford B. Dole, the "pineapple king," negotiated to have Hawaii annexed, but anti-imperialist President Grover Cleveland refused to allow annexation to take place. The Dole government continued in power until 1898, when, in the enthusiasm for expansion created by the Spanish-American War, Hawaii was annexed by a joint resolution of Congress. Although Hawaii had a population and economy worthy of statehood at the time of annexation, racism kept it in territorial status until 1959. American politicians rightly assumed that polyethnic Hawaii would send non-white representatives to Congress. As one southern legislator put it during a hearing on Hawaiian statehood in the 1930s, if Hawaii became a state, we'd have "a senator named Moto!"[19]

Fuchs indicates that there were at least three Hawaiis at the time of annexation. One was the monogamous haole society, characterized by private ownership of land, by Western dress, music, and recreation, and by Christianity. Whites owned most of the land, were in control of the economy, and ran the political system. Plantation life was primarily Asian—languages, games, worship, and attitudes toward family, property, and authority had the flavor of the Orient. Asians provided the labor; but, although the most numerous, they were divided by ethnicity and were economically dependent. Then there was what remained of the native Hawaiian culture, found in the more remote villages. The villagers prayed to Madam Pele, the Fire Goddess, asking her to spread lava over the land in order to wash the foreigners into the sea. The relative power of each of the groups was a good predictor of the type of Hawaii that was to emerge.

20th-Century Hawaii

Hawaii at the start of the 20th century was full of contradictions, yet the oligarchy lived and managed the contradictions up to the time of the Japanese attack on Pearl Harbor, when the cumulative effect of public education, universal suffrage (which was decreed under American annexation), and World War II began to alter its structure. As Fuchs writes:

> A handful of haoles, intolerant of opposition, ran the Islands, but discontent was openly expressed in uncensored ethnic papers. The oligarchy, self-consciously Caucasian, made few open appeals to racial prejudice. The small group ... nevertheless helped foster education. The small aristocracy, reaping the benefits of a plantation system, with its ruthlessness, was constantly torn between the desire for power and profit and the evangelism of both the

Congregational church and the American dream of freedom and opportunity for all.[20]

But the toilers on the plantations and the native Hawaiians did not see the conflict. Power and profit always seemed to prevail.

There were some openings in the stratification system. One was the emphasis on education—a New England value—and children of former plantation workers acquired an education. Foremost were the children of Asian background; native Hawaiians were less so inclined. Another was that of miscegenation and intermarriage; even the early haoles married Hawaiian women of high rank. Members of important haole families—Bishop, Wilcox, Shipman, Campbell, and others—married Hawaiian women. As Fuchs speculates, their own traditions of intermarriage may have prevented them from attacking the marital practices of other groups. Native Hawaiians joined in this practice fully.

Although there were strikes and other symptoms of discontent, the haole oligarchy dominated the islands for the next forty years. Ethnicity became the primary means of identification—people thought of themselves as haoles, Hawaiians, Portuguese, Chinese, Japanese, or Filipinos. Each ethnic group, shaped initially by the historical circumstances of its immigration, developed distinctive ways of life. The haole goal was to maintain control. The goal for the Portuguese was to be considered as haole; for the Chinese, to be economically independent; and for the Japanese, to be accepted. The goal for the Hawaiians was to recapture the past.[21]

Of all the groups, the native Hawaiians had the most difficulty in adjusting to the competitive haole culture. Much of their past behavior did not fit into the newer society. For example, their sexual behavior and casual use of property were looked upon as criminal by haole norms. The islands had undergone too much change, and a retreat to the past left the Hawaiians further behind.

An attempt was made in 1920 to set aside public lands at nominal rentals and leases to persons of at least one-half Hawaiian "blood" through the Hawaiian Homes Commission. The legislation was an attempt to "rehabilitate" the Hawaiian people and to enable them to regain possession of their land. But as Fuchs says,

> The rehabilitation idea did not produce a Hawaiian renaissance. It was, after all, too much to ask. The haole religion, family structure, sex mores, land system, property relationships ... were fundamentally different from what was known in ancient Hawaii. The Hawaiian Homes Commission Act represented one more, perhaps the major, futile Hawaiian effort to recapture the past.[22]

An understandable and all-too-common response to frustrated lives is the phenomenon of scapegoating. Hawaiians were no exception. Rather than venting their hostility against the powerful haole, the natives began blaming the "orientals" for their plight. They helped the haoles write land laws discriminating against the Chinese, and then they turned their animus against the Japanese. But, although they disliked both the haoles and Asians as groups, the natives kept many individual friendships and continued their traditions of sex and marriage without discrimination.

Intermarriage meant that Hawaiians and part-Hawaiians became diffused throughout the population. They carried on the spirit of "aloha," in spite of animosity and hostility toward groups, individuals were treated with friendliness and generosity. As a consequence, the picture of Hawaii as a racial paradise has a degree of validity, given the ethnic and racial diversity of its population.

Howard reports a rise in ethnic militancy in the 1970s, led by younger, relatively well-educated Hawaiians.[23] There is an interest in the native language and in traditional art and music, and there is a revitalized ethnic identity. The basic theme lies in the Hawaiians' alienation from their lands and the abuse of the environment by the "foreigners." It includes a greater concern for group affiliation than for individual achievement. Accumulation of wealth is secondary to maintaining social relations.

At a conference sponsored by the Council of Hawaiian Organizations, the following goals were listed. First was to achieve self-determination, followed by establishing a land base for use by native Hawaiians. Other goals were to address their educational needs, to acheive economic independence, and to strengthen the family and the old spirit of cooperation. The leaders saw the mainland white, haole immigration as the primary cause for the disruption of the Hawaiian life-style.[24]

Hawaiians have emigrated to the mainland, but their actual numbers are difficult to assess. Most are of mixed ancestry, and their experiences are as diverse as the diversity that they represent. There are places in California that even carry such names as Hawaiian Gardens, but whether these represent more than just names is open to question.

PROBLEMS

It is clear that a number of similar problems are faced by immigrants from all the Pacific Islands. For most, the problems are more pronounced as they leave their homes for life on the mainland. The native Hawaiians are unique in that they face the problem of being "invaded"; they have lost their lands, power, culture, and identity because they did not have restrictive immigration laws and failed to inaugurate practices that would have kept them as the dominant group. Rather, they integrated and assimilated at a rapid pace; now, at the end of the 1980s, very few of the "pure" remain.

Some of the problems shared by all Pacific Islanders are:

1. The vast differences between the education and skills necessary to survive in a modern technological society and the culture of the islands.

2. Loss of status, rank, and prestige. Former leaders may end up in unskilled laboring jobs; very few find employment in the white-collar and professional sector.

3. Low wages and high expenses. Many islanders have large families and are obligated to take care of them. Most contribute regularly to church.

4. Problems of roles and identity. Identity that is closely tied to the family, kinship groups, and villages is weakened in the new culture. Hierarchical roles, especially of the male, are threatened.

5. Unrealistic stereotypes of the islands that foster an exotic, romantic image or an image of heavy-drinking revelers.

6. Placement in a group titled "Asians," often expanded to include Pacific Islanders. The backgrounds are vastly diferent and place the islanders at a disadvantage when competing for federal funds and other forms of assistance.

7. Attempts to recapture a past that may be beyond their ability to control.

The problem for the Pacific Islanders is more sociocultural than based on discrimination and oppression. What was functional in a small island economy may not be that helpful in an urban, technological society. Further, unlike some of the other Asian groups, their numbers are too small and their resources too slim to develop a structurally separate community and a parallel "opportunity structure." Community resources that may have been useful in the islands may not be effective in helping them to capitalize on opportunities available in the outside mainstream community.

The most encouraging sign is that islander immigration comes at a time when most overt discrimination has disappeared. There are still problems associated with membership in a different "race" in a race-conscious society, but the relatively small size of the group should enable them to acculturate at a rapid pace. Their cultural ties, especially in terms of their language, are not functional in any international sense, so by the second and third generations, it may quietly disappear. However, their strong family ties and the ethos of helping one another will, we hope, be retained and become integrated into the larger society.

NOTES

1. Ramsey Shu, "Kinship Systems and Migrant Adaptation: Samoans in the United States," *Amerasia Journal* 12, no. 1 (1985): 23–47.

2. Sereisa Milford, "Imperialism and Samoan National Identity," *Amerasia Journal* 12, no. 1 (1985): 48–56.

3. Bernard Pierce, "Acculturation of Samoans in the Mormon Village of Laie, Territory of Hawaii" (master's thesis, University of Hawaii, 1956).

4. Ibid.

5. Interview with Sereisa Milford, Sept. 9, 1986, at UCLA.

6. Ramsey Shu and Adele Satele, *The Samoan Community in Southern California: Conditions and Needs* (Chicago: Asian American Mental Health Research Center, 1977).

7. Lydia Kotchek, "Of Course We Respect Our Old People, But ... : Aging Among Samoan Migrants," *California Sociologist* 3, no. 2 (1980):197–212.

8. Ibid.

9. Ibid.

10. Interview with Milford.

11. Faye Munoz, "An Exploratory Study of Island Migration: Chamorros of Guam" (Ph.D. diss., UCLA, 1979).

12. Ibid.

13. Ibid.

14. Alan Howard, "Hawaiians," in Stephan Thernstrom et al., eds. *The Harvard Encyclopedia of American Ethnic Groups* (Cambridge, Mass.: Harvard University Press, 1980), pp. 449–52.

15. Lawrence Fuchs, *Hawaii Pono: A Social History of Hawaii* (New York: Harcourt, Brace and World, 1961).

16. Ibid.

17. Ibid., p. 13.

18. Ibid., p. 24.

19. For details, see Roger Daniels, *Asian America: Chinese and Japanese in the United States Since 1850* (Seattle: University of Washington Press, forthcoming).

20. Fuchs, *Hawaii Pono,* p. 38.

21. Ibid., p. 42.

22. Ibid., p. 72.

23. Alan Howard, "Hawaiians."

24. Bradd Shore, "Pacific Islanders," in *Harvard Encyclopedia,* pp. 763–68.

11

Southeast Asians

Southeast Asians who have entered the United States as refugees include the Vietnamese, Laotians, Cambodians (Kampucheans), Hmong, and the ethnic Chinese. Their refugee status was one result of U.S. intervention in Vietnam after World War II and the subsequent fall of South Vietnam to the communist forces from Hanoi. Before we examine each of these Southeast Asian groups, we will study the differences between a refugee and a "regular" immigrant and discuss briefly the history of U.S. policy toward refugees.

WHO IS A REFUGEE?

A refugee is a person who flees his or her native country for safety in a time of distress. Thus, refugees are a special kind of immigrant; however, they face the same questions that all newcomers must address. Do they attempt to become a part of the mainstream? Are their goals acculturation, integration, and assimilation? Or do they wish to retain a separate identity, maintaining pluralistic structures and awaiting the day that they can return to their homelands? What are the attitudes of the majority group toward them? What are the reactions of other minorities?

Although the major difference between the refugee and the immigrant relates to the type of entry into our country, there are other differences worth noting. In a push-pull model of migration, the refugee is more likely to be "pushed" out of his or her home. There is often a move from one site to another; an additional element is some type of persecution, based on race, religion, or political ideology. There is a strong dimension of fear and crisis. Very few refugees have the luxury of thinking about the long-term consequences of their migration. Many harbor the hope of eventually returning to their homes, and thus there is a temporary quality to their migration.

But, if past behavior of Russians, Jews, and Cubans is any indication, few refugees will return home. Most students of migration, beginning with Ravenstein, argue that "push" immigrants are less likely to return than "pull."

There is general agreement that the term "refugee" was first applied in the late 1600s.[1] However, the sight of populations fleeing from political and other disasters was a common one long before that time. At one period, refugees were regarded as desirable and made welcome since they brought with them technological, industrial, military, commercial, and agricultural skills. At present, it appears that refugees representing less wealthy and less skilled populations are less desired, especially if they are racially and culturally different from the host society. But the rapid changes in the political and economic spheres over the past several decades has created a massive refugee population, so it can be justifiably argued that the twentieth century is the century of the refugee.

The increased use of the passport during World War I, identified by Ascherson as one of the more noxious, but lasting mementos of that war,[2] created "stateless persons" and compounded problems of mobility across national boundaries. The Russian Revolution and the steady stream of refugees fleeing from German fascism in the 1930s further contributed to population movement. World War II saw the displacement of many populations from their previous homes; current conditions creating refugees include changes in government, wars, civil strife, and instability.

Although there is general agreement that a refugee is one who flees a country in a time of distress, the question of who is a "true" refugee remains difficult to ascertain. Economic migrants, fortune hunters, opportunists, and those who have consciously planned on immigration are mixed with those who were forced to flee for their lives because of a change in the political structure. Grant acknowledges the crisis conditions leading to forced migration, but he also notes that some refugees fled to the United States and other countries for a reason common to most immigration—the hope for a better life, when compared to limited opportunities at home.[3] But no matter what the circumstances, refugees share a common background. They have cut off ties with the country of their birth, and they are venturing into a new land with little formal preparation. There are questions of how to make a living, how to fit, and how to manage. Will their norms and values be congruent and functional in the new setting? How helpful will their new hosts be in the transition?

U.S. POLICY TOWARD REFUGEES

Prior to 1980, the United States policy toward refugees was on an ad hoc basis. The Displaced Persons Act of 1948 allowed individuals uprooted by World War II and those fleeing Soviet persecution to immigrate; the Refugee Relief Act of 1953 offered asylum to victims of national calamities and those fleeing communism. After the Bay of Pigs incident, Congress acted to regularize and make permanent the immigration status of all Cubans who had arrived in this country since January 1, 1959, by granting them refugee eligibility through the Migration and Refugee Assistance Act of 1962. Amendments to the Immigration and Nationality Act of 1965 established parole authority for granting asylum on an individual basis. Cuban refugees entering the country between 1961 and 1971 and 100,000 refugees from Indochina in 1976 came under the parole provisions.

In 1980, President Carter signed the Refugee Assistance Act, which for the first time formulated an explicit policy for refugees. It moved beyond Cold War priorities and established annual admission levels of 50,000 and allowances for upward increases. It recognized the principle of asylum and regularized mechanisms for distributing federal aid to refugees and for reimbursing states, local governments, and private voluntary agencies for their refugee-related expenses.

THE TWO WAVES OF SOUTHEAST ASIAN REFUGEES

Two waves of refugees are generally identified.[4] Many in the first wave were military personnel, civil servants, teachers, farmers, fishermen, employees of the Americans, and Catholics. They recognized that their middle- and upper-class life-styles would not be compatible with a communist regime; they feared reprisals and personal harm, so escape was a necessity. Educational attainment was generally high; nearly half of the household heads were born in northern Vietnam and had fled to the south after the French defeat at Dienbienphu in 1954. The immigration was primarily in family groups, although there was also a sizable number of unaccompanied single males. There were extremes in wealth; some came with substantial sums of money, while others fled with scarcely more than the clothes on their backs.[5]

The second wave consisted of those refugees who arrived in the United States after 1975. Poor agricultural harvests, the economic drain of continued fighting in Laos and Cambodia, loss of jobs, and generally poor economic conditions contributed to the push. Many also feared being sent to "re-education" centers and work camps and being forcibly moved away from their urban environment. Increased hostilities between Vietnam and China created an additional problem for the ethnic Chinese residing in Southeast Asia; their loyalty was questioned, and their property was expropriated.

In summary, the first wave was generally composed of refugees from the more "advantaged" backgrounds. Nguyen and Henkin compared the two groups.[6] In the first wave, 49 percent were under 36 years of age; in the second wave, 58 percent. The family size was four in the first group, and four to five in the second. Forty-one percent were Catholic and 40 percent Buddhist in the first wave; 29 percent were Catholic and 47 percent Buddhist in the second. In terms of education, 48.8 percent of the first wave attended over four years of college, compared to 29.1 percent of the second. The first wave was generally more familiar with Western ways and culture than the second, although the latter also included members of the intelligentsia who had been unable to leave earlier.

The recency of the migration of Southeast Asians can be garnered from the following statistics. Prior to 1970, there were approximately 20,000 Vietnamese in the United States, and the number of Cambodians and Laotians was too small to be counted. By 1980 there were 415,235 Indochinese, of which 78 percent were Vietnamese, 16 percent Cambodians, and 6 percent Laotians. The Population Reference Bureau estimated that in 1985 there were 634,200 Vietnamese, 218,400 Laotians, and 160,800 Cambodians, in the United States. Although there were initial attempts to scatter the refugees throughout the country, the majority have migrated to the sunbelt states. California has the most Southeast Asian refugees (135,308), followed by Texas (36,198) and Washington (16,286).[7]

THE VIETNAMESE

Background

Foreign influences on Vietnam have included the Chinese, French, Japanese, and the Americans. The history of Chinese immigration to Southeast Asia extends over 2,000 years. Some came by land, to Cochinchina and Cambodia; more came by sea, to Vietnam. The Chinese influence has been long and pervasive, yet relationships between the two cultures have seldom been positive. The Chinese lived in their own segregated communities and were subject to numerous repressive measures.[8]

The French entered Vietnam in 1777, at a time when European powers were colonizing most of the world. Their initial influence was primarily cultural and religious. Their conquest of the region began in 1858 under Napoleon III. France saw the growing influence of the British and Dutch in this area and seized the opportunity by aiding the ruling families to suppress peasant uprisings. The Treaty of 1787 gave the French exclusive trading rights and access to the ports. French Catholic missionaries became a significant factor in the country, and the ruling group, fearing a foreign takeover, passed an edict of death against the missionaries. The French responded by landing troops but did not gain control over the country until the 1890s. Civil liberties, such as the freedom of speech, participation in the political process, and travel, were denied the Vietnamese.[9]

There were continuous rebellions against French rule. The most significant was the Revolutionary Youth Movement, which was founded by Ho Chi Minh in 1925 and which evolved into the Vietnamese Communist Party in 1930. The strikes and rebellions that occurred during the worldwide depression were crushed by the French; most of the surviving resistance leaders went underground.

The Japanese moved into Vietnam in 1940. For the most part they tolerated and cooperated with existing French colonial institutions, substituting Asian imperialism for European. The defeat of Japan in August 1945, the last episode of World War II, left a power vacuum that was partially filled by the Viet Minh, led by Ho Chi Minh, who had resisted the Japanese and would resist the French, the Americans, and, eventually, his ideological cousins, the Chinese. All, in his eyes, were foreign intruders.[10]

The French, with American assistance, reoccupied Vietnam, but their defeat at Dienbienphu accelerated a departure that had been sure to come. In an international conference at Geneva, Switzerland, in 1954, France conceded the independence of Vietnam and the neighboring countries of Laos and Cambodia. Free elections were to be held in all of Vietnam in 1956, but these never took place. Instead two rival regimes, the Republic of Viet Nam (South Vietnam) and the Democratic Republic of Viet Nam (North Vietnam), evolved under a Catholic Nationalist, Ngo Dinh Diem, and Ho, respectively. An artificial division at the seventeenth parallel with a demilitarized zone, similar to the Korean model, was declared but proved unavailing. In both North and South Vietnam separate but highly suspect elections were held, although few scholars now doubt that Ho had much more support throughout the country than did Diem, whose religion in a nation overwhelmingly Buddhist and whose Western support in a highly nationalistic country tarnished his credentials. Throughout the period from 1945 to 1975 a bloody civil war went on in Vietnam, with each side receiving significant foreign support.

The United States entered this conflict almost imperceptibly. Aid was given to the French by the Truman administration (1945–1949), and by the end of the Eisenhower administration (January 1961) there were approximately 600 American advisors in Vietnam. When John Kennedy died in

November 1963, there were more than 16,000 American soldiers in Vietnam, and they were beyond the advising stage. Under Lyndon Johnson the number grew to almost 475,000 at the end of 1967, not counting perhaps 60,000 men in the offshore fleet and another 33,000 stationed in Thailand. Only when the generals asked for another 206,000 men did Johnson stop the troop buildup, but not the war or the bombing that went with it. Although it was clear by 1968, if not before, that the war could not be won without sacrifices that neither the American government nor its people were willing to make, the fighting went on until April 1975 and was extended into the former French colonies of Laos and Cambodia.

Loss of life was tremendous. In addition to more than 50,000 Americans, perhaps two or even three million Vietnamese were killed. (These figures do not count the postwar bloodbath in Cambodia.) This carnage created many millions of refugees, internal and external. Within South Vietnam one official estimate was that just between 1965 and 1968, three million people became refugees. Many were housed in squalid refugee camps with minimal sanitary facilities; others crowded into Saigon and other cities. By 1969, South Vietnam had changed from a 85 percent rural country to one that was nearly half urban.[11]

While tens of thousands of Vietnamese had come to the United States before 1975, our total withdrawal from Vietnam in early 1975 set off the first part of the second wave of Southeast Asian refugees. Between then and the end of the year, more than 130,000 were admitted. That number dropped to 17,000 over the next two years. Then, starting in 1978, it surged again, as hundreds of thousands of so-called boat people sought desperately to leave Southeast Asia. Not only Vietnamese and ethnic Chinese but also Cambodians and Laotians began to fill the refugee camps in the countries of first asylum, particularly Thailand. The United States agreed at first to accept 7,000 a month from the camps and then doubled this to 14,000. This second part of the second wave peaked in the fiscal year October 1, 1979–September 30, 1980, when over 166,000 Southeast Asian refugees were admitted, some 70,000 of whom were not from Vietnam. In all, from April 1975 to September 1984, more than 700,000 Southeast Asians were admitted. They represented about one Asian American in seven at that time. And, it should be noted, only about half of Southeastern Asian refugees came to the United States. At the end of 1981, according to the United Nations High Commissioner for Refugees, China had taken more than a quarter of a million, France and Canada more than 80,000 each, Australia nearly 60,000, West Germany over 20,000, and Great Britain 16,000.[12]

In Transit

Rose describes a number of ways that refugees arrived in the United States.[13] For some, there was an initial move from their homes to first-asylum camps in Thailand, Malaysia, and the Philippines. Papers had to be checked and essential information transmitted to New York. Next came a search for sponsors. The selection of a sponsoring agency was more or less arbitrary, unless friends and relatives could be found. When a match was made and medical clearances obtained, the next move was to a transit center. Special chartered planes would then take the refugees to West Coast airports. A final trip would then be made to a prearranged residence in a nearby city.

For others, there were additional way stations prior to reaching America, such as the Refugee Processing Centers in Indonesia and the Philippines. The purpose of these stations was to regulate the flow of refugees and to orient them to the manners and mores of their future homes. For example, at Bataan in the Philippines, caseworkers updated files and assigned all refugees between the ages of sixteen and fifty-five to English-as-a-second-language (ESL) classes. Refugees were required to attend eight weeks of ESL classes, as well as four weeks of cultural orientation classes, before moving on to their final destination.

These temporary centers were under the jurisdiction of the United Nations High Commission for Refugees (UNHCR) and the local governments, with the United States playing no official role, although providing the bulk of the funding. Since other countries were also involved, the curriculum was not limited to the English language and the American culture. Language training and learning a new culture are difficult steps under the best of conditions; an evaluation of the courses indicates neither outstanding success nor dismal failure.[14]

A recital of the bureaucratic steps that a refugee must go through hides the pain, the suffering, and the anxiety that each person experiences. Stories about the boat people and their experiences of starvation, drowning, rape, and robbery were not uncommon. While almost every refugee has undergone terrible experiences, those of the boat people, escapees from Vietnam trying to get to Thailand or Malaysia by sea, are perhaps the worst. In 1981 the vicious attacks on these helpless people by pirates reached epidemic proportions; some 80 percent of all boats were apparently attacked at least once. One survivor later told her story in Seattle. Vo Thi Tam was the wife of a former officer in the South Vietnamese Air Force. After he had been released from "re-education" by the new government, he and Vo, who was pregnant, decided to try to escape. Somehow they became separated; Vo still does not know what happened to him or whether he is dead or alive. Here is her story:

> When we reached the high seas, we discovered, unfortunately, that the water container was leaking and only a little bit of the water was left. So we had to ration the water from then on. We had brought some rice and other food that we could cook, but it was so wavy that we could not cook anything at all. So

all we had was raw rice and a few lemons and very little water. After seven days we ran out of water, so all we had to drink was the sea water, plus lemon juice.

Everyone was sick and, at one point, my mother and my little boy, four years old, were in agony, about to die. And the other people on the boat said that if they were agonizing like that, it would be better to throw them overboard so as to save them pain.

During this time we had seen several boats on the sea and had waved to them to help us, but they never stopped. But that morning, while we were discussing throwing my mother and son overboard, we could see another ship coming and we were very happy, thinking maybe it was people coming to save us. When the two boats were close together, the people came on board from there—it happened to be a Thai boat—and they said all of us had to go on the bigger boat. They made us all go there and then they began to search us—cutting off our blouses, our bras, looking everywhere. One woman, she had some rings she hid in her bra, they undressed her and took out everything. My mother had a statue of Our Lady, a very precious one, you know, that she had had all her life—she begged them just to leave the statue to her. But they didn't want to. They slapped her and grabbed the statue away.

Finally they pried up the planks of our boat, trying to see if there was any gold or jewelry hidden there. And when they had taken everything, they put us back on our boat and pushed us away.

They had taken all our maps and compasses, so we didn't even know which way to go. And because they had pried up the planks of our boat to look for jewelry, the water started getting in. We were very weak by then. But we had no pump, so we had to use empty cans to bail the water out, over and over again.

That same day we were boarded again by two other boats, and these too, were pirates. They came aboard with hammers and knives and everything . . . we could only beg them for mercy. . . . So these boats let us go and pointed the way to Malaysia for us.

That night at about 9:00 P.M. we arrived on the shore and we were so happy finally to land somewhere that we knelt down on the beach and prayed, you know, to thank God.

While we were kneeling there, some people came out of the woods and began to throw rocks at us. They took a doctor who was with us and they beat him up and broke his glasses, so that from that time on he couldn't see anything. . . . They searched us for anything precious that they could find, but there was nothing left except our few clothes and our documents. They took these and scattered them all over the beach.

Then five of the Malaysian men grabbed the doctor's wife, a young woman with three children, and they took her back into the woods and raped her—all five of them. Later, they sent her back, completely naked, to the beach.

After this the Malaysians forced us back into the boat and tried to push us out to sea. But the tide was out and the boat was so heavy with all of us on board that it just sank in the sand. And so they left us. . . .

In the morning, happily, the local police came, and Vo and the other survivors were taken to a refugee camp from which she—one of the lucky ones with relatives already in the United States—was soon able to come to the United States as a refugee.[15]

Liu interviewed refugees who discussed their experiences in temporary camps in Guam and Camp Pendleton.[16] Problems included boredom and the lack of counseling and guidance. One of the most serious complaints was the lack of serious concern about mental health needs. The refugees also criticized the assumption that they would assimilate to American ways without difficulty; they feared that resettlement policies might lead to the breakup of family and extended family units; and they resented the lack of sensitivity to Vietnamese cultural values and existing social networks.

In summarizing the experiences of the first wave, Liu indicated that from the point of view of education and skills, the refugees were desirable immigrants. However, he predicted that they would face problems of status loss since many would have to settle for lesser jobs than in their presettlement lives.[17]

Early Adaptation

Nguyen and Henkin surveyed the heads of households of the boat people.[18] The respondents came from strong, traditional families, including an extended kinship pattern rather than the nuclear family. There was marked improvement in employment from 1975 to 1979. However, improvement in the employment picture was not necessarily related to social and emotional satisfaction. The great majority felt that their children should learn their native language and absorb the Vietnamese culture.

It is interesting to note that after one year in the United States refugees still had difficulty in dealing with cultural differences such as the breakup of family and extended family units, the limits placed on the number of people living in a home, the lack of respect toward the elderly, the absence of friendly people, the hectic pace at work, the dependence on the automobile and other means of transportation, and the high value placed on work and achievement over interpersonal relationships.[19]

But for all, the critical question remains: Would they have been better off remaining in Vietnam? Part of the answer would be intimately related to their ability to cope with the new environment.

OTHER SOUTHEAST ASIAN REFUGEES

Not all Southeast Asian refugees are from Vietnam; some come from Laos and Cambodia. And even within these smaller groups there are a variety of subdivisions. For example, in a current study of Southeast Asian refugees, the following ethnic groups are identified: Blue, White, and Striped

Hmong; Chinese, Krom, and Mi Khmer (Cambodians); Chinese, Mien, Thai
Dam, and Khmu Laotians; and Lowlander and Highlander Vietnamese.[20]

LAOTIANS (HMONG)

Refugees from Laos are primarily the Hmong, a people indigenous to
China who spread southward into the hills of Laos early in the 19th century.
Some Hmong, which means "free man," also populated parts of Thailand
and Vietnam. They are referred to in Chinese history as a race who lived
in the mountains, speaking a particular language, wearing special clothes
seen nowhere else, and dating as far back as 3,000 years. Modern authorities
have described them as an industrious, independent, and peace-loving
people who became involved in the Vietnamese War primarily because of
their strategic location.[21]

Background

Laos was influenced by the French brand of colonialism, though the
French invested even less in terms of transportation, education, or health
care in Laos than they did in Vietnam. The Japanese occupied the nation
briefly during World War II, but it was reoccupied by the French in 1946.
In 1954 the Geneva Accords established Laotian independence under the
Royal Lao Government. However, a political split in 1949 resulted in the
creation of the Progressive People's Organization, a forerunner of the Pathet Lao and an ally of the Viet Minh. Thus, by the time the Royal Lao
Government came to power, the Pathet Lao were in control of perhaps half
the countryside.

The escalation of the war in Vietnam affected Laos; the country was
used as a major supply line for North Vietnam (the Ho Chi Minh trail ran
the length of eastern Laos). There was massive American bombing there,
and by 1970 two-thirds of Laos had been bombed, creating more than
600,000 refugees. The CIA created counter-guerrilla forces among the
Hmong; their missions included collecting intelligence on North Vietnamese movements and rescuing American personnel, especially downed American pilots. An estimated 15,000 Hmong were killed in combat. They gained
the reputation of being courageous and knowledgeable jungle fighters.[22]

The fall of Vietnam and the withdrawal of American forces saw thousands of Hmong fleeing Laos. They fled to different parts of the world—to
the United States, to France, to French Guiana, a few to Canada and Australia, and many more to Thailand. As late as 1983, more than 76,000 Laotians
were in Thai refugee camps; more than 75 percent of these were the mountain people.[23]

Resettlement

The experiences of the Hmong in transit were similar to those of other Southeast Asian refugees. At first the resettlement programs attempted to scatter them throughout the United States, but most voluntarily moved to the warm-weather states, though a group of perhaps 10,000 has settled in and around Minneapolis. The northeastern cities were too cold, and rents were too high. Other areas proved too isolated and lonely. Even understanding sponsors could not take the place of extended family and familiar faces.

One story—no doubt true—relates how many Hmong relocated to the Fresno area. There was a rumor that a Hmong family became prosperous through raising cherry tomatoes in Fresno. Word got around, and the combination of climate, fertile agricultural land, and a community of fellow ethnics drew many Hmong to the San Joaquin Valley. In 1985 an estimated 20,000 of the 60,000 Hmong were reported as living in the valley, with approximately 15,000 living in Fresno.[24] The story is familiar to groups who have little access to reliable information and are dependent on rumors and personal information networks. Stories of one of their group "making it" are often followed by a mass migration to that area, with the hope that similar good fortune awaits them.

King and Holly in 1985 focused on some of the problems faced by the newcomers.[25] The Hmong came as an immigrant group with very few tools with which to adapt to the American society. They had no written language until about three decades ago, when missionaries came to their villages. They strongly believe in evil spirits, they trust their shamans, and they distrust modern medicine. The arrival of the Hmong has strained social service agencies. Nearly nine out of ten Hmong were reported to be on welfare, and the clustering of the population has created several ethnic ghettos. Although Fresno lies in the heart of an agricultural area, it is the home of agribusiness, and not the site of the kinds of small family plots that characterized the former Hmong homes in the highlands. Furthermore, in the old country, there were no taxes and few bills. In Fresno, at the first of the month, everything comes due.

The situation has reached the point where no direct resettlement is allowed from Thailand to Fresno, yet it is estimated that perhaps one-half of the Hmong refugees who enter the United States will end up in the Fresno area. Bad feeling against the refugees runs high; minority groups who previously suffered prejudice and discrimination also feel threatened by the newcomers.

King and Holley also report several unusual cases involving the Hmong.[26] One was a suicide of a Hmong who was apparently overcome with shame and confusion following arrest for a traffic violation; another was the attempted prosecution of some Hmong men as criminals in what to them was the customary way of claiming a bride. There were also mysterious deaths of middle-aged men who just went to sleep and never woke up.

Vang offers a more cheery perspective.[27] He reported in 1981 that on the whole the Hmong were being successfully resettled. Goals of self-sufficiency had been accomplished, and the majority were holding manual jobs. The major problem was the English language; Vang emphasized that long-term goals could not be fulfilled unless there was a mastery of English.

The Hmong arrive with a strong family and clan system. By tradition the families are large, and they follow a model of male dominance, where the role of the wife is devotion to her husband and where clan and kinship ties are strong. The clans serve as mutual aid associations, and the household, rather than the individual, serves as the primary unit.

Older Hmong still dream of going home to the southeastern Asian highlands. Many are forced to rely on their children for an understanding of American ways, of which they do not necessarily approve. It is likely that the younger Hmong will take the initial steps toward understanding the new society, while the older ones may be forced to tolerate the new ways or simply give up.

CAMBODIANS (KAMPUCHEANS)

The Khmer are the majority group in Cambodia, constituting about 85 percent of the population, and Chinese and Vietnamese make up most of the rest. They are primarily Buddhist and similar to the Laotians in terms of their kinship systems, animist beliefs, modes of production, and world views.[28]

Background

Khmer culture has been influenced by the Thais, Vietnamese, Chinese, and the Burmese. It was also influenced by the West, first through the Spanish and the Portuguese, later the French, and then the Americans.[29]

Cambodia was at one time one of the great civilizations in Southeast Asia. Centered in the royal city of Angkor, the empire lasted from 802 to 1432, when it became a part of the Vietnamese and Siamese kingdoms. It remained a vassal state until the French took control in 1863. The French rule was indirect and used native authorities when possible. French investment was very small. By 1939 only four Cambodians had graduated from senior high school, and in 1941, of a population of nearly three million, there were only 537 students in the secondary schools. There were a number of rebellions against the French; in 1916 as many as 100,000 peasants demonstrated against the French in Phnom Penh.[30]

Cambodian independence was declared by Prince Norodom Sihanouk in 1944 when Southeast Asia was still controlled by the Japanese. In 1946, Cambodia was declared an autonomous state within the French union, but the French retained control. In 1955, Sihanouk defeated a French-backed candidate and remained prime minister. Problems with the United States led to an increased dependence on Russian and Chinese aid. There was also increased cooperation with the North Vietnamese, and by 1966, Cambodia was indirectly involved in the Vietnam War. The North Vietnamese and the Vietcong were regularly using the border area for food and as a sanctuary from South Vietnamese and American air attacks. Prince Sihanouk was aware of the situation but tried to pursue a course of neutrality. His country was caught between Communist China and North Vietnam on one side, and the United States and South Vietnam on the other. However, according to Shaplen,[31] Sihanouk's gravest fear was to be taken over by the Vietnamese.[32] When Cambodia came under formal control of the Provisional Revolutionary Government in 1969, the American response was to begin bombing Cambodia, including a program to defoliate the rubber trees.

In 1970, General Lon Nol, with the approval of the United States, overthrew Prince Sihanouk's government. Relations with North Vietnam and the Viet Minh were broken off. Between 1970 and 1975 the United States dropped over half a million tons of bombs. The war created more than three million refugees.

Lon Nol's rightist government controlled the urban areas, but the extreme left-wing Khmer Rouge controlled the countryside. In 1975, just before the American exodus from Vietnam, the Khmer Rouge under Pol Pot entered Phnom Penh and overthrew Lon Nol. Pol Pot, born Saloth Sar, remains a somewhat mysterious figure. He spent some years in Paris with a Khmer student group called the Marxist Circle, which had loose ties with the French Communist Party. He took over leadership of the Vietnamese Communist Party's Cambodian branch in 1962 and charted a course that would be independent from Vietnam.

Pol Pot's victory was followed by a reign of terror, which ended with the murder of at least one million Cambodians by Cambodians and the forced relocation of many others. The book *The Killing Fields* and the motion picture made from it depict this horror graphically. More than 150,000 fled to Vietnam and 33,000 to Thailand. Pol Pot's primary targets were intellectuals, government officials, and urban dwellers, but Cambodians of all classes suffered.

In 1978, Vietnam, by then under communist control and aided by the Soviet Union, which sought to control Chinese expansion in the area, invaded Cambodia and replaced the Pol Pot regime with a new puppet government. The invasion was followed by another mass exodus from Cambodia. An estimated 100,000, fearing the traditional enmity between the Khmer and the Vietnamese, fled to Thailand. Continued famine, along with the Vietnamese offensive, drove nearly 500,000 to first-asylum refugee camps along the Thai border.

In Transit

Strand and Jones estimated that in 1985 close to 300,000 Cambodians remained in Thailand and along its borders, another 94,000 were in Thai holding centers, and another 200,000 lived in border camps under the control of three Cambodian resistance factions.[33] There are also about 30,000 refugees, most of them ethnic Chinese, living in Vietnam.

Kong, a refugee herself, describes the incidents leading to the removal of her upper-class family from Phnom Penh.[34] She was attending a private school for girls run by Catholic nuns when the 1970 overthrow of Sihanouk occurred. The majority of the students at the school were Vietnamese, and because of the enmity between the Cambodians and Vietnamese, the school was closed. Kong was not Vietnamese and was able to transfer to a high school in Cambodia. She planned to go to France for a college education. In 1975 the Khmer Rouge began to move forces into Phnom Penh, already overcrowded with refugees. Foreigners and upper-class Cambodians began to leave. Kong's father sent her and the rest of the family to Saigon. Kong arrived there in March 1975, when the South Vietnamese government was disintegrating and the American Embassy was evacuating its employees. Her father rejoined the family by taking the last plane out of Phnom Penh, just as the Khmer Rouge took over the city.

But the situation in Saigon became critical, so the family then moved to Vientiane, the capital of Laos. Life there was described as peaceful, but because the future seemed uncertain, Kong's father decided to leave Laos. The entire family "sneaked out" of Laos into Thailand—they had been informed that Cambodian passports would not be recognized. They were able to make it safely to Oudong Air Base and then to Outapao Air Base, where many Cambodian refugees lived. From there, it was a wait of several weeks before boarding a plane in June 1975 for El Toro Air Base, then to the Marine Corps Base at Camp Pendleton, and finally to a small town on the outskirts of Los Angeles under the sponsorship of the Presbyterian church.

Early Adaptation

The change from a peaceful, privileged life in Cambodia to eventual arrival in the United States covered almost every life situation that a person could experience. There was danger, anxiety, and fear, interspersed with happy moments and new experiences. The clash between norms, life-styles, and cultures was constant. No matter where Kong and her family went, it called for adjustment and adaptation. Homesickness was a problem, and even today she feels that her real home is Phnom Penh.

Pasternak describes the life of Tea Chamrath, who is also a refugee from Cambodia but holds a different orientation.[35] Tea learned English, got a job as a mapmaker, saved money, and brought his family to America. But Tea, a former marine commander in Cambodia, is not a typical immigrant. His plans do not include a future in the United States; his desire is to go back to Cambodia to fight a war. He reads everything that he can about current events in Southeast Asia and has joined with other Cambodians who plan to topple the current regime in Phnom Penh. Many of his fellow refugees were former high-ranking military officers under Prince Sihanouk.

Resisters such as Tea, although fiercely militant in their desire to retake their homeland, are generally seen by Americans as doughnut makers, welfare counselors, and owners of small markets and jewelry stores. They appear as regular immigrants, just trying to make a living. Tea has been reported to have left for Southeast Asia, but no word has been heard from him since the fall of the city of his destination to the Vietnamese.

The situation in Cambodia is a case study of frustration and failure. No one seems to have "won." The Khmer Rouge under Pol Pot carried out mass executions but now survives in refugee camps. Prince Sihanouk lives in exile in Beijing, while Lon Nol waits impatiently in Fullerton, California, hoping to return to Cambodia and power. Vietnam now dominates Cambodia, but its sway seems shaky. The biggest losers have been the peasants. Millions have died or fled; those who remain exist under conditions of extreme hardship.

ADAPTATION

Since the arrival of the refugees is so recent, it is difficult to provide systematic evidence about their adaptation. We hypothesize seven interrelated factors that will affect the adaptation of the Vietnamese, as well as the other Southeast Asian refugees, to the United States:

1. Goals.
2. Cohesion of the ethnic community and family.
3. Compatibility of the ethnic culture with host society norms and values.
4. Role of the federal government and voluntary agencies.
5. Reception by the host society.
6. Ethnic identity.
7. Occupation and education.

Goals

The goals of a group are related to motivations for immigration and subsequent experiences upon arrival in the new country. Refugees, as discussed earlier, are not voluntary immigrants and therefore may look upon their stay in a country as temporary, awaiting the day that they can return to their homes. However, the return to their homes is obviously quite different from the quest of the sojourners; refugees must await the reinstatement of a favorable political regime. In many ways, they may represent a government in exile, although for most the term may be too formal and unrealistic. The government-in-exile model, an experience that was a part of the early Korean migration, has also seen its counterparts in the Lithuanian, Latvian, Polish, and Cuban experiences, as well as that of the White Russian refugees from the Bolshevik Revolution of 1917. We have talked to members of several of these communities who have attempted to keep alive the native culture through the celebration of historic events and rituals. Some have even formed cabinets and appointed ministers, and carry on as if they were part of a government. The strongest incentive to retain their old ways is the hope that one day they will be able to return to their homeland in triumph.

The initial policy of the U.S. government was to settle the refugees in widely scattered sites so that they would assimilate rapidly. This policy also sought to avoid intense competition for jobs in specific localities, which would arouse a backlash by American workers. There was also pressure to resettle the refugees as rapidly as possible, however unsuitable the situation, in order to place them in the category of "voluntary migrants" who would be able to take care of themselves and become "American."[36] Policymakers ignored the possible social and psychological consequences of separation, although there is little question that scattered individuals will integrate and assimilate at a higher rate than those residing in ethnic enclaves. The separation policy generally did not work; after a few months many refugees moved away from their sponsors and opted for living in California, Texas, and Louisiana. Their concentration in urban areas has provided the social networks that have been characteristic of the development of other Asian groups.

Baldwin reports on two separate surveys conducted of the Indochinese in Orange County in California in 1981 and 1984.[37] The 1984 report indicates that the longing to return to their native countries had not decreased and that a lesser percentage had applied for citizenship in 1984 than in 1981. There was a higher tendency to identify themselves in ethnic terms, such as Vietnamese, Lao, or Cambodian, rather than American. The author speculates that the changes may be due to a difference in stages, whereby concerns for survival, which were of high priority at the beginning, have been superseded by questions of their past heritage.

For many old-timers the desire to return to their homelands will remain paramount, and thus acculturation and integration may be unrealistic goals. However, the younger refugees are acculturating more rapidly, are more desirous of becoming American citizens, and are more optimistic about their future in the United States.[38]

It is likely that those refugees who have done well economically, educationally, and socially will be more likely to set goals of integration and assimilation. Younger refugees will also acculturate and become "American" at a rapid pace, and they will question the norms and values of their parents, just as children of other immigrants have done. It may be difficult for parents to teach their children "Vietnamese ways" and even more difficult to socialize them for a return to the old country as time in America lengthens.

It should be noted that one can be a "success" without acculturating, integrating, and assimilating. An individual can retain an ethnic identity, practice the ethnic culture, and participate primarily with fellow ethnics and still be a good American citizen or resident alien.

Cohesion of Ethnic Community and Family

The initial attempt by the federal establishment to separate and scatter the refugees throughout the country may have been based on good intentions (i.e., integration), but it failed to take into consideration the valuable functions played by ethnic communities and families. Initially there were no established Southeast Asian communities, but since 1975 over 500 mutual assistance associations have been created within the refugee communities.[39] They encompass cultural, religious, and political groups. Other organizations fulfill professional needs and serve senior citizen and youth groups. They provide social, religious, and fraternal support; education and language development; job training; and cultural orientation. As resources are meager, they have not developed to the point of providing jobs and business opportunities on a large scale to fellow refugees, yet there are signs of the development of such economic assistance. For example, Day and Holly report on the development in Orange County, California, of Little Saigon.[40] This area is made up of Vietnamese noodle shops, grocery stores carrying Asian foodstuffs, boutiques, Chinese herbal medicine shops, and a variety of professional offices. Little Saigon provides a place where the refugees can speak the same language and experience the ambience of their home country. DeVoss describes a burgeoning community in Anaheim, where there are shops and a club with the ambience of Saigon, including Vietnamese music and familiar food.[41]

Perhaps the most important function of an ethnic community is to provide social and psychological support for a population that has been forced to adapt to a strange land with different customs. It is a familiar story; most immigrants have gone through this stage. At one time the development of such communities was frowned upon. The ethnic ghetto was considered a hindrance to Americanization and the "melting pot," but recent trends have been toward the encouragement of ethnic diversity and pluralistic structures. However, these ethnic communities are not all peaceful enclaves; there are intra-group conflicts based on political ideology, competing ambitions for leadership, status distinctions, and the question of who can serve as spokespersons for the group.

Those refugees who arrived in family units—extended family in-cluded—had a number of practical advantages, such as emotional support and multiple incomes. They came from a culture, similar to other Asian groups we have discussed, with hierarchical family structures with the male at the head. A constant problem with such structures is that the role of the male head may be threatened. If the man who used to be the head of the family can't find a job or obtains one inferior to his employment in Viet-nam, his role and status are threatened. In addition, the wife may be forced to work and may end up in a better-paying job than her husband. One Vietnamese wife believes that the "new pressures, the new roles, the new equality have caused the divorce rate among Vietnamese couples in Amer-ica to rise rapidly."[42] She added that in order to be successful in the business world she had to be aggressive, assertive, and efficient, but when she was with her own people she wished to be a Vietnamese woman—shy, patient, and resilient.

Children are also caught in the familiar conflict between disparate cultural norms. In school they are taught to express opinions and ask why, whereas at home their parents want them to be more traditional and do what they are told. It will be interesting to see how the children will handle the question of "culture conflict"; it may well be that the experiences of previous Asian groups such as the Chinese and the Japanese will serve as the model. Generational differences will no doubt appear as length of time in the United States increases.

Compatibility of Ethnic Culture with Host Society Norms and Values

Asian cultures generally fit into the dominant society through con-formity and lack of overt conflict. Rose notes that, in addition, the Vietnam-ese brought with them cultural values that were highly adaptive to the Amer-ican society.[43] They came with a strong sense of the family, they wanted a better life for their children, and they had a high degree of achievement motivation. Vietnamese culture encourages responsibility, discipline, and hard work; prefers that adversity be faced with courage and stoicism; and places a high value on education.

Role of the Federal Government and Voluntary Agencies

One of the features of the resettlement of the refugees has been the role played by the federal government and the private, voluntary agencies (Volags). Without the cooperation between the public and private sectors, the enormous job of moving, then placing, the refugees could not have been done.

Sponsorship has included commitments to provide food, clothing, and shelter until the refugees became self-supporting. Sponsors were to help in finding employment, arranging for schools and medical services, and providing advice and counsel.

Liu, although acknowledging the positive contributions by both the public and private sectors, writes that government bureaucracies, operating in their customary fashion, showed little sensitivity to the culture of the Vietnamese, partly because very few Asians were involved in the program.[44] Further, they adopted an assimilation strategy and delegated the resettlement task to a variety of private agencies who operated in a nonuniform manner. The lack of coordination often caused confusion and conflict, both among the refugees and among the various agencies.

Federal financial assistance to the refugees has been helpful in the period of transition but has caused a variety of problems for the states, since it involved a time limit. McMillan reports that in 1984, California had 300,000 to 350,000 of the 696,000 refugees taken into the United States since the 1975 fall of Saigon.[45] A significant portion of the California refugees—some 140,000—were on welfare. The state's cost climbed from zero in 1980 to $84 million in 1983 and an estimated $140 million in 1984. It should be recalled that the federal government provided total reimbursement for public assistance for the first three years, after which it was left to the state and local authorities to assume up to one-half of the costs, the same share that they assume for nonrefugee populations on welfare.

Yet, despite their handicaps and problems, many if not most refugees have become self-supporting. One 1982 survey of families that had arrived in the previous four years found that virtually all the Southeast Asian refugees in this group began their American lives on welfare. At the time of the survey, 35 percent of all families were totally off public assistance, and, for those here forty months or more, half were. Similarly, in the period just after arrival, 86 percent of adults were unemployed; after four years the figure was 30 percent. The shift toward employment and away from welfare shows that Vietnamese, like most other Americans, would rather be self-sufficient.

The same survey showed that the household was key. Most self-sufficient households became so only when a second family member found a job. In the survey, families with two or more workers—93 percent—were above the poverty line. Therefore, it is not individuals, but households functioning as income-generating units, that permit even the most disadvantaged groups of recent immigrants to begin the rise toward middle-class consumption patterns—the goal of most Americans.[46]

Reception by the Host Society

One of the most critical factors in the adaptation of any migrating group is related to its reception by the host culture. In comparison to the racism faced by early arrivals from Asia, the Indochinese have entered the

United States when most of its overt anti-Asian practices are no longer in existence. It has been an era of civil rights, of equal opportunity and affirmative action.

However, the Indochinese arrived at a period when most of the public wished to forget about Vietnam; not all anti-Asian prejudices had disappeared, and it was a time where Americans seemed to be more concerned about fulfilling their own needs and destinies, rather than helping others, especially Asians from Vietnam.

There have been instances of marked conflict between Americans and Vietnamese. In Texas and Florida, American fishermen have been upset by the fishing techniques of the Vietnamese;[47] blacks and Chicanos have complained about the special assistance given to the refugees, thereby decreasing the resources available to their own minority communities.[48] Baldwin's survey indicates that Orange County residents were just as dissatisfied with refugee resettlement in 1984 as they were in 1981.[49] The feeling that "they must be getting a government handout" is strong,[50] and there remains a resentment that American taxpayers have paid for the progress or the nonprogress of the refugees.

Skinner and Hendricks noted that a number of conflicts involved the Vietnamese with other ethnic minorities.[51] In a number of universities, blacks and Chicanos confronted school officials with complaints that the refugees were receiving a disproportionate amount of financial aid, thereby decreasing their share. Similar conflicts have arisen in the area of public housing and other governmental services.

The experience of the refugees supports the views of Lipset and Raab, who identified several groups who would feel threatened by an influx of refugees.[52] The "once hads," often labeled as nativists, would be threatened by any influx of foreigners, whereas the "never hads," made up of the disadvantaged, including minority groups, would complain of a double standard in funding priorities and competition for jobs.

Ethnic Identity

Identification as an ethnic minority provides certain advantages in the areas of employment, housing, health, education, and access to loans. It is what Gordon labels corporate pluralism.[53] Skinner and Hendricks cite a 1979 speech by Shearer before the National Coalition for Refugee Resettlement in Washington, D.C., which examines some of the negative effects of ethnic minority labeling.[54] Are the Vietnamese expected to assimilate as a minority group, which includes low-level jobs and a "job ceiling" above which they are not expected to compete? Does minority status reinforce a designation as outsiders? Does the categorization maintain a status quo, rather than bring about fundamental social change? Without ethnic minor-

ity status, groups are free to compete with each other and to confront established economic and political institutions.

But it should also be emphasized that the Vietnamese, like other migrants from Asia, are physically identifiable and cannot merge into the
dominant culture as easily as have those of European descent. Minority status may be forced upon them, just as being "recognized" as an Asian remains a reality for the Chinese and the Japanese, even of the fourth and
fifth generations.

Occupation and Education

The most obvious sources of satisfaction for any migrating group will
be to find decent jobs and a good education for the next generation. Baldwin reported that in the prime employment group, defined as those between the ages of 25 and 54, 45 percent of the men and 28 percent of the
women were employed full time in Orange County.[55] Lack of English skills
and the unavailability of child care were cited as the main obstacles to employment. Vietnamese have found employment as assembly line workers,
technicians, machine operators, and office workers.

There have been problems of underemployment and the lack of Vietnamese in supervisory positions. Intra-ethnic conflict can occur—previous
lower-status employees in the home country giving orders to former high-
ranking army officers, or of males taking orders from females. Prior to the
influx of refugees, Hispanics held many of the local assembly line positions,
and accusations of job infringement have been reported by employers.[56]

Stein compared the occupational adjustment of the Vietnamese refugee with other non-Asian refugee groups.[57] Given the same period of four
to eight years after arrival, he found that the Vietnamese were doing better
than Cuban refugees and less well than the 1956 Hungarian refugees and
the refugees from Nazi Germany. There was much downward mobility, but
he believed that this pattern would be ameliorated by time, acculturation,
language improvement, retraining programs, hard work, and determina-
tion. The early years are the most critical, for if problems are not solved
early, discouragement follows and the refugee may begin to accept dependence on the public welfare system.

The language barrier appears to be the most immediate problem for
the refugees. It creates misunderstandings and hinders effective communication. Futher, because refugee status arose from political-military decisions
and events and not from conscious decisions to emigrate, solutions may
have to include more than individual motivation. The economic disadvantage and the psychological struggles of populations caught in events beyond
their control place them in a position different from the "normal," voluntary immigrant.

Precise data about education are difficult to obtain because of the newness of the migration, but there is a general belief that the Southeast Asians, especially the Vietnamese, will do well in school. One young girl has even won a national spelling contest, and there are enough students attending major universities to form a Vietnamese Students Association. We are personally acquainted with several ethnic Chinese families from Vietnam whose children are attending or have graduated from four-year universities. It is a remarkable educational record for families that entered the country so recently and with a language handicap.

SUMMARY

The one common generalization concerning the Southeast Asian refugees is that of diversity. They bring with them a variety of backgrounds, differences in culture and history, and a heterogeneity of skills and experiences. Yet there is a tendency to view them as "refugees from Southeast Asia," and whatever stereotype this label brings to mind. The image may be that of the refugee girl who won the national spelling bee contest and was honored by the president of the United States, or the image may be of those who are struggling to make ends meet in urban slums.

There are some common elements, however. The usual combination of variables that have affected all newcomers to the United States—motivations, skills and aspirations, and the strength of their communities and families—will determine part of their future. Another part of the equation, as it is for all migrating groups, will be the reaction of the dominant community, which also includes other minorities, both Asian and non-Asian.

What little evidence we have concerning the refugees indicates that many are having a difficult time. Chapter 12, in which we cover empirical data on such variables as employment and income, shows that the Southeast Asians are below the whites and the more established Asian groups. It would be surprising if such were not the case. The conditions of emigration—panic, inadequate time, little planning; problems in transit; life in temporary centers; then entrance into a modern, industrial society—would strain the adaptive capacities of most individuals.

Owan, in discussing the problem of refugees with human services workers, suggests three themes—all relevant to how we deal with *all* people who are different.[58] First is the ability to be sensitive to the various cultures and life experiences and to recognize both the similarities and the differences. Communication patterns, feelings, and emotions may not be expressed in the American manner, so assumptions based on the American culture may be misleading. Second, culturally relevant frames for understanding must be studied, identified, and used. Patience and flexibility will be rewarded. Finally, there is a need for competent and well-trained personnel who can provide the assistance that the newcomers need. The "sink or swim" philosophy that has guided much of our policies for immigrants in previous eras may have to be rethought as our country moves from a "resource-rich" to a "resource-limited" society.

NOTES

1. Michael Marrus, *The Unwanted: European Refugees in the Twentieth Century* (New York: Oxford University Press, 1985).
2. Neal Ascherson, "No Place for Them," *New York Review of Books,* Feb. 27, 1986, p. 5.
3. Bruce Grant, *The Boat People* (New York: Penguin Books, 1980).
4. Liem T. Nguyen and Alan B. Henkin, "Refugees from Vietnam," *Journal of Ethnic Studies* 9, no. 4 (1982): 101–16.
5. William Liu, *Transition to Nowhere* (Nashville, Tenn.: Charter House, 1979); Darrel Montero, *Vietnamese-Americans: Patterns of Settlement and Socioeconomic Adaptation in the United States* (Boulder, Colo.: Westview, 1982).
6. Nguyen and Henkin, "Refugees."
7. Darrel Montero and Ismael Dieppa, "Resettling Vietnamese Refugees: The Service Agency's Role," *Social Work* 27, no. 1 (1982): 74–82.
8. Paul J. Strand and Woodrow Jones, Jr., *Indochinese Refugees in America* (Durham, N.C.: Duke University Press, 1985).
9. Ibid.
10. Jean Lacouture, *Ho Chi Minh: A Political Biography* (New York: Viking Press, 1968).
11. Strand and Jones, *Indochinese.*
12. George Herring, *America's Longest War,* 2nd ed. (New York: Knopf, 1986).
13. Peter I. Rose, "Southeast Asia to America: Links in a Chain, Part II," *Catholic Mind,* March/April 1982, pp. 11–25.
14. Ibid.
15. Joan Morrison and Charlotte Fox Zabusky, *American Mosaic: The Immigrant Experience in the Words of Those Who Lived It* (New York: Dutton, 1980), pp. 447–48.
16. Liu, *Transition,* p. 118.
17. Ibid., p. 170.
18. Nguyen and Henkin, "Refugees."
19. Ibid.
20. State Department of Mental Health Refugee Project, *Asian Community Mental Health Services* (Oakland, Calif., 1986).
21. Tou-Fou Vang, "The Hmong of Laos," in *Bridging Cultures: Southeast Asian Refugees in America* (Los Angeles: Asian American Community Mental Health Training Center, 1981).
22. Peter H. King, "From Laos to Fresno: Hmong Try to Adjust," Los Angeles *Times,* Apr. 7, 1985; Strand and Jones, *Indochinese.*
23. Strand and Jones, *Indochinese.*
24. Peter H. King, "From Laos to Fresno."
25. Peter H. King and David Holley, "Indochinese Find Haven, Pain in the U.S.," Los Angeles *Times,* May 1, 1985.
26. Ibid.
27. Tou-Fou Vang, "The Hmong of Laos."
28. Strand and Jones, *Indochinese.*
29. Ibid.

158   SOUTHEAST ASIANS

30. Carole Chan, "Aspects of Khmer Culture and Cambodians in America," in *Bridging Cultures*, p. 91.
31. Robert Shaplen, "A Reporter at Large, the Captivity of Cambodia," *The New Yorker*, May 5, 1986, pp. 66–105.
32. Ibid.
33. Strand and Jones, *Indochinese*.
34. Bosseba Kong, "The Resettlement of a Cambodian Family in the United States" (Master's thesis, University of California, Los Angeles, 1984).
35. Judy Pasternak, "For Cambodian Refugees, War Is Still Going On," Los Angeles *Times*, Mar. 24, 1985 (Westside Section).
36. Liu, *Transition*.
37. Beth C. Baldwin, *Capturing the Change* (Santa Ana, Calif.: Immigrant and Refugee Planning Center, 1982).
38. Ibid.
39. Beth C. Baldwin, *Patterns of Adjustment* (Orange, Calif.: Immigrant and Refugee Planning Center, 1984).
40. Kathleen Day and David Holley, "Vietnamese Create Their Own Saigon," Los Angeles *Times*, Sept. 30, 1984.
41. David DeVoss, "A Long Way From Home," Los Angeles *Times*, Jan. 5, 1986.
42. Day and Holley, "Vietnamese Create Their Own Saigon."
43. Peter I. Rose, "Links in a Chain: Observations of the American Refugee Program in Southeast Asia," *Catholic Mind* March 1982: 2–25, and "Southeast Asia to America," *Catholic Mind*, March-April 1984: 11–25.
44. William Liu, *Transition*, p. 173.
45. Penelope McMillan, "Indochinese Refugees a Costly Load for Counties," Los Angeles *Times*, Sept. 16, 1984.
46. Ibid.
47. Paul D. Starr, "Troubled Waters: Vietnamese Fisherfolk on America's Gulf Coast," *International Migration Review* 15(1981): 1–2.
48. Kenneth Skinner and Glenn Hendrick, "The Shaping of Ethnic Self-Identity among Indochinese Refugees," *The Journal of Ethnic Studies* 7, no. 3 (1977): 25–41.
49. Baldwin, *Capturing the Change* and *Patterns of Adjustment*.
50. Day and Holley, "Vietnamese Create Their Own Saigon."
51. Skinner and Hendricks, "The Shaping of Self-Identity."
52. Seymour M. Lipset and Earl Raab, *The Politics of Unreason* (New York: Harper and Row, 1969), p. 23–24.
53. Milton Gordon, *Human Nature, Class and Ethnicity* (New York: Oxford University Press, 1984).
54. Skinner and Hendricks, "The Shaping of Self-Identity."
55. Baldwin, *Patterns of Adjustment*.
56. Day and Holley, "Vietnamese Create Their Own Saigon."
57. Barry N. Stein, "Occupational Adjustment of Refugees: the Vietnamese in the United States," *International Migration Review* 13, no. 1 (1979): 25–45.
58. Tom Owan, ed., *Southeast Asian Mental Health* (Bethesda, Md.: National Institute of Mental Health, 1985).

12

Present Status of Asian Americans

It is difficult to discuss the adaptation of Asian Americans without the use of value-laden terms. "Entering the mainstream," "learning the American way," "maintaining an ethnic identity," and a variety of descriptive adjectives (good, successful, poor, marginal) reflect points of view that evaluate how a group is doing. One problem associated with these judgments is that they often reflect a dominant group perspective, while giving less credence to minority group perceptions. Further, it is difficult to talk about success without a reference to goals, and there may be differences between both dominant and Asian American groups about what constitutes a "successful" American. Finally, there will be individual differences about what constitutes a good adaptation; thus, glib generalizations concerning Asian Americans as a "model minority" reflect a narrow perspective.

For example, if Asian Americans wish to "become American as rapidly as possible," then acculturation, integration, amalgamation, and assimilation can be seen as positive signs of progress. If, however, there are those who desire to maintain a strong ethnic identity, with the retention of ethnic traditions and culture, the same variables will be interpreted differently. In addition, there is often conflict within a group; one individual may applaud signs of integration, while another may strongly disapprove. Such conflicts can even arise within the same family.

The same can be said of the dominant group. As we enter into the last years of the twentieth century, there may be more enlightened definitions of what constitutes a "successful minority." Dominant group notions do change. At one time, a good Indian was a dead Indian; a common goal regarding Asian Americans was that of total exclusion from the American society; and blacks were supposed to be almost totally segregated. Or on a more subtle level, Asian Americans and blacks who behaved according to dominant group role prescriptions, such as those who "knew" their place, might be considered as more successful than their more nonconforming counterparts. Even today, success may be equated with those who have opted to become more like members of the dominant group or those who have adjusted to minority status through conflict-free behavior. Therefore, it would be appropriate in this chapter concerning adaptation to keep these different perspectives in mind.

POPULATION

One of the most fundamental facts concerning Asian Americans is their small number. For even with current large percentage increases, they remain a tiny fraction of the total U.S. population. Table 12-1 shows that in the year 1900, the 204,462 Asian Americans constituted only 0.3 percent of the American population whereas the 5,147,900 in 1985 constituted 2.1 percent. The estimate of 10 million by the year 2000 means that they would make up 4.0 percent of the total U.S. population.

TABLE 12-1   Numbers and Percent of Asian Pacific Americans (APA) in the United States 1900–2000

YEAR	APA	PERCENT OF TOTAL POPULATION
1900	204,462	.3
1920	332,432	.3
1940	489,984	.4
1960	877,934	.5
1980	3,466,421	1.5
1985 (est.)	5,147,900	2.1
1990 (projection)	6,533,608	2.6
2000 (projection)	9,850,364	4.0

Source: Robert W. Gardner, Bryant Robey, and Peter C. Smith, "Asian Americans: Growth, Change and Diversity," *Population Bulletin* 40, no. 4 (Oct. 1985): Tables 1, 2, and 16, pp. 5, 2, 37.

TABLE 12-2   Projected Numbers and Percents of Asian Americans in the United States by Group in the Year 2000

GROUP	NUMBER	PERCENT OF TOTAL ASIAN POPULATION
Filipino	2,070,571	21.0
Chinese	1,683,537	17.1
Vietnamese	1,574,385	16.0
Korean	1,320,759	13.4
Asian Indian	1,006,305	10.2
Japanese	856,619	8.7
Other Asian	1,338,188	13.6
Total	9,850,364*	

*This projection assumes a total U.S. population of about 268 million in 2000; Asian Americans would represent 3.7% of the total population, up from 1.5% (actual) in 1980.

Source: Robert W. Gardner, Bryant Robey, and Peter C. Smith, "Asian Americans: Growth, Change and Diversity," *Population Bulletin* 40, no. 4 (Oct. 1985): 37, Table 16, Asian American Population:1980 and Projected for 1990 and 2000.

ETHNIC GROUP

Table 12-2 shows one population projection of Asians by ethnic group. By the year 2000 it is estimated that the Filipinos will be the most numerous, followed by the Chinese, Vietnamese, Korean, Indian, and the Japanese. The figures emphasize growth through immigration; it should be recalled that in the 1970 census the Japanese were the most numerous and that there were very few Vietnamese and Korean residents. But immigration from Japan has been negligible, while migration from other Asian countries has been high.

California remains the most popular state for Asians. One estimate by Cain and Kiewiet is that Asian Americans will constitute 14 percent of that state's population by 2000.[1]

IMMIGRATION

The growth of Asian Americans by immigration is illustrated in Table 12-3. Prior to 1970 the majority of immigrants came from Europe; since 1970, the rise of Hispanic and Asian immigrants has been the largest. The percentage increase of Asians from 6 percent in 1950-1960 to 36 percent in 1970-1980 and 48 percent in 1980-1984 is the steepest of any of the groups. The rise has been the result of changes in immigration legislation; discriminatory laws against Asian immigrants were an important part of our national policy until the Immigration Act of 1965.

TABLE 12-3   Comparison of U.S. Legal Immigration by Continent, 1950–1960, 1970–1980, 1980–1984 (in percent)

	1950–1960	1970–1980	1980–1984
Europe	59	18	12
Latin America	22	41	35
Asia	6	36	48

Source: Bruce E. Cain and D. Roderick Kiewiet, *Minorities in California* (Pasadena, Calif.: The California Institute of Technology, Division of Humanities, 1986), pp. 1–3. Data for 1980–1984 are from Gardner, Robey, and Smith, "Asian Americans," p. 2, Figure 1.

The recency of Asian immigration can be inferred from a survey of Asian/Pacifics in Los Angeles County. Over 65 percent of the group were foreign-born; 50 percent had arrived since 1970; and 21 percent spoke little English.[2]

DISTRIBUTION BY REGION

Table 12–4 shows the distribution of Asian Americans in the United States. The majority live in the West, especially the Japanese and the Filipino. Asian Indians and, to a lesser extent, the Koreans are spread more evenly throughout the country. Because of their small numbers and their uneven distribution, chances for majority group members to meet more than an occasional Asian American are slim. Therefore, their appearance in the mass media takes on an additional importance.

TABLE 12-4   Total U.S. and Asian American Population, by Region, 1980

POPULATION	PERCENT DISTRIBUTION			
	Northeast	Midwest	South	West
Total U.S.	21.7	26.0	33.3	19.1
Total Asian*	17.1	12.3	14.2	56.4
Japanese	6.5	6.5	6.6	80.3
Chinese	26.8	9.2	11.3	52.7
Filipino	9.9	10.4	11.0	68.8
Korean	19.1	18.1	19.9	42.9
Asian Indian	34.2	23.1	23.4	19.2
Vietnamese	9.0	13.4	31.4	46.2

*Includes all Asian Americans; not just those listed separately.

Sources: Bureau of the Census, 1980 Census of Population, PC80-1-B1, General Population Characteristics, Table 53, and PC80-S1-12, Asian and Pacific Islander Population by State, Tables 1 and 4.

TABLE 12-5 Children Born per 1,000 Women Aged 15-44 by Ethnicity, United States, 1980

GROUP	CHILDREN
All United States	1.43
White	1.35
Black	1.80
Hispanic	1.81
Asian	1.16

Source: Robert W. Gardner, Bryant Robey, and Peter C. Smith, "Asian Americans: Growth, Change and Diversity," *Population Bulletin* 40, no. 4 (Oct. 1985): Figure 4.

FERTILITY AND LIFE EXPECTANCY

Table 12-5 shows the number of children born by ethnic group. The Asian average of 1.16 is lower than the U.S. mean (1.43) and lower than the figure for whites (1.36). In fact, it is the lowest among all comparison groups.

The life expectancy of various Asian groups is high; in 1980, the white mean was 76.4 years; the Japanese, 79.7; the Chinese, 80.2; and the Filipino, 78.8.[3]

EDUCATION

Table 12-6 shows the percentage of high school graduates by sex and age categories. All Asian males, except the Vietnamese, were equal to or above white norms in the percent completing high school. Female figures were

TABLE 12-6 High School Graduates Among White, Black, Hispanics, and Asian American Adults, 1980 (Percent of persons aged 25-29 and 45-54 who had completed high school)

	MALE		FEMALE	
POPULATION	25-29	45-54	25-29	45-54
White	87.0	68.7	87.2	70.1
Black	73.8	42.9	76.5	45.9
Hispanic	58.4	38.4	59.2	35.5
Japanese	96.4	88.1	96.3	82.5
Chinese	90.2	68.7	87.4	57.7
Filipino	88.8	79.6	85.0	71.3
Korean	93.5	90.4	79.0	68.5
Asian Indian	93.5	86.1	87.9	62.0
Vietnamese	75.5	63.6	63.4	41.4

Sources: Bureau of the Census, 1980 Census of Population, PC80-1-D1-A, Detailed Population Characteristics, Table 262, and special unpublished tabulations of the Asian American population.

less consistent, especially in the 45–54-year-old group, where the Chinese, Korean, Asian Indian, and Vietnamese were below white norms.

Data from Cain and Kiewiet on California males 25 years or older who have four years or more of college, show the educational advantage of the Asians.[4] For example, 24 percent of male Californians had four or more years of college, whereas 37 percent of the Japanese, 42 percent of the Chinese, 30 percent of the Filipino, and 50 percent of the Koreans had similar educational achievement.

DOCTORAL DEGREES

Table 12–7 shows the number of doctoral degrees by race for 1975–1984. The number of Asians receiving doctorates nationwide has remained constant—approximately 1,000 per year. This figure is comparable to the number of black Ph.D.s and higher than the number earned by Hispanics and American Indians. When analyzed in the context of their small population base, the percentage of Asians receiving the credential leading to college teaching is the highest among all of the minority groups. However, Trombly adds the sobering note that the faculties of colleges and universities are primarily white and will continue to be unless there is a drastic change in the production of Ph.D.s.[5]

SCHOLASTIC APTITUDE

College entrance is influenced strongly by a number of tests, the most common of which is the Scholastic Aptitude Test (SAT), low scores on which are

TABLE 12–7   California Degree Recipients by Ethnic Background, 1975–1984

YEAR	BLACK	LATINO	ASIAN	AMERICAN INDIAN	WHITE	TOTAL
1975	1,057	337	1,025	36	24,961	27,416
1976	1,149	363	975	40	24,943	27,470
1977	1,194	474	910	77	23,654	26,309
1978	1,106	538	1,032	60	22,342	25,078
1979	1,114	539	1,102	81	22,396	25,232
1980	1,106	485	1,102	75	22,461	25,229
1981	1,116	526	1,072	85	22,469	25,268
1982	1,143	614	1,004	77	22,135	24,973
1983	1,004	607	1,043	81	22,216	24,951
1984	1,049	605	1,017	73	21,792	24,536

Source: William Trombley, "Faculty: Graduate Student Aid," in Los Angeles *Times*, Part I, July 6, 1986, p. 1.

thus a barrier to higher education. Asian Americans do extremely well on the quantitative part of the examination, in fact better than any other group. In 1985 all Asian American math scores averaged 520. The comparable figure for non-Hispanic whites was 490, and all other groups were lower. Not surprisingly, Asian American verbal scores were not as high. In 1985 they averaged 404, well below the 449 of non-Hispanic whites, but still ahead of other groups. The ability of Asian Americans to do well on the SAT is one important factor in their mobility through the educational system.

The stereotype that all Asians do well in school may be pleasing to some but is a disservice to those who do not conform to the image. Some Asians do well, but the price paid for "success" is sometimes very high. For example, Tong indicates a strong "pushy parent" syndrome where children are forced into the hard sciences and emphasis is on continual study.[6] We have heard from students that instead of praise for a report card of all As and one B, there is criticism concerning the B grade. Then there is the critical comparison of the achievement of children from other Asian American families. Parents also give mixed messages. Good children are supposed to stay in touch with their parents and remain dependent, but they are also supposed to become independent and earn money while in school.

The movement of Asian Americans into higher education can be seen in the enrollment figures of the University of California at Berkeley. In 1972 they made up 13.3 percent of the incoming freshmen; in the fall of 1986 they made up 26 percent of the entering class. Projections indicate that they may soon constitute one-third of the student body.[7]

THE FAMILY

A common perception is that Asian Americans come from cohesive, intact families. There is evidence to support this contention; the number of divorces is small, especially among the first-generation immigrants. For example, census figures indicate that Asian American divorce rates are well below their proportion in the population.[8]

However, acculturation and generational changes have led to different expectations and motives for marriage, resulting in a rise in the number of separations and divorces. Table 12–8 shows the percent of households headed by a woman based on the 1980 census. The white and Japanese figures were identical (10.1 percent); the Indian percentage was much lower (6.4 percent); and the Chinese (11.1 percent), the Filipino (12.3 percent), and the Korean (11.2 percent) figures were slightly higher.

Asian American households include the employment of several workers. White households with three or more workers totaled 12 percent, whereas the Japanese (19 percent), the Chinese (20 percent), the Korean (14 percent) and the Filipino (24 percent) all had higher percentages.[9] These

TABLE 12-8   Percent of Households Headed by a Woman, by Ethnic Group, 1980

GROUP	PERCENT
White	10.1
Black	29.8
Latino	18.1
Japanese	10.1
Chinese	11.1
Filipino	12.3
Korean	11.2
Indian	6.4
Vietnamese	14.2

Source: Gardner, Robey, and Smith, "Asian Americans," p. 21, Table 8, Household Composition of White, Black, Hispanic, and Asian American Populations, 1980.

figures are reflected in family income data. Thus, although Asian American household income may be high, it often includes the income of several individuals.

It should be noted that Asians have come from societies where the employment of women for wages outside the home was not a common practice. The need for additional income, better job opportunities for females and youngsters, and changing norms through acculturation have influenced the change in household employment patterns.

There have been some negative consequences of multiple family employment. Aside from the lack of time and energy to devote to child rearing, there has been a rise in the number of latchkey children, a term used to describe the children of working parents who can't be home after school and, therefore, give the children the keys to the family apartment or home.

Problems of intergenerational conflict between "old-fashioned parents" and their Americanized children are as old as the story of immigrants themselves. But Asian American families generally do not ask for outside counseling, which can lead to an assumption that they are "problem free."

OCCUPATION AND EMPLOYMENT

One of the most critical areas for evaluating the adaptation of Asian Americans is that of occupation and employment. The primary goal of most immigrants has been to better their economic status; thus, one measure of their success lies in their ability to find jobs. The problem for many newly arrived immigrants, especially those with advanced or professional degrees, is the initial inability to find employment appropriate to their past experiences.

Figures from the 1980 census on selected occupational categories indicate a wide variation within the group (see Table 12–9). For example, 49 percent of the Asian Indians were in the managerial group, compared to only 12 percent of the Samoans. There were relatively even distributions in most of the other categories. In general, the older, more established Asians—the Chinese, Japanese, and Indians—were distributed in more prestigious and higher-paying occupations than the newly arrived Pacific Islanders and Vietnamese. In terms of modal employment, the Japanese, Filipino, Korean, Hawaiian, and Guamanian were in the "technical" sector; the Chinese and the Indian in the "professional" sector; and the Vietnamese and Samoan in the "laborer" sector.

The overrepresentation of Asian Americans in the small business sector continues. Thirty-seven percent of Asian American businesses are in California, and of these, 76 percent have no paid employees, that is, they are run by "family" members. Sixty-eight percent of the Asian American firms are in retail or in services.

Cain and Kiewiet in their study of minority-owned businesses in California make the following generalizations about Asian Americans.[10] The businesses are primarily sole proprietorships, using family and other nonpaid employees, and profits are generally small. They tend to be concentrated in eating or drinking establishments (8 percent), food stores (6 percent), and health services (11.8 percent). The Chinese are disproportionately in the retail, wholesale, and finance areas and are not found in transportation and construction. The Japanese businesses are more concentrated in construction and finance and less in the areas of retail and service. Filipino firms are in transportation, finance, and services. Korean enterprises are primarily in retail and not in finance. The Koreans have also become greengrocers—they operate about 1,000 of the 1,200 independent grocery stores in New York City.[11] In another virtual monopoly, a Los Angeles Police Department vice detective reports that twenty-two of the twenty-five massage parlors in Los Angeles (a figure that seems somewhat low) are operated by Koreans.[12] Asian Indians are noticeable in motels and newsstands.

The basic advantage of Asian American business owners over Hispanics and blacks is that they have greater family resources, including labor and income, and are therefore able to draw upon a larger capital and employee base. They also serve a wealthier ethnic constituency.

However, there have also been drawbacks to business in the Asian American community. Language problems and dependence on ethnic clientele have limited growth and expansion. Concentration in traditional minority areas where per capita wealth is lower is another limiting factor, and the general reluctance of some Asians to take advantage of Small Business Administration (SBA) government loans is another handicap.[13]

The phenomenon of "ethnic succession" can be observed in the small business sector. A small "mom and pop" grocery store may have been

TABLE 12–9 Percent Employment in Selected Categories, 1980

	MANAGERIAL PROFESSIONAL	TECHNICAL SALES AND ADMINISTRATIVE SUPPORT	SERVICE OCCUPATIONS	FARMING, FORESTRY, FISHING	PRECISION PRODUCTION	OPERATORS, LABORERS
Japanese $N = 382,534$	28.5	34.2	12.8	4.4	10.0	10.1
Chinese $N = 399,964$	32.6	30.0	18.6	0.5	5.6	12.7
Filipino $N = 361,469$	25.1	33.3	16.5	2.8	8.3	14.0
Korean $N = 140,748$	24.9	27.4	16.5	0.9	9.9	20.4
Asian Indian $N = 170,855$	48.5	28.0	7.8	0.9	5.2	9.6
Vietnamese $N = 80,715$	13.3	26.7	15.3	0.9	14.5	29.3
Hawaiian $N = 68,399$	16.6	28.3	21.7	3.3	11.6	18.5
Guamanian $N = 11,966$	13.6	34.4	18.3	1.5	13.8	18.4
Samoan $N = 11,098$	12.5	26.4	19.8	1.8	12.5	27.0

Source: Bureau of the Census, 1980 Census of Population, PC80-1-C1, General Social and Economic Characteristics, U.S., Summary 1-160, Table 163.

started by a Jewish couple, then sold to a Japanese American, who in turn sold the business to a Korean couple. Older, more established minorities tend to move out as better opportunities arise; their place is then taken by newer immigrant groups.

UNEMPLOYMENT

Unemployment figures based on "men in the labor force who reported some unemployment during 1979" and drawn from the 1980 census show that some Asians do better than whites, while others do not. Compared to white norms (17 percent), the Japanese (14 percent) and the Indian (14 percent) had lower figures of unemployment, whereas the Chinese (19 percent), Filipino (19 percent), and Korean (21 percent) had higher figures. The exceptionally high rate of unemployment for the Vietnamese (33 percent) indicates serious problems in that refugee community. The average length of time for Asian unemployment was generally less than for non-Asians. With the exception of the Vietnamese, the Asian rates were lower than the rates for the black (26 percent) and Hispanic (24 percent) minorities.[14]

INCOME AND POVERTY

There are a variety of income figures that can be drawn from the U.S. census. There is individual income and family income, and there are figures based on the mean and the median. It should also be noted that Asian Americans are concentrated in high-income states, such as California and New York, where the cost of living is also high.

Table 12–10 compares full-time Asian American worker median in-

TABLE 12–10 White, Black, Hispanic, and Asian American Worker Incomes and Family Poverty Levels, 1979

POPULATION	MEDIAN INCOME OF A FULL-TIME WORKER	PERCENT OF FAMILIES BELOW POVERTY LEVEL
White	$15,572	7.0
Black	11,327	26.5
Hispanic	11,650	21.3
Japanese	16,829	4.2
Chinese	15,753	10.5
Filipino	13,690	6.2
Korean	14,224	13.1
Asian Indian	18,707	7.4
Vietnamese	11,641	35.1

Source: Bureau of the Census, 1980 Census of the Population, PC80-1-C1, General Social and Economic Characteristics, Tables 148, 149, 158, 159, 164, and 165.

come for 1979 as reported in the 1980 census.[15] Compared to white workers ($15,572), the Japanese, Chinese, and Asian Indian had higher median incomes, whereas the Filipino, Korean, and Vietnamese had lower median incomes. The percent of families at the poverty level also showed differences. The Japanese and Filipino had lower rates of poverty; the Asian Indian about the same; and the Chinese, Korean, and Vietnamese higher.

In terms of median family income, when compared to the white median, Asian American income was as follows; the Japanese, Asian Indians, Filipino, and Chinese above; the Koreans about equal; and the Vietnamese and Pacific Islanders below. As we have previously noted, family income figures are related to higher labor force participation by family members.

The basic generalization is that, with the exception of the newly arrived refugees, Asian Americans are doing relatively well in terms of income. However, as with any group, there are many who live on marginal incomes. There are the aging populations, dependent on Social Security (there are some who are not eligible because of employment in noncovered areas and others who came here too late in life to be covered); individuals without families; the chronically sick; and those who cannot work for a variety of reasons. The image that "Asians have made it" makes it extremely difficult for those on the margins to get the care and the attention that they sorely need.

CORPORATE REPRESENTATION

By corporate representation, we refer to Asian Americans in positions of some authority and power. Figures of such distributions are difficult to obtain; however, a major complaint among Asian Americans has been the lack of upward mobility into positions of power.

Table 12–11 shows the number of Asian American officers and directors in the largest U.S. business firms. Of the 29,000 officer and director positions, 159, or 0.5 percent, were occupied by Asians. Asians made up 3 percent of the members of the Board of Directors of Chambers of Commerce in selected California sites. It is interesting to note that in Gardena, a suburb of Los Angeles with a high concentration of Japanese, including businesses from Japan, there is a high proportion of Asians as board members.

POLITICS

Asian Americans, especially the Japanese, have exercised political power through the Democratic party in Hawaii. Both of the state's senators, Daniel Inouye and Spark Matsunaga, are Japanese Americans and Democrats, as is

TABLE 12-11   Corporate Success of Asian Americans: High-level Management Positions Held

POSITION	NUMBER OF POSITIONS	NUMBER HELD BY ASIAN AMERICANS	PERCENT
Officers and directors of 1,000 largest U.S. firms	29,000	159	0.5
Board of directors of chambers of commerce			
State of California	26	0	0.0
Los Angeles	41	2	4.8
San Diego	76	1	1.3
San Jose	27	0	0.0
Monterey Park	22	7	31.8
Gardena	27	3	11.1

Sources: *The Corporate 1000: A Directory of Who Runs the Top 1,000 U.S. Corporations* (Washington, D.C., The Washington, D.C. Monitor, Inc., 1985); rosters received from each Chamber of Commerce.

its governor, George Ariyoshi. Patricia Saiki, a Republican, was elected to the House of Representatives in 1986. However, the heavy influx of whites from the mainland and new immigrants from the Philippines, as well as the increased political consciousness of native Hawaiians and Pacific Islanders, will probably affect the political power of Japanese Americans.

Two Japanese Americans, Democrats Norman Mineta from San Jose and Robert Matsui from Sacramento, currently represent California in the U.S. House of Representatives. None represent the state in the U.S. Senate (S. I. Hayakawa served one term there), and there are no Asian Americans in the California State Senate or Assembly. A Chinese American woman, March Fong-Eu, holds statewide office, having been elected secretary of state in 1974 and reelected three times. Michael Woo became the first Asian American elected to the Los Angeles City Council in 1986.

Although almost all elected Asian Americans have been from western states, Shien Biau Woo, a Shanghai-born physics professor-turned-politician, was elected lieutenant governor of Delaware in 1984 and holds the highest state office won by an Asian American on the mainland. At a national convention of Chinese Americans held in 1986, Arthur Wong, an elected member of the Washington state legislature, answered the question, "When will we see an Asian president of the United States?" with "Only when we have a political infrastructure...."

Thus, increasing numbers of Asian Americans are running for office, and it is no longer a surprise to see Asian American names on the ballot.

Although the majority of Asian Americans are registered Democrats, in Los Angeles County they are less predominantly so than are blacks and Hispanics. In common with these other minorities, they tend to have a relatively low voter registration. However, as a group they appear to be more politically conservative than other minorities.[16]

NATURALIZATION

Many have argued, implicitly or explicitly, that because of their attachment to their homeland and difficulty in acculturating, Asians coming to the United States have been reluctant to make what seems to many to be the final break with their past—becoming American citizens. The one sophisticated study we have of recent naturalization data suggests exactly the opposite. Elliott Barkan has recently examined American naturalization patterns between 1951 and 1978 (see Table 12–12).[17] His results show that Asians in general have been more likely than most other persons to become naturalized American citizens within a short time after their eligibility. The tendency for Japanese immigrants to have a lower naturalization percentage than the other four main groups most probably reflects the fact that, unlike many recent immigrants from elsewhere in Asia, few Japanese are involved in contemporary chain migration. For persons so engaged, of course, citizenship is a valuable tool, placing one's relatives in a higher preference category than that of relatives of a resident alien and making a wider group of relatives eligible to come to the United States. There is also the desire to become "American" as quickly as possible; loyalty and patriotism are not uncommon qualities among many immigrants from Asia.

SOCIAL PROBLEMS

By social problems, we refer to crime, delinquency, alcohol abuse, mental disorders, mental illness, and similar behaviors that are generally viewed

TABLE 12–12   Response to Citizenship: Percentage of Aliens Nationalized During Their Fifth to Eighth Year of Residence, Fiscal Years 1958–1978

SAMPLES	1958–1968	1969–1978	1958–1978
All Persons	50.98	50.16	50.56
Europeans	54.71	44.57	51.00
North Americans	41.12	42.81	42.17
South Americans	58.24	40.93	45.06
All Persons but Asians	51.96	44.42	48.46
Asians	43.28	64.50	58.80
Chinese	43.90	75.70	66.17
Japanese	37.94	42.85	39.62
Koreans	28.84	58.20	53.11
Filipinos	28.74	60.93	55.18
Indians	53.61	81.11	78.56

Source: Department of Justice, *Annual Report of the Immigration and Naturalization Service* (Washington, D.C., 1951–1978), Table 44; Elliott R. Barkan, "Whom Shall We Integrate?: A Comparative Analysis of the Immigration and Naturalization Trends of Asians Before and After the 1965 Immigration Act (1951–1978)," *Journal of American Ethnic History* 3 (1983): 29–57, at p. 48.

as "bad" or dysfunctional. The reasons behind these problems may vary widely.

Crime and Delinquency

The early Chinese and Japanese were victims of a number of negative stereotypes. They were accused of living in dirt, being diseased, being heathens, and, worst of all, being less than human. Their sexual habits were compared to those of animals; questions of their character and honesty were constantly raised. Yet a scholarly study by Strong and others in 1934 showed low rates of crime and delinquency among "orientals" in California.[18] Recent statistics from the FBI (see Table 12–13) show that the arrest rates of Asian Americans for serious crime from 1980 to 1985 remain well below their proportion in the population.[19]

Despite this, there has been recent concern about crime and delinquency in the Asian American communities. Unemployed youth with limited language facility and minimal skills may be more prone to illegal actions, and publicity about "criminal elements," such as the *yakuza* of Japan, the triads from China, and Korean and Vietnamese gangs, indicates that Asian American communities are not problem-free.

A California Youth Authority training seminar titled "Asian Gangs" discussed current gang activity among Asian Americans.[20] A member of the Los Angeles Police Department claimed that there were close tie-ins between gang activity in California and organized crime from some Asian countries. In addition, as noted in Chapter 8, white-collar entrepreneurial crime has surfaced in the Asian Indian community.

Alcohol Abuse

The abuse of alcohol is a social problem. There is heavy drinking among Japanese, Korean, and Filipino males, but very little seems to spill out into major problem behavior.[21] Since drinking mostly is done with friends and occurs during rituals and celebrations, it may have a different meaning than drinking to combat frustration, anger, and alienation. However, it is a cause of concern, particularly continued heavy drinking among young adult males (see Table 12–14). Research evidence concerning drug addiction among Asian Americans is scarce; it is probable that drug use will more or less reflect the ambience of the local communities.

Mental Health

A major problem in discussing mental health and mental illness is the lack of valid empirical data. What information is available generally supports the notion that although Asian Americans have as many problems as any other group, very few use mental health facilities. There is a definite

TABLE 12–13 Total Arrests,* Percent,† and Rate Distribution‡ by Race, United States, 1980–1985

	1980	1981	1982	1983	1984	1985
Total	2,195,746	2,291,169	2,138,015	2,145,411	1,831,683	2,118,524
White	1,438,098	1,472,421	1,340,866	1,343,607	1,194,229	1,365,558
	(65.5)	(64.3)	(62.7)	(62.6)	(65.2)	(64.5)
Black	720,739	781,983	761,544	766,312	606,443	713,326
	(32.8)	(34.1)	(35.6)	(35.7)	(33.1)	(33.7)
American In-dian	20,194	18,820	16,940	17,208	17,070	21,581
	(.9)	(.8)	(.8)	(.8)	(.9)	(1.0)
Asian/Pacific	16,715	17,945	18,665	18,284	13,941	18,059
	(.8)	(.8)	(.9)	(.9)	(.8)	(.9)
Rate Distribution						
White	81.9	80.4	69.7	69.6	81.5	71.7
Black	41.0	42.6	39.6	39.7	41.4	37.4
American In-dian	1.1	1.0	0.9	0.9	1.1	1.1
Asian/Pacific	1.0	1.0	1.0	1.0	1.0	1.0

*Offenses charged for the arrests are violent crimes (murder, forcible rape, robbery, and aggravated assault) and property crimes (burglarly, larceny-theft, motor vehicle theft, and arson).

†The percent distribution is indicated in parentheses. Because of rounding, the percentage may not add to total.

‡The rate distribution (Asian/Pacific vs. other racial group) is calculated by dividing the percentage of non-Asian racial group by that of Asian/Pacific group.

Source: *Uniform Crime Reports for the United States, 1980–1985* (Washington, D.C.: Federal Bureau of Investigation), Tables, Total Arrests, Distribution by Race, U.S.

TABLE 12-14 Alcohol Consumption by Asian American Males (in percent)

	CHINESE (N = 122)	FILIPINO (N = 81)	JAPANESE (N = 75)	KOREAN (N = 57)
Heavy drinkers	17.2	33.3	44.0	26.3
Moderate to light	61.5	41.9	41.3	33.3
Infrequent/abstainers	21.3	24.7	14.6	40.4

Distribution is significant at the .001 level; N = number

Source: James Lubben, Harry H. Kitano and Iris Chi, "Heavy Drinking Among Young Adult Males" (Paper presented at the Fourth Conference in Asian American Studies, San Francisco State University, Mar. 20, 1987).

cultural element in the way that most Asians are seen by mental health professionals and why Asian Americans, as well as most other minority groups, do not use professional facilities at a higher rate.[22]

Tung, writing from a Southeast Asian perspective, indicates some of the problems of diagnosis when seeing Asian patients.[23]

1. Asians do not freely discuss emotional conditions, especially when they are negative. Grief and depression may be expressed in muted form—oblique, indirect messages may be the norm. Problems are often understated.

2. Asians may appear as modest, discreet, and self-deprecating. They may not volunteer details about themselves and do not want to be seen as boastful. They may be reticent about negative items pertaining to self, family, or community.

3. There is special discretion when talking about one's family. A description of relationships and the emotional interplay among family members is difficult to obtain. Direct accusatory or hostile comments about parents or elders will be unusual.

4. Very little voluntary information on sex life and sexual matters will be given: There will be special difficulty between females and male professionals. Indirect information will be more easily handled.

5. Physical symptoms and bodily discomfort are more acceptable areas for discussion than psychosexual matters.

6. All symptoms should be carefully examined for cultural relevance and meaning. Talking with dead parents and ancestors is not necessarily a sign of mental illness.

As can be seen, cross-cultural differences complicate any assessment of mental health. Immigrants and refugees face enormous problems of adjustment; it is surprising how most of them adapt to culture shock with few signs of overt breakdown. It may very well be that negative conditions, no matter how bad, may still be seen as relatively better than what they left behind. For some, there is also the option of returning home.

MASS MEDIA

One of the "least successful" aspects of the Asian American experience is the portrayal of Asian Americans in the media, both in print and film. Starting with the villainous stereotypes in early movies, progress can only be measured in inches. The evil Jap of World War II and the Communist gooks in Korea, China, and Vietnam—faceless, fanatic, maniacal, willing to die because life is not valued—are endlessly recycled with changes in nationality as our foreign policy changes.[24]

There have been attempts by Asian American filmmakers to portray the Asian American experience in more realistic terms; films such as *Dim Sum, Chan is Missing,* and *Hito Hata* have achieved a limited success. The dilemma for Asian Americans in show business relates primarily to their visibility; non-Asian audiences may not accept Asian Americans in dominant group roles. In addition, productions that are relevant to minority group life may appeal to a limited audience.

The stereotypes of the dominant culture are not always negative—one author, when approached for his picture by a national newspaper, was asked if he would put on a kimono—but still they are stereotypes. Perhaps it is unrealistic to expect Asian Americans eventually to appear randomly in American productions as heroes, villains, lovers, and ordinary people, but it certainly would be a sign of progress to move in this direction.

Marital Assimilation

A common rhetorical question—But do you want your daughter to marry one?—was once a critical item in maintaining the separation between races. The expected answer was no, and for years the question reflected the deep-seated fears of mongrelization from both the dominant and minority groups. To reinforce this belief, there were antimiscegenation laws; prejudice, reinforced by stereotypes, discrimination, and segregation, maintained the separation between races. But today, the question has lost its symbolic meaning, and its answer might even be, why not?

Table 12–15 shows the rates of outmarriage, or marriage out of one's own ethnic group, of the Chinese, Japanese, Koreans, and Vietnamese (1984 only) in Los Angeles for 1975, 1977, 1979, and 1984. The highest rates of outmarriage occurred in 1977 for all groups. The highest rates were by the Japanese (60 percent), Chinese (49.7 percent), and Koreans (34.1 percent). Several other generalizations can be made from this data: (1) Females consistently outmarried at a higher rate than males, (2) the number of marriages among Asian groups has increased, and (3) there has been a decrease in outmarriages by all groups since 1977. This decrease probably represents the growing incidence of new immigrants in the Asian American population.

TABLE 12–15 Outmarriage Rates of Chinese, Japanese, Koreans, and Vietnamese, Total and by Sex, for 1975, 1977, 1979, and 1985, Los Angeles County

CHINESE

YEAR	MARRIAGES	OUTMARRIAGES		PERCENT OUTMARRIAGES	
		Number	Percent	Men	Women
1984	1,881	564	30.0	43.4	56.6
1979	716	295	41.2	43.7	56.3
1977	650	323	49.7	43.7	56.3
1975	596	250	44.0	37.8	62.2

KOREAN

YEAR	MARRIAGES	OUTMARRIAGES		PERCENT OUTMARRIAGES	
		Number	Percent	Men	Women
1984	543	47	8.7	21.4	78.6
1979	334	92	27.6	20.4	79.6
1977	232	79	34.1	26.6	73.4
1975	250	65	26.0	36.9	63.1

JAPANESE

MARRIAGES	OUTMARRIAGES		PERCENT OUTMARRIAGES	
	Number	Percent	Men	Women
1,404	719	51.2	39.8	60.2
764	463	60.6	47.3	52.7
756	477	63.1	39.4	60.6
664	364	54.8	46.4	53.6

VIETNAMESE

MARRIAGES	OUTMARRIAGES		PERCENT OUTMARRIAGES	
	Number	Percent	Men	Women
560	34	6.0	25.3	74.7
—	—	—	—	—
—	—	—	—	—
—	—	—	—	—

Source: Los Angeles County Marriage License Bureau.

Table 12–16 also shows the actual number of outmarriages by ethnic group for the four years. Percentage increases may be deceptive since they are a proportion of such marriages. The actual number of outmarriages increased from 1979 to 1984 for the Chinese (295 to 564) and the Japanese (463 to 719), but decreased for the Koreans (92 to 47).

Figure 12–1 shows the direction of marriages by Japanese Americans in Los Angeles County from 1924 to 1984.[25] It should be noted that interracial marriages were illegal in California prior to 1948 (*Perez v. Lippold*). Yet there were recorded instances of such unions, and, as far as we can tell, there were no legal repercussions. (Interracial marriages effected in other states were valid in California.) Starting from a low of 2 percent in 1924, there was a slow but steady rise in Japanese American outmarriages through the 1950s, followed by a dramatic spurt in 1971 to 1979, with outmarriages in the 50 to 60 percent range. The drop to 51.2 percent does not reflect the continued rise in such marriages.

The direction of marriage for the children of interracial marriages shows that whether part-Chinese, part-Japanese, or part-Korean, the individual will usually marry a non-Asian. Therefore, there is a further merging or melting into the dominant group. It is our impression that many individuals from mixed marriages feel that they are not fully accepted by either the majority or minority community. We have heard of attempts to start their own organizations (i.e., for part–Filipino-Americans) in Los Angeles, but none has yet been successful. It seems to be only a matter of time before their numbers will be sufficient to warrant such groupings.

The majority of out-of-group marriages by Asian Americans are to whites. Only 5 to 10 percent of the outmarriages are between Asian groups. Therefore, the great majority of such marriages in Los Angeles are interracial.[26]

Data from Hawaii indicate the following rates of outmarriage between 1970 and 1980: the Chinese between 75 and 82 percent, the Japanese between 47 and 59 percent, and the Koreans between 83 and 92 percent. Between 17 and 34 percent of outmarriages in Hawaii were to other Asians.[27]

The rise in marital integration is due to a combination of historical factors, demographic variables, the overthrow of discriminatory legislation, loosening controls of the family, better opportunities in employment and education, gaining of more equal status, desegregation of housing, and the rise of individual preferences in marital choices. The most powerful predictors of outmarriage were generation and sex. A female of at least the third generation tends to outmarry at a high rate.

One other phenomenon that is on the rise is the purchase of "Oriental brides" by non-Asians through mail order, a practice that is reported to be a booming business.[28] Lonely American males pay a fee and are given pictures of prospective brides from Asian countries, especially the Philippines. Some Asian groups have reacted quite negatively to the practice, charging

TABLE 12-16 English Only, Birthplace, Arrival in the United States, Median Household Income, and Home Ownership by Ethnicity, Los Angeles County

	NUMBER	PERCENT ENGLISH ONLY	PERCENT BORN IN THE U.S.	PERCENT ARRIVED SINCE 1970	MEDIAN HOUSEHOLD INCOME*	PERCENT HOME OWN-ERSHIP
Chinese	94,200	14	28	49	$19,820	63
Filipino	100,040	24	26	53	23,693	66
Hawaiian	6,220	80	96	2	17,145	52
Indian (Asian)	17,720	27	23	61	17,810	53
Japanese	117,020	49	70	14	22,368	64
Korean	64,500	8	13	77	16,610	48
Vietnamese	26,040	4	7	91	9,610	19
White, Non-Hispanic					19,830	62
Black					12,190	46
Hispanic					14,505	42

Source: *Pacific Rim Profiles* (Los Angeles: United Way, November 1985), pp. 80, 103, 146–160.
*Bureau of the Census, 1980 Census of Population and Housing, PCH 80-2-226.

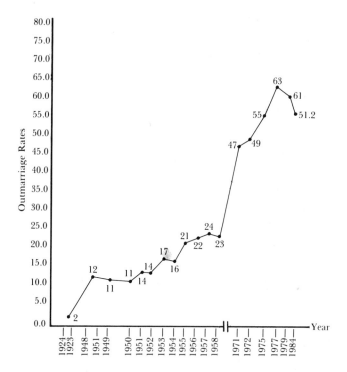

FIGURE 12-1   Outmarriage Rates of Japanese in Los Angeles County, 1924–1984
Source: Based on Burma (1963), Panurzio (1942), Risdon (1954), and Kikumura and Kitano (1973). For 1948 through 1959, total marriages with at least one Japanese partner include all interracial marriages recorded for those years; 1972 data are for January–June; 1975, 1977, 1979, and 1984 data are from the Los Angeles County Marriage License Bureau. (See note 25.)

that foreign women are dehumanized and exploited. Defenders of the system maintain that it gives the women an alternative to a life of poverty.

There also are social clubs where majority group males can meet "lovely Oriental females." Ads in Los Angeles newspapers advertise such clubs; male members include a high proportion of middle- to upper-status professional whites.[29] It may well be that males are looking for the stereotyped Asian female—good at housekeeping, service oriented, willing to stay at home, and sexy.

LOS ANGELES DATA

Los Angeles County has large numbers of Asian Americans, about whom much data has been gathered. From these data we will present an acculturation variable (English only), as well as information concerning "equality" (income, home ownership, infant mortality) to give an idea about the present status of Asian Americans. Generalizations from Los Angeles should be read with caution: They do not necessarily apply elsewhere.

Table 12-16 presents data on Asian Americans in terms of speaking English only, birthplace, arrival since 1970, median household income and home ownership. The majority of the groups are relatively recent arrivals and are more at home with their native languages. Nevertheless, they are well on their way towards income equality and home ownership. The most "Americanized" groups are the Japanese and the Hawaiians; our chapters on these groups show a high degree of acculturation, especially by generation for the Japanese.

Death Rates

Death rates provide another measure of inequality (Table 12-17). Dominated groups generally have higher rates of infant mortality, as well as shorter life expectancies. Asian infant deaths fall below whites rates, 6.7 percent to 8.2 percent; the highest rates of infant mortality are among blacks. Adult deaths are a reflection of age: Asian adult deaths fall below white figures, while the lowest death rates are with the Hispanics, who are a very young population.

SUMMARY

In summary, there are a variety of ways of assessing where Asian Americans are. For those sympathetic to goals of amalgamation and participation in the mainstream, there has been progress, especially when compared to previous decades. Incomes have risen, occupational levels have advanced, immigration laws have been liberalized. Many Asian Americans have entered colleges and universities. Marital assimilation has taken place, and each generation appears to be more American than the next. The repeal of discriminatory laws has allowed Asian Americans to become naturalized, to generally live where they wish, and to run for and be elected to public office. Many own homes. Infant deaths are low, and Asian Americans live longer.

Discrimination exists, but it is subtle. Mobility to the upper echelons of management and power have yet to be broached in any consistent fashion. Instances of "isolate discrimination" serve as reminders that all is not fully well—that Asian Americans can still be the targets of racial attacks and scapegoating.

For the pluralist, continued immigration has reinvigorated ethnic communities. English is not the preferred language for many, especially since such a large percentage are foreign born and are recent arrivals. There are areas in the country where one can remain comfortably ethnic, where ethnic newspapers, ethnic television, ethnic churches, and a large number of ethnic organizations continue to thrive. One can retain the eth-

TABLE 12-17 Death Rates by Ethnicity, Los Angeles County, 1980 and 1983

	INFANT DEATHS (BY PERCENT)				ADULT DEATHS (BY PERCENT)			
	NUMBER	1980	NUMBER	1983	NUMBER	1980	NUMBER	1983
Asian	61	8.1	64	6.7	1,339	3.4	1,732	4.3
White (Non-Hispanic)	541	12.8	454	10.4	45,109	11.4	42,445	10.7
Hispanic	518	8.8	509	8.2	5,677	2.7	6,665	3.2
Black	391	21.0	374	19.5	7,252	7.7	7,287	7.9

Source: County of Los Angeles Department of Health Service, Public Health Programs, "Vital Statistics Report," 1980–1981, 1983.

nic culture, speak the ethnic language, share ethnic foods, and live a life within an ethnic enclave, with minimal contact with the dominant community. The most significant change is that the current pluralism is voluntary in nature, whereas in previous eras ethnic communities were a response to a lack of opportunities in the larger community.

Asian American communities are as dynamic as dominant communities, and thus changes are a part of life. American-born youngsters will change the "culture" of their communities. There will be those who will integrate and amalgamate, others will follow a bicultural path, and some may opt for remaining primarily ethnic. Some new immigrants will remain in their enclaves; others will use the ethnic community as a way station toward eventual participation in the mainstream. In the final analysis, ethnic communities have served and will continue to serve many purposes, just as they have played a significant role for other immigrant groups. But the major key to their survival is the dominant community. Assimilation or pluralism lies primarily in the hands of the more powerful larger community. Their immigration laws will determine the make-up of future populations; their control of laws, wealth, resources, and power will be the primary impetus for whatever changes that may occur.

NOTES

1. Bruce E. Cain and D. Roderick Kiewiet, *Minorities in California* (Pasadena, Calif.: The California Institute of Technology, Division of Humanities, 1986).

2. *Pacific Rim Profiles* (Los Angeles: Asian Pacific Research and Development Council, United Way, Inc., n.d.).

3. Robert W. Gardner, Bryant Robey, and Peter C. Smith, "Asian Americans: Growth, Change and Diversity," *Population Bulletin* 40, no. 4 (Oct. 1985): 1–44.

4. Cain and Kiewiet, *Minorities in California.*

5. William Trombley, "Faculties Still Largely White," Los Angeles *Times,* July 6, 1986, p. 1.

6. Ann Cherian, "Reorientations," *California Monthly* (Sept. 1986) 32–38.

7. Fox Butterfield, "Why Asians Are Going to the Head of the Class," *New York Times,* Aug. 3, 1986, p. 18; Cherian "Reorientation."

8. See "Divorces," in *Vital Statistics of the U.S., 1982:* vol. III, *Marriage and Divorce* (Hyattsville, Md.: U.S. Dept. of Health and Human Services, 1986) Table 2–18.

9. Cain and Kiewiet, *Minorities in California.*

10. Ibid.

11. John Greenwald, "Finding Niches in a New Land," *Time,* July 8, 1985, (Special Immigrants Issue), pp. 32–33.

12. Miles Corwin, "Prostitution: The Far East Link Is Growing in Los Angeles," Los Angeles *Times,* Sept. 15, 1986, part II, p. 1.

13. Cain and Kiewiet, *Minorities in California.*

14. Gardner, Robey and Smith, "Asian Americans."

15. Ibid.

16. Don Nakanishi, *The UCLA Asian Pacific American Voter Registration Study,* (Los Angeles: UCLA

Department of Education, 1986). Marvine Howe, "Attain More Political Power, Chinese-Americans Are Told," *New York Times,* July 13, 1986.

17. Elliott Barkan, "Whom Shall We Integrate?: A Comparative Analysis of the Immigration and Naturalization Trends of Asians Before and After the 1965 Immigration Act (1951–1978)," *Journal of American Ethnic History* 3 (1983): 29–57.

18. See Walter G. Beach, *Oriental Crime in California* (Stanford, Calif.: 1932, Stanford University Press); Harry H. L. Kitano, "Japanese American Crime and Delinquency," *The Journal of Psychology* 66 (1967): 253–63; H. K. Misaki, *Delinquency of Japanese in California* (Stanford, Calif.: Stanford University Series in Education-Psychology, 1933); Edward K. Strong, Jr., *The Second-Generation Japanese Problem* (Stanford, Calif.: Stanford University Press, 1934).

19. *Uniform Crime Reports for the United States 1980–1985* (Washington, D.C.: Federal Bureau of Investigation, 1986).

20. "Asian Gangs," (Camarillo, Calif.: California Youth Authority Training Seminar), March 4, 1986.

21. See Harry H. L. Kitano, Herb Hatanaka, Wai-tsang Yeung and Stanley Sue, "Japanese American Drinking Patterns," in Linda Bennett and Genevieve Ames, eds., *The American Experience with Alcohol* (New York: Plenum Press, 1985), pp. 359–71; Stanley Sue, Harry H. L. Kitano, Herb Hatanaka, and Wai-tsang Yeung, "Alcohol Consumption Among Chinese in the United States," in Linda Bennett and Genevieve Ames, eds., *The American Experience with Alcohol* (New York: Plenum Press, 1985), pp. 359–71; Joseph Westermeyer, "Hmong Drinking Practices in the United States," in Linda Bennett and Genevieve Ames, eds., *The American Experience with Alcohol* (New York: Plenum Press, 1985), pp. 373–91.

22. Stanley Sue and H. McKinney, "Asian Americans in the Community Mental Health Care System," *American Journal of Orthopsychiatry* 45, no. 1 (1975): 11–118.

23. Tran Minh Tung, "Psychiatric Care for Southeast Asians: How Different is Different?" in Tom Owan, ed., *Southeast Asian Mental Health* (Bethesda, Md.: National Institute of Mental Health, 1985), pp. 5–40.

24. Patti Iiyama and Harry H. L. Kitano, "Asian Americans and the Media," in G. Barry and C. Mitchell-Kernan, eds., *Television and the Socialization of the Minority Child* (New York: Academic Press, 1982), pp. 66–90.

25. J. H. Burma, "Interracial Marriage in Los Angeles, 1948–1959," *Social Forces* 42 (Dec. 1963): 156–65; C. Panunzio, "Intermarriage in Los Angeles, 1924–33," *American Journal of Sociology* 47 (Mar. 1942): 690–701; R. Risdon, "A Study of Interracial Marriages Based on Data for Los Angeles County," *Sociology and Social Research* 39 (1954): 92–95; A. Kikumura and H. Kitano, "Interracial Marriage: A Picture of the Japanese Americans," *Journal of Social Issues,* 29, no. 2 (1973): 67–81.

26. H. Kitano, W. Young, L. Chai, and H. Hatanoka, "Asian American Interracial Marriage," *Journal of Marriage and the Family* 46, no. 1 (1984): 179–90.

27. Ibid.

28. "Asian American Women" (Seminar, UCLA, Nov. 3, 1986).

29. Ibid.

13

Adaptations of Asian Americans

Income, employment, political participation, the relative absence of certain social problems, and marital practices provide evidence of the adaptation of Asian Americans to the United States. However, individual factors without a theoretical framework can be deceptive. In this final chapter, we will review some of the more common models and propose a model for predicting future adaptation.

Bogardus, in his study of Chinese, Japanese, Filipino, and Mexican immigrants in the 1920s and 1930s, proposed a race relations cycle.[1] The cycle began with curiosity, followed by economic welcome, industrial and social antagonism, legislative antagonism, fair play tendencies, quiescence, and second-generation difficulties. The model closely fits the experiences of the early Asian immigrants, especially the Chinese and the Japanese.

Park also proposed a cycle consisting of competition, conflict, accomodation, assimilation, and amalgamation.[2] However, after studying race relations in Hawaii in the 1930s, he concluded that there were three possible outcomes of the relations between groups; a caste system, complete assimilation, or the creation of a permanent minority. His model also described the experiences of Asian groups up to that time, but it did not accurately foresee the changes that eventually occurred, especially in Hawaii.

Shibutani and Kwan in 1956 indicated that assimilation—defined as a change of mental perspective whereby the immigrant perceives the world from an American rather than from his or her previous national background—is inevitable, unless one group exterminates the other.[3] Given the relative degree of power of the dominant group and "voluntary immigration," the model has a degree of validity, although conditions such as an open society, equality, and length of time should also be considered. Societal barriers, such as legislative discrimination, can maintain inequality indefinitely.

Gordon in 1964 provided a more detailed schema concerning assimilation into American society.[4] He saw seven stages—cultural, structural, marital, identificational, attitude receptional, behavioral receptional, and civic assimilation. Therefore, the variables leading to assimilation are taking on American ways, or acculturation; integrating into the structures of the dominant society; marrying into the dominant group; identifying as an American; and acceptance without prejudice, discrimination, and value conflict. Although criticized for advocating an assimilationist perspective, many of Gordon's variables are appropriate in any analysis of immigrant group adaptation.

There are a number of other models that differentiate between European immigrants and those of color. Blauner in 1972 wrote about these differences.[5] Colonized minorities did not immigrate voluntarily (i.e., native Americans, black slaves); there was "forced" acculturation; the minorities were ruled and controlled by outsiders; and there was racism. Therefore, the model of voluntary immigration, acculturation, integration, and eventual assimilation, which was the experience for many Europeans, is limited when dealing with "colored" minorities.

Pluralism emphasizes the maintenance of ethnicity and sees America as composed of a mixture of various groups. Analogies to a symphony orchestra or to a salad bowl are used to illustrate the model. Walzer in 1980 saw racism as the barrier to a fully developed pluralism; ethnic groups are not all equal so that pluralism can mean continued disadvantage and inequality.[6] A country committed to pluralism is limited to providing opportunities to ensure that all citizens, without reference to their respective groups, share equally. It cannot, however, prevent people from moving from a more disadvantaged ethnic group to the resource-rich dominant group.

Gleason in 1980 focused on some of the difficulties associated with a pluralistic position.[7] The notion of achieving a rich and harmonious society, where each ethnic group is spending time and money to advocate its own needs and priorities, is yet to be achieved. Further, the notion of a common good or common goals is difficult to achieve under this model.

Cheng and Bonacich in 1983 viewed race and ethnic relations in the context of the world economy.[8] Capitalistic economies require cheap labor; cheap labor lies in the periphery (i.e., migrant workers, immigrant laborers) of the economic system. Racial and ethnic minorities are often located on the periphery; those on the "outside" have little economic control over their lives; they are at the mercy of economic currents and political decisions. Race relations, from this perspective, are less a result of white racism and more a function of political and economic decisions.

Most models reflect a dominant group perspective and assume that assimilation into the mainstream is a desired goal. Terms such as "cultural deprivation" reflect this bias—that somehow minority groups have less and therefore have to be brought up to par, whereas other explanations, such as "being different" or victims of inequality, may be just as plausible.

PREJUDICE AND DISCRIMINATION

The variables most closely tied to shunting the adaptation of minority groups away from "straight line theory"[9]—that is, the process that culminates in the eventual absorption of the ethnic group into the larger culture and general population—are prejudice and discrimination. Prejudice, often maintained through stereotypes, means avoidance; discrimination, often tied to legislation, leads to disadvantage.[10]

Myrdal in 1944 used discrimination and the principle of cumulation to explain the plight of the blacks in the 1930s.[11] Discrimination keeps the minority in a state of inequality—low income, poor housing, inferior education. This in turn is related to family disorganization and criminal and deviant behavior, which in turn leads the discriminator to justify more discrimination, which then leads to more deprivation, more disorganization, and more inequality. It should also be noted that the spiral is not only related to a downward path; it can also move upward with the removal or lessening of racial discrimination.

The cumulation process can also be seen in the historical development of Asian American communities. Prejudice and discrimination led to segregated housing and the exclusion of Asians from organizations and services of the dominant community. Therefore, Asians were forced to rely on their own resources—hospitals, jobs, insurance companies, social clubs—which led to segregated ethnic organizations and communities. These developments led in turn to cries about the unassimilability of Asians by the dominant community. But this situation can be reversed. Since World War II the importance of ethnic community organizations has declined, as opportunities in the dominant community have increased for most Asian American groups.

Generally, prejudice, because it is an attitude, is viewed as less damaging to a minority group than discrimination, although there is an assumed link between the two. Prejudice is much more widespread—Can we control people's minds?—and therefore, a difficult target to eradicate, whereas an

TABLE 13-1   **Degree of Prejudice Directed Toward One's Racial/Ethnic Group (in percent) (Los Angeles, 1984)**

AMERICAN'S DEGREE OF PREJUDICE TOWARD	RACE/ETHNICITY OF RESPONDENT		
	BLACK	HISPANIC	ASIAN
Most are prejudiced	17	10	5
Some are prejudiced	63	54	52
Most are not prejudiced	21	36	42

Source: Bruce E. Cain and D. Roderick Kiewiet, *Minorities in California* (Pasadena, Calif.: The California Institute of Technology, Division of Humanities, 1986), p. III–115.

attempt to control behavior, especially through legislation, is looked upon as a more effective way of gaining equality.

Table 13-1 shows the responses by blacks, Hispanics, and Asians in Los Angeles regarding prejudice that has been directed toward them. Among the groups, the Asians responded the most liberally; they perceived less prejudice than the other groups from the white community.

Table 13-2 shows the responses of the three groups to questions regarding reported instances of discrimination. Asians reported the highest percentage of social discrimination and the lowest percentage of economic discrimination.

A more comprehensive overview of discrimination from a national perspective is available in a 1986 publication by the U.S. Commission on Civil Rights.[12] It reports a wide number of incidents against Asian Americans:

> Seattle, Washington—shots being fired into homes of Southeast Asian refugees;
>
> New York City—a Chinese woman pushed in front of a subway train;

TABLE 13-2   **Personally Experienced Discrimination Reported by Blacks, Latinos, and Asian-Americans (in percent) (Los Angeles, 1984)**

MOST SERIOUS DISCRIMINATION PERSONALLY EXPERIENCED:	RACE/ETHNICITY OF RESPONDENT		
	Black	Hispanic	Asian
Most Serious Discrimination Personally Experienced:			
None	39	65	55
Social	19	16	30
Economic	42	19	15

Source: Cain and Kiewiet, p. III–114.

California—the word "Jap" spray painted on the garage door of an Asian American legislator;

Houston—public health official characterizes Chinese and Vietnamese restaurants as having different standards of cleanliness;

Los Angeles—bumper stickers reading Toyota-Datsun ... Pearl Harbor and Unemployment, Made in Japan;

Davis, California—fatal stabbing of a Vietnamese student by a white high school student;

Fort Dodge, Iowa—Laotian immigrant assaulted by a twenty-three-year-old white male;

Massachusetts—at least twenty complaints concerning acts against Southeast Asian refugees in 1983;

Texas—conflict between Vietnamese and local fishermen culminates in death of a white crab fisherman.

Other incidents included vandalism of cars, misdemeanor assaults, graffiti, harassment, and intimidation. The most dramatic case was that of Vincent Chin,[13] a twenty-seven-year-old, American-born draftsman of Chinese ancestry. On the night of June 19, 1982, Chin went with three friends to a topless bar, the Fancy Pants Tavern in the Detroit suburb of Highland Park, to celebrate his impending marriage. Some racial slurs were made by a forty-three-year-old automobile industry foreman, who thought that Chin was Japanese and somehow responsible for his unemployment. A scuffle ensued, and all were asked to leave the night spot. Later that night, the white foreman and his twenty-three-year-old stepson saw Chin in a fast food restaurant, waited for him to leave, and, while the stepson held Chin, the older man beat him with a baseball bat. Chin died four days later. Originally charged with second-degree murder, the white pair, in a plea bargain, were allowed to plead guilty to manslaughter. Wayne County Circuit Judge Charles Kaufman fined each white man $3,780 and placed them on three years probation.

The Asian American community was outraged. The lenient sentences were interpreted by Asian Americans as an indication that they were unequal in the eyes of the law. The protests eventually forced an investigation, which produced a federal indictment of the older man for depriving Chin of his civil rights. Tried and found guilty, the prime assailant was sentenced to twenty-five years in prison in September 1984. That conviction was reversed on appeal. In April 1987—almost five years after the event—conflicting testimony and blurred memories of witnesses resulted in an acquittal of the killer on the federal charge. The issue in question was not the homicide but whether the motivation was "racial."

But if we select a few headlines from other years—1924, Congress passes a law denying immigration of Asians, 1942, President Roosevelt signs Executive Order 9066, removing all persons of Japanese ancestry from the

West Coast—then the current rash of anti-Asian actions takes on a different tone.

The current incidents reflect what Feagin refers to as "isolate discrimination"—actions taken by individuals against other individuals.[14] This type of discrimination, which can be directly linked to prejudice, has minor societal impact, although it serves as a reminder to the minority group member that prejudice and discrimination have not been eliminated and that one has to remain on guard. On the other hand, the examples of 1924 and 1942 represent institutionalized discrimination—actions taken by groups against other groups, which have far-ranging effects and are therefore much more damaging to the minority group. However, the distinction may mean very little to the victims of current, isolated attacks.

"Isolate discrimination" may not be as benign and minor in terms of societal effects when linked to power. A racially prejudiced individual holding a position of power can influence policy and programs, even if only through negative votes or decisions. However, on an overall level, the diminution of institutionalized discrimination can be looked upon as an optimistic sign concerning the relationship between Asians and the dominant community, and one hopes that behavior on the "isolate" level will also undergo change.

CIVIC ASSIMILATION

One of the last stages in the assimilationist perspective occurs when the ethnic minority no longer uses the ethnic variable in civic affairs. Bell sees indications of this process in the political arena, although there still are, of course Asian issues—immigration, redress for wartime mistreatment, and equal opportunity for disadvantaged Asians.[15] But Asian American politicians—outside of Hawaii—cannot run solely on an Asian American agenda, they are forced to embrace wider platforms. The linkage to wider issues has kept Asian politicians from playing "typical minority politics." Similarly, Asian Americans are often excluded from affirmative action programs, and there are fears that they may become the targets of unofficial quotas.

THE ASIAN AMERICAN MODEL

From the data, we perceive certain patterns in the adaptation of Asians to the United States. Variables such as time of immigration, motives, and demographic factors—all relating to what the immigrants brought with them—are important, just as is the welcome that they received upon their arrival. But after their initial entrance, a number of adaptive patterns have emerged.

The two most often mentioned variables are assimilation and ethnic identity. The assimilation variable, as previously mentioned, includes integration into the schools, the work place, the social groupings, as well as identification with the majority and marital assimilation. The ethnic identity dimension is essentially a pluralistic adaptation, focusing on the retention of ethnic ways. Figure 13–1 illustrates the model and the four types associated with the model.

Cell A: High Assimilation, Low Ethnic Identity

Cell A shows an Asian American, high in assimilation and low in ethnic identity. The individual is more American than ethnic; many members of the third generation and Asian Americans isolated from ethnic communities fall into this category. Language, life-styles, and expectations will be American; the ethnic language and culture will be all but forgotten. High rates of marriage to non-Asians can be predicted; more females than males may belong to this category. Individuals who desire to become "American," no matter what the generation, will also fit into this cell.

Friendship and social patterns will also show a high proportion of non-Asian contacts. Friends will be from the majority culture; membership will be in dominant group organizations, such as fraternities and sororities. Ethnic identity, if present, will be primarily symbolic;[16] there may be occasional participation in ethnic holidays and ethnic festivals, the partaking of ethnic foods and an occasional ethnic movie. But for Asian Americans in this category, the one inescapable fact is that of ethnic visibility, and reactions from the outside world force the retention of an ethnic identity, no matter how slight. Canadians currently use the term "visible minority" to describe those whose ethnicity is signaled by skin color.

FIGURE 13-1 Assimilation Model

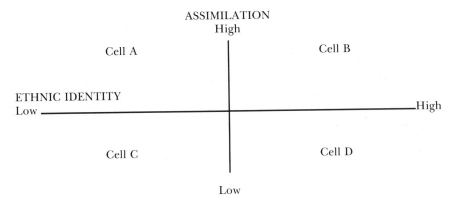

Cell B: High Assimilation, High Ethnic Identity

The individuals who fit into this category will be similar in the assimilation category to those in Cell A, but will differ from those in the previous model by retaining a strong ethnic identity. Friendship patterns, membership in organizations, and interests show a strong bicultural perspective; the individual moves easily in and out of both cultures. Further, the person is knowledgeable about ethnicity and the ethnic culture and is comfortable with a strong ethnic identity. The category is a bicultural one; it may include some academics and some older individuals brought up with a multicultural perspective. The hyphenated Asian-American will fit under this category, although it will probably be difficult to maintain an even balance between the two.

Cell C: Low Assimilation, Low Ethnic Identity

This cell describes the alienated, the disenchanted, and the disillusioned. They have acquired very little of the American culture and are also uncomfortable with an ethnic identity. We see a small proportion of Asian Americans in this category.

Cell D: Low Assimilation, High Ethnic Identity

This cell includes a large number of newly arrived immigrants, as well as Asian Americans who have spent much of their lives in ethnic communities. The latter may have achieved a "functional level" of adaptation to the American culture but are more comfortable within the ethnic enclaves. Marriage will tend to be within the ethnic group; the person is more ethnic than American. Members of the first generation, especially those who emigrated at an advanced age, are likely to be in this category. Asian Americans who feel that the white society will never treat them as equals may also opt for a pluralistic adaptation.

Variations in assimilation were observed by Hansen, who saw a third-generation reawakening of ethnic identity—what the second generation tries to forget, the third generation remembers.[17] There are, for example, significant numbers of third- and fourth-generation Japanese Americans enrolled in the Education Abroad Program of the University of California Tokyo Study Center, but we find, so far, few other such manifestations. Perhaps it is not just a coincidence that the most observable example occurs among a group whose immigration has largely stopped.

The underlying assumption of assimilation theory is that the American mainstream has the power, the organization, and the resources that "pull" immigrant groups in its direction. It is incumbent upon the less powerful to come to grips with the "American culture," lest they remain outsiders looking in. At one time, the dominant society practiced a policy of selective exclusion. Asians were unwelcome, so there were modifications and a delay in assimilation. It is no accident that the call for pluralism, for separate identities, and a reevaluation of assimilationist models were led by ethnic groups who were excluded from equal participation in the society. Now that exclusionary policies have been modified, it will be interesting to see if newer Asian immigrants, including American-born generations who have faced a minimal amount of institutionalized barriers, follow an assimilationist model.

As Gans indicates, the third and succeeding generations grow up without assigned roles or groups that anchor identity.[18] Thus, ethnicity is no longer taken for granted. Most of them are acculturated participants in the mainstream; the primary, but sill powerful, reminder of their "Asian-ness" remains their visibility. Other reminders, such as overt discrimination and the politics of exclusion, are no longer in vogue; ethnic organizations, especially those that stress civil rights and equality, have a difficult time attracting younger members without an ethnic "cause." One symptom of the progress of a group toward assimilation would be the disappearance of ethnic organizations devoted to civil rights and equality; the existence of such groups, especially in the third world communities, indicates that much is yet to be achieved.

Studies focusing on the importance of social class in the Asian American communities are lacking. Even though many of the early immigrants would have been classified as lower class in terms of their income and education, their expectations were more middle class—higher education for their children, saving for the future, ownership of land, starting their own business. Conversely, those who might have been classified as upper class were not viewed as such by their peers in the dominant community. Views of class solidarity did not develop, especially across ethnic lines, so class consciousness in terms of social action to redress grievances was not a common phenomenon.

There is little question that social class and other status variables operate within each Asian community and that length of time in America is accompanied by an increased differentiation in income, education, mobility, housing, and life-styles. Good marriages and good prospects are commonly defined in social class terms; many parents search diligently for marital partners for their children in terms of good education, a good house in a good neighborhood, good family, and good income. The definition of desirability has even cut across ethnic boundaries—whereas in a previous era, the question might have been, "But is your fiancé Asian?", a more common question might now be, "But is he a doctor?" Ethnic parents who often deny the importance of such variables when judging others appear to have developed finely honed procedures to discover the "really eligible." And many are disappointed when their acculturated children marry for love, which means partners without the desired characteristics.

194   *ADAPTATION OF ASIAN AMERICANS*

In conclusion, Asians, purveyors of the well-known Rashomon perspective—that views of reality are dependent on the position of the observer—provide a number of such perceptions. For those in business and economics they are viewed as busy entrepreneurs, focusing on small business and the professions and generally doing well. For those in the mental health fields—psychiatry, psychology, counseling, and social work—Asian Americans are a cause of concern. They appear to have as many problems as others but do not avail themselves of professional services. For educators, Asian Americans are a source of delight—good, hard-working students—although the image is changing. For politicians, they are an unknown group, but a group to be considered because of their growing numbers. For some frustrated Americans, Asian Americans are a convenient scapegoat—easy to stereotype, easy to blame.

In the final analysis, we agree with the assessment of Bell, who believes that immigrant groups, and specifically Asian immigrants, have been good for America.[19] Asian immigrants and their children have enriched and improved every field that they have entered. Their grocery stores provide fresh produce, their doctors enrich the health field, and their students enhance the quality of scholarship at our universities. But such credit should not be reserved solely for them—Asian Americans have followed the path that has been characteristic of other immigrant groups and, like them, they have added much more to the society than they have taken away.

NOTES

1. Emory Bogardus, "A Race Relations Cycle," *American Journal of Sociology* 35 (1930):612–17.
2. Robert E. Park, *Race and Culture* (New York: Free Press, 1950).
3. Tamotsu Shibutani and Kian Kwan, *Ethnic Stratification* (New York: Macmillan, 1965).
4. Milton Gordon, *Assimilation in American Life* (New York: Oxford University Press, 1964).
5. Robert Blauner, *Racial Oppression in America* (New York: Harper and Row, 1972).
6. Michael Walzer, "Pluralism: A Political Perspective," in Stephan Thernstrom et al., eds., *The Harvard Encyclopedia of American Ethnic Groups* (Cambridge, Mass.: Harvard University Press, 1980), pp. 781–87.
7. Philip Gleason, "American Identity and Americanization," in Stephan Thernstrom et al., eds., *The Harvard Encyclopedia of American Ethnic Groups* (Cambridge, Mass.: Harvard University Press, 1980), pp. 31–58.
8. Lucie Cheng and Edna Bonacich, eds., *Labor Immigration Under Capitalism: Asian Workers in the United States Before World War II* (Berkeley and Los Angeles: University of California Press, 1983).
9. Neil Sandberg, *Jewish Life in Los Angeles* (Lanham, Md.: University Press of America, 1986), p. 134.
10. Harry H. L. Kitano, *Race Relations*, 3rd ed. (Englewood Cliffs, N.J.: Prentice-Hall, 1985).
11. Gunnar Myrdal, *An American Dilemma* (New York: Harper, 1944).
12. United States Commission on Civil Rights, *Recent Activities Against Citizens and Residents of Asian Descent* (Washington, D.C.: Government Printing Office, 1986).

13. Ibid., p. 4.

14. Joe Feagin, *Racial and Ethnic Relations* (Englewood Cliffs, N.J.: Prentice Hall, 1978).

15. David Bell, The Triumph of Asian Americans," *The New Republic,* July 15 and 22, 1985, pp. 24–31.

16. Herbert Gans, "Symbolic Ethnicity: The Future of Ethnic Groups and Cultures in America," in Norman Yetman, ed., *Majority and Minority* (Boston: Allyn and Bacon, 1985), pp. 429–442.

17. Marcus L. Hansen, *The Problems of the Third Generation* (Rock Island, Ill.: Augustana Historical Society, 1938).

18. Gans, "Symbolic Ethnicity."

19. Bell, "The Triumph of Asian Americans."

Suggestions for Further Reading

The following books will serve as an introduction to many of the topics that we have discussed in this book. Some, but not all, have been cited in the end notes; most contain bibliographies.

RACE RELATIONS AND ACCULTURATION

Banton, Michael. *Racial and Ethnic Competition.* Cambridge: Cambridge University Press, 1983.
Blauner, Robert. *Racial Oppression in America.* New York: Harper and Row, 1972.
Daniels, Roger, and Harry H. L. Kitano. *American Racism: Exploration of the Nature of Prejudice.* Englewood Cliffs, N.J.: Prentice-Hall, 1970.
Gordon, Milton M. *Assimilation in American Life: The Role of Race, Religion and National Origins.* New York: Oxford University Press, 1964.
Kitano, Harry H. L. *Race Relations,* 3rd ed. Englewood Cliffs, N.J.: Prentice-Hall, 1970.

HISTORIES OF IMMIGRATION

Archdeacon, Thomas J. *Becoming American: An Ethnic History.* New York: The Free Press, 1983.
Daniels, Roger, "Changes in Immigration Law and Nativism Since 1924," *American Jewish History* 76 (1986): 159–80.

Reimers, David M. *Still the Golden Door: The Third World Comes to America.* New York: Columbia University Press, 1985.

CHINESE AMERICANS

Chan, Sucheng. *This Bittersweet Soil: The Chinese in California Agriculture, 1860–1910.* Berkeley and Los Angeles: University of California Press, 1986.
Lyman, Stanford M. *Chinese Americans.* New York: Random House, 1974.
Tsai, Shih-san Henry. *The Chinese Experience in America.* Bloomington, Ind.: Indiana University Press, 1986.
Yung, Judy. *Chinese Women of America: A Pictorial History.* Seattle: University of Washington Press, 1986.

JAPANESE AMERICANS

Daniels, Roger. *Asian America: Chinese and Japanese in the United States Since 1850.* Seattle: University of Washington Press, 1988.
Daniels, Roger. *Concentration Camps, North America: Japanese in the United States and Canada During World War II.* Melbourne, Fla.: Krieger, 1981.
Kitano, Harry H. L. *Japanese Americans: The Evolution of a Subculture.* Englewood Cliffs, N.J.: Prentice-Hall, 1969.
Petersen, William. *Japanese Americans: Oppression and Success.* New York: Random House, 1971.

KOREAN AMERICANS

Choy, Bong-youn. *Koreans in America.* Chicago: Nelson-Hall, 1979.
Kim, Hyung-chan, ed. *The Korean Diaspora.* Santa Barbara, Calif.: Clio Press, 1977.
Patterson, Wayne, and Hyung-chan Kim. *The Koreans in America.* Minneapolis: Lerner Publications, 1977.

FILIPINO AMERICANS

Bulosan, Carlos. *America is in the Heart.* Seattle: University of Washington Press, 1973.
Lasker, Bruno. *Filipino Immigration to the Continental United States and Hawaii.* Chicago: University of Chicago Press, 1931.
Melendy, H. Brett. *Asians in America: Filipinos, Koreans, and East Indians.* Boston: Twayne, 1977.
Quinsaat, Jesse, ed. *Letters in Exile: A Reader on the History of Filipinos in America.* Los Angeles: University of California, 1976.

ASIAN INDIANS

Chandrasekhar, S., ed. *From India to America.* La Jolla, Calif.: Population Institute, 1984.
Hess, Gary. "The Forgotten Asian Americans: The East Indian Community in the United States," in Norris Hundley, ed. *The Asian American.* Santa Barbara, Calif.: Clio Press, 1976, pp. 157–78.

Jensen, Joan M. "East Indians," in Stephan Thernstrom, ed., *The Harvard Encyclopedia of American Ethnic Groups*. Cambridge, Mass.: Harvard University Press, 1980, pp. 296–301.

Jensen, Joan M. *Passage from India*. New Haven: Yale University Press, 1988.

Saran, Parmata. *The Asian Indian Experience in the United States*. Cambridge, Mass.: Schenkman, 1985.

THE REFUGEE EXPERIENCE

Daniels, Roger. "American Refugee Policy in Historical Perspective," in J. C. Jackman and C. Borden, eds., *The Muses Flee Hitler: Cultural Transfer and Adaptation, 1930–1945*. Washington, D.C.: Smithsonian Institution, 1983, pp. 61–77.

Loescher, Gil, and John A. Scanlan. *Calculated Kindness: Refugees and America's Half-Open Door, 1945 to the Present*. New York: Free Press, 1986.

Marrus, Michael. *The Unwanted: European Refugees in the Twentieth Century*. New York: Oxford University Press, 1985.

Stein, Barry, and Sylvano Tomasi, eds. "Refugees Today," special issue of *International Migration Review* 15 (1981): 1–393.

Wain, Barry. *The Refused: The Agony of the Indochina Refugees*. New York: Simon and Schuster, 1982.

SOUTHEAST ASIANS

Kelly, Gail Paradise. *From Vietnam to America*. Boulder, Colo.: Westview Press, 1979.

Liu, William T. *Transition to Nowhere: Vietnamese Refugees in America*. Nashville, Tenn.: Charter House, 1979.

Montero, Darrel. *Vietnamese Americans: Patterns of Resettlement and Adaptation*. Boulder, Colo.: Westview Press, 1979.

Strand, Paul J., and Woodrow Jones, Jr. *Indochinese Refugees in America*. Durham, N.C.: Duke University Press, 1985.

PACIFIC ISLANDERS

Joan Ablon. "The Social Organization of an Urban Samoan Community," *Southwestern Journal of Anthropology* 27 (1971): 75–96.

Fuchs, Lawrence. *Hawaii Pono: A Social History of Hawaii*. New York: Harcourt, Brace and World, 1961.

Lewthwaite, Gorden R., Christine Mainzer, and Patrick J. Holland. "From Polynesia to California: Samoan Migration and Its Sequel," *Journal of Pacific History* 8 (1973): 133–57.

Lind, Andrew. *Hawaii's People*. Honolulu: University of Hawaii Press, 1967.

Macpherson, Cluny, Bradd Shore, and Robert Franco, eds. *New Neighbors: Islanders in Adaptation*. Santa Cruz, Calif.: University of California, 1978.

REFERENCE WORKS

Kim, Hyung-chan, ed. *Dictionary of Asian American History*. Westport, Conn.: Greenwood Press, 1986.

Thernstrom, Stephan, ed. *The Harvard Encyclopedia of American Ethnic Groups*. Cambridge, Mass.: Harvard University Press, 1980.

*A*PPENDIX

1980 Census Data

TABLE A-1 Asian American Population, by State, 1980.

UNITED STATES REGIONS (STATES WITH 10,000 OR MORE ASIANS)	TOTAL ASIAN POPULATION	ASIAN INDIAN	BANGLADESHI	BURMESE	CAMBODIAN (KAMPUCHEAN)	SRI LANKAN (CEYLONESE)	CHINESE	FILIPINO	HMONG	INDONESIAN
United States	3,466,421	387,223	1,314	2,756	16,044	2,923	812,178	781,894	5,204	9,618
Total, selected States	3,373,604	372,793	1,296	2,647	15,370	2,793	794,750	765,664	4,877	9,411
Percent of Asians in selected states	97.3	96.3	98.6	96.0	95.8	95.6	97.9	97.9	93.7	97.8
Northeast	591,844	132,560	692	421	2,288	842	217,624	77,051	354	1,888
Massachusetts	51,882	8,943	87	50	198	109	24,882	3,180	46	208
Connecticut	20,742	5,426	29	—	228	81	4,948	3,049	35	79
New York	327,499	67,636	393	278	496	421	147,250	35,630	10	1,212
New Jersey	108,417	30,684	167	56	52	140	23,492	24,470	—	172
Pennsylvania	69,211	17,230	16	37	885	80	13,769	8,640	79	175
North Central	426,081	89,588	138	476	2,258	442	74,944	80,928	2,780	1,087
Ohio	52,070	13,602	13	20	87	47	10,584	7,966	27	124
Indiana	23,612	4,746	—	7	172	10	4,491	3,507	—	94
Illinois	170,614	37,438	25	269	554	132	28,847	44,317	433	229
Michigan	61,313	15,363	37	30	280	144	10,824	11,132	127	280
Wisconsin	21,465	3,902	12	13	95	2	4,835	3,036	408	163

State	Total									
Minnesota	31,647	3,734	—	5	555	85	4,558	2,628	1,331	93
Iowa	13,358	2,424	—	41	183	6	1,973	1,058	266	40
Missouri	23,516	4,276	32	91	104	11	4,520	3,883	—	12
Kansas	16,755	2,588	19	—	169	5	2,440	1,648	159	40
South	493,744	90,602	292	734	2,570	423	91,415	85,626	123	1,235
Maryland	66,849	13,788	38	251	232	28	15,037	11,763	19	234
Virginia	68,619	9,046	100	94	450	40	9,495	19,111	—	112
North Carolina	21,530	4,855	—	20	94	9	3,229	2,869	—	127
South Carolina	12,641	2,572	—	—	21	—	1,204	3,797	6	—
Georgia	24,510	4,725	—	54	—	8	4,258	2,825	—	13
Florida	60,211	11,039	2	51	357	40	12,930	15,252	—	219
Kentucky	11,090	2,669	—	8	—	—	1,381	1,417	—	6
Tennessee	14,624	3,392	—	—	116	17	2,904	1,761	—	27
Louisiana	24,174	3,036	—	14	55	10	3,091	2,650	—	32
Oklahoma	18,553	3,168	20	36	91	5	2,384	1,681	34	46
Texas	129,972	23,395	114	97	1,025	160	26,714	15,952	7	325
West	1,954,752	74,473	192	1,125	8,928	1,216	428,195	538,289	1,947	5,408
Colorado	32,733	2,565	—	33	273	17	4,224	2,764	110	215
Arizona	22,968	2,078	32	39	111	—	6,681	3,799	4	21
Utah	15,874	932	—	—	342	—	2,913	1,138	364	16
Nevada	14,458	527	46	12	—	—	3,192	3,826	—	—
Washington	104,662	4,267	—	87	1,752	108	17,984	25,662	89	238
Oregon	38,430	2,265	114	5	749	12	7,918	4,800	538	171
California	1,246,654	59,774	—	933	5,586	1,040	325,882	358,378	733	4,535
Hawaii	452,951	708	—	16	58	26	55,916	132,075	52	153

(continued)

TABLE A–1 (Continued)

UNITED STATES REGIONS (STATES WITH 10,000 OR MORE ASIANS)	JAPANESE	KOREAN	LAOTIAN	MALAYAN	OKINAWAN	PAKISTANI	THAI	VIETNAMESE	ASIAN NOT SPECIFIED[1]	ALL OTHER ASIAN
United States	716,331	357,393	47,683	4,075	1,415	15,792	45,279	245,025	12,897	1,377
Total, selected States	701,251	345,679	44,745	3,944	1,362	15,344	42,612	235,238	12,518	1,310
Percent of Asians in selected states	97.9	96.7	93.8	96.8	96.3	97.2	94.1	96.0	97.1	95.1
Northeast	46,913	68,357	4,666	589	42	5,166	7,214	22,021	2,884	272
Massachusetts	4,290	5,369	570	107	—	198	549	2,847	230	19
Connecticut	1,841	2,015	873	32	—	123	254	1,575	124	30
New York	24,754	33,260	1,357	261	—	3,214	4,028	5,849	1,261	189
New Jersey	10,263	13,173	230	52	—	1,109	921	2,846	565	25
Pennsylvania	4,422	12,597	926	108	—	516	943	8,127	652	9
North Central	46,254	64,573	13,371	1,986	32	3,355	8,433	32,949	2,178	309
Ohio	6,271	7,756	1,080	209	4	268	950	2,751	303	8
Indiana	2,503	3,940	817	382	6	224	469	2,137	104	3
Illinois	18,432	24,351	3,086	666	4	1,760	3,265	6,287	462	57
Michigan	6,460	8,948	1,031	328	10	481	938	4,364	436	100
Wisconsin	2,123	2,900	1,472	137	5	104	309	1,699	196	54
Minnesota	3,191	6,676	3,012	21	—	77	167	5,316	173	25
Iowa	1,024	2,057	1,162	105	3	55	741	2,101	106	13
Missouri	2,897	3,356	202	28	—	125	648	3,134	148	49
Kansas	1,611	2,701	1,176	74	—	172	461	3,331	161	—

South	47,631	70,999	7,846	535	115	3,565	10,184	76,916	2,633	300
Maryland	4,656	14,783	105	12	—	378	944	4,162	398	40
Virginia	5,173	12,797	597	97	13	658	913	9,451	345	108
North Carolina	3,594	3,694	419	27	—	26	454	1,966	121	26
South Carolina	1,584	1,766	203	4	—	31	277	1,113	47	22
Georgia	3,596	5,590	290	21	20	29	603	2,339	159	—
Florida	5,667	4,948	542	42	—	392	1,441	7,077	169	19
Kentucky	1,170	2,170	336	6	—	—	327	1,461	137	—
Tennessee	1,752	2,405	720	55	—	59	220	1,158	38	—
Louisiana	1,671	2,009	201	68	—	136	265	10,853	57	26
Oklahoma	2,249	2,757	824	93	2	277	533	4,174	179	—
Texas	12,084	13,772	2,872	73	69	1,302	3,373	27,791	835	12
West	575,533	153,464	21,800	965	1,226	3,706	19,448	113,139	5,202	496
Colorado	10,841	5,143	1,839	50	7	209	812	3,247	308	76
Arizona	4,629	2,543	264	6	13	78	744	1,756	139	31
Utah	5,508	1,397	730	—	—	11	409	1,991	119	4
Nevada	2,478	2,332	246	13	—	73	675	1,018	58	8
Washington	27,389	13,441	2,479	76	53	104	1,329	8,933	618	16
Oregon	8,580	4,998	1,779	84	12	74	473	5,743	129	100
California	268,814	102,582	11,945	648	206	3,022	13,412	85,238	3,611	201
Hawaii	239,734	17,453	1,369	59	935	59	765	3,403	130	40

¹Includes write-in entries such as Asian American, Asian, and Asiatic.

Source: Bureau of the Census, 1980 Census of Population: Asian and Pacific Islander Population by State, 1980, Supplementary Report PC80-S1-12, Table 4.

TABLE A-2 Pacific Islander Population, by State, 1980

UNITED STATES REGIONS (STATES WITH 400 OR MORE PACIFIC ISLANDERS)	TOTAL PACIFIC ISLANDER POPULATION	POLYNESIAN						
		Total	Hawaiian	Samoan	Tahitian	Tongan	All Other	Total
United States	259,566	220,278	172,346	39,520	791	6,226	1,395	35,508
Total, selected states	256,804	218,361	170,762	39,212	789	6,219	1,379	34,723
Percent of Pacific Islanders in selected states	98.9	99.1	99.1	99.2	99.7	99.9	98.9	97.8
Northeast	7,426	4,960	4,273	522	77	44	44	2,302
Massachusetts	733	445	352	93	—	—	—	276
New York	3,459	2,192	1,950	151	30	29	32	1,211
New Jersey	966	691	579	112	47	—	—	225
Pennsylvania	1,293	1,064	909	87	9	15	6	220
North Central	9,192	6,547	5,476	991	9	17	54	2,506
Ohio	1,096	890	823	64	—	2	1	195
Indiana	743	583	503	60	—	4	16	154
Illinois	1,546	1,052	964	88	—	—	—	471
Michigan	1,321	990	894	90	—	6	—	323
Wisconsin	560	350	258	87	—	—	5	176
Minnesota	579	379	315	51	—	—	13	163
Iowa	489	375	301	50	—	5	19	114

Missouri	1,440	780	357	7	—	—	290
Nebraska	424	177	48	—	—	—	192
Kansas	772	351	57	—	—	—	364
South	19,186	11,427	1,784	82	68	109	5,520
Maryland	1,097	630	86	—	—	15	333
Virginia	1,939	1,033	194	12	19	2	645
North Carolina	1,620	954	132	—	—	—	534
South Carolina	729	467	57	8	—	—	197
Georgia	1,492	795	134	6	—	7	538
Florida	2,298	1,484	222	56	9	41	470
Kentucky	733	378	122	—	—	—	233
Tennessee	628	438	111	—	8	—	71
Alabama	683	583	38	—	—	—	62
Mississippi	508	401	20	—	—	—	87
Louisiana	949	626	69	—	—	—	242
Oklahoma	1,204	695	117	—	—	—	385
Texas	4,422	2,375	401	—	32	44	1,488
West	223,762	151,170	36,223	623	6,097	1,188	25,180
Idaho	523	293	103	—	54	7	66
Colorado	1,524	825	135	13	7	5	523
Arizona	1,594	854	179	—	24	26	503
Utah	4,350	913	1,171	48	1,809	265	139
Nevada	1,148	552	54	13	148	45	336
Washington	6,925	2,840	1,837	7	88	67	1,931
Oregon	2,472	1,555	97	6	122	5	561
California	66,171	24,245	18,087	260	2,356	418	18,211
Alaska	678	419	102	7	—	4	146
Hawaii	137,696	118,251	14,349	269	1,482	336	2,648

(continued)

TABLE A-2 (Continued)

UNITED STATES REGIONS (STATES WITH 400 OR MORE PACIFIC ISLANDERS)	MICRONESIAN					MELANESIAN			PACIFIC ISLANDER NOT SPECIFIED[1]
	Guamanian	Northern Mariana Islander	Marshallese	Palauan	All Other	Total	Fijian	All Other	
United States									
Total, selected states	30,695	698	474	692	2,949	3,311	2,834	477	469
	30,018	672	474	668	2,891	3,258	2,797	461	462
Percent of Pacific Islanders in selected states	97.8	96.3	100.0	96.5	98.0	98.4	98.7	96.6	98.5
Northeast	1,952	19	33	43	255	135	127	8	29
Massachusetts	251	—	18	7	—	4	4	—	8
New York	1,017	—	10	—	184	35	35	—	21
New Jersey	199	—	5	14	7	50	50	—	—
Pennsylvania	164	—	—	10	46	9	1	8	—
North Central	1,816	30	78	9	573	117	20	97	22
Ohio	137	—	20	6	32	11	3	8	—
Indiana	119	—	16	—	19	6	—	6	—
Illinois	367	14	18	3	69	23	17	6	—
Michigan	199	2	—	—	122	—	—	—	8
Wisconsin	162	—	—	—	14	34	—	34	—
Minnesota	102	2	5	—	59	37	—	37	—
Iowa	95	—	5	—	14	—	—	—	—
Missouri	203	—	—	—	87	6	—	6	—

Nebraska	109	—	—	—	83	—	—	—	7
Kansas	259	12	19	—	74	—	—	—	—
South	4,757	147	160	50	406	166	92	74	30
Maryland	323	14	—	—	10	33	10	23	—
Virginia	548	—	60	13	70	21	21	—	13
North Carolina	388	—	—	7	79	—	—	—	—
South Carolina	182	21	—	—	15	—	—	—	—
Georgia	503	—	—	—	14	12	12	16	—
Florida	442	4	—	—	28	16	—	—	—
Kentucky	208	—	—	—	21	—	—	—	—
Tennessee	66	—	—	—	5	—	—	—	—
Alabama	62	—	—	—	—	—	—	—	—
Mississippi	87	—	—	—	—	—	—	—	—
Louisiana	230	6	—	—	6	12	—	12	—
Oklahoma	261	—	32	—	92	—	—	—	7
Texas	1,229	95	68	30	66	72	49	23	10
West	22,170	502	203	590	1,715	2,893	2,595	298	388
Idaho	42	15	—	—	9	—	—	—	—
Colorado	506	—	2	—	15	16	—	16	—
Arizona	346	—	32	6	119	8	—	8	—
Utah	64	17	—	—	58	—	—	—	5
Nevada	275	13	—	43	5	—	—	—	—
Washington	1,739	34	5	14	139	155	147	8	—
Oregon	366	34	—	6	155	126	126	—	—
California	17,009	322	86	204	590	2,217	2,062	155	377
Alaska	129	11	—	—	6	355	260	95	—
Hawaii	1,630	56	78	305	579	—	—	—	6

[1]Includes persons who did not provide a specific written entry but reported "Pacific Islander."

Source: Bureau of the Census, 1980 Census of Population: Asian and Pacific Islander Population by State, 1980, Supplementary Report PC80-S1-12, Table 5.

Index